Advanced Interdisciplinary Applications of Machine Learning Python Libraries for Data Science

Soly Mathew Biju
University of Wollongong in Dubai, UAE

Ashutosh Mishra
Yonsei University, South Korea

Manoj Kumar
University of Wollongong in Dubai, UAE

A volume in the Advances in
Computational Intelligence and
Robotics (ACIR) Book Series

Published in the United States of America by
IGI Global
Engineering Science Reference (an imprint of IGI Global)
701 E. Chocolate Avenue
Hershey PA, USA 17033
Tel: 717-533-8845
Fax: 717-533-8661
E-mail: cust@igi-global.com
Web site: http://www.igi-global.com

Library of Congress Cataloging-in-Publication Data

Names: Biju, Soly, 1976- editor. | Mishra, Ashutosh, 1986- editor. | Kumar, Manoj, 1986- editor.
Title: Advanced interdisciplinary applications of machine learning Python libraries for data science / edited by Soly Biju, Ashutosh Mishra, Manoj Kumar.
Description: Hershey, PA : Engineering Science Reference, [2023] | Includes bibliographical references and index. | Summary: "This book will help emerging data scientist to gain hands on skills needed through real world data and completely up to date Python code. This book covers all the technical details right from installing the needed software to importing libraries and using latest data sets, deciding on the right model, training and testing, evaluation of the model. It will also cover NumPy, Pandas and matplotlib. It covers various machine learning like Regression, linear and logical Regression, Classification, SVM (support Vector Machine), clustering, KNearest Neighbor, Market basket analysis, Apriori, K Means clustering, Visualization using Seaborne. None of the existing books in the field covers all the essential algorithms with practical implementation and code in Python with all needed libraries and provides links to datasets used"-- Provided by publisher.
Identifiers: LCCN 2023017275 (print) | LCCN 2023017276 (ebook) | ISBN 9781668486962 (h/c) | ISBN 9781668486979 (s/c) | ISBN 9781668486986 (eISBN)
Subjects: LCSH: Python (Computer program language) | Quantitative research--Data processing. | Computer programming. | Machine learning.
Classification: LCC QA76.73.P98 A375 2023 (print) | LCC QA76.73.P98 (ebook) | DDC 005.13/3--dc23/eng/20230911
LC record available at https://lccn.loc.gov/2023017275
LC ebook record available at https://lccn.loc.gov/2023017276

This book is published in the IGI Global book series Advances in Computational Intelligence and Robotics (ACIR) (ISSN: 2327-0411; eISSN: 2327-042X)

British Cataloguing in Publication Data
A Cataloguing in Publication record for this book is available from the British Library.
All work contributed to this book is new, previously-unpublished material.

The views expressed in this book are those of the authors, but not necessarily of the publisher.
For electronic access to this publication, please contact: eresources@igi-global.com.

Advances in Computational Intelligence and Robotics (ACIR) Book Series

Ivan Giannoccaro
University of Salento, Italy

ISSN:2327-0411
EISSN:2327-042X

MISSION

While intelligence is traditionally a term applied to humans and human cognition, technology has progressed in such a way to allow for the development of intelligent systems able to simulate many human traits. With this new era of simulated and artificial intelligence, much research is needed in order to continue to advance the field and also to evaluate the ethical and societal concerns of the existence of artificial life and machine learning.

The **Advances in Computational Intelligence and Robotics (ACIR) Book Series** encourages scholarly discourse on all topics pertaining to evolutionary computing, artificial life, computational intelligence, machine learning, and robotics. ACIR presents the latest research being conducted on diverse topics in intelligence technologies with the goal of advancing knowledge and applications in this rapidly evolving field.

COVERAGE

- Neural Networks
- Synthetic Emotions
- Computational Intelligence
- Pattern Recognition
- Heuristics
- Adaptive and Complex Systems
- Algorithmic Learning
- Cyborgs
- Computer Vision
- Computational Logic

IGI Global is currently accepting manuscripts for publication within this series. To submit a proposal for a volume in this series, please contact our Acquisition Editors at Acquisitions@igi-global.com or visit: http://www.igi-global.com/publish/.

Titles in this Series

Handbook of Research on Thrust Technologies' Effect on Image Processing
Binay Kumar Pandey (Department of Information Technology, College of Technology, Govind Ballabh Pant University of Agriculture and Technology, India) Digvijay Pandey (Department of Technical Education, Government of Uttar Pradesh, India) Rohit Anand (G.B. Pant DSEU Okhla-1 Campus, India & Government of NCT of Delhi, New Delhi, India) Deepak S. Mane (Performance Engineering Lab, Tata Research, Development, and Design Center, Australia) and Vinay Kumar Nassa (Rajarambapu Institute of Technology, India)
Engineering Science Reference • © 2023 • 542pp • H/C (ISBN: 9781668486184) • US $350.00

Multi-Disciplinary Applications of Fog Computing Responsiveness in Real-Time
Debi Prasanna Acharjya (Vellore Institute of Technology, India) and Kauser Ahmed P. (Vellore Institute of Technology, India)
Engineering Science Reference • © 2023 • 280pp • H/C (ISBN: 9781668444665) • US $270.00

Global Perspectives on Robotics and Autonomous Systems Development and Applications
Maki K. Habib (The American University in Cairo, Egypt)
Engineering Science Reference • © 2023 • 405pp • H/C (ISBN: 9781668477915) • US $360.00

Stochastic Processes and Their Applications in Artificial Intelligence
Christo Ananth (Samarkand State University, Uzbekistan) N. Anbazhagan (Alagappa University, India) and Mark Goh (National University of Singapore, Singapore)
Engineering Science Reference • © 2023 • 220pp • H/C (ISBN: 9781668476796) • US $270.00

Handbook of Research on Deep Learning Techniques for Cloud-Based Industrial IoT
P. Swarnalatha (Department of Information Security, School of Computer Science and Engineering, Vellore Institute of Technology, India) and S. Prabu (Department Banking Technology, Pondicherry University, India)
Engineering Science Reference • © 2023 • 432pp • H/C (ISBN: 9781668480984) • US $335.00

701 East Chocolate Avenue, Hershey, PA 17033, USA
Tel: 717-533-8845 x100 • Fax: 717-533-8661
E-Mail: cust@igi-global.com • www.igi-global.com

Table of Contents

Chapter 11

Detailed Table of Contents

Chapter 1
An Exploration of Python Libraries in Machine Learning Models for Data

Jawahar Sundaram, CHRIST University (Deemed), India
K. Gowri, Sri Ramakrishna College of Arts and Science, India
S. Devaraju, VIT Bhopal University, India
S. Gokuldev, Rathinam College of Arts and Science, India
Sujith Jayaprakash, BlueCrest University College, Ghana
Harishchander Anandaram, Amrita Vishwa Vidyapeetham, India
C. Manivasagan, Rathnavel Subramaniam College of Arts and Science, India
M. Thenmozhi, Sri Eshwar College of Engineering, India

Python libraries are used in this chapter to create data science models. Data science is the construction of models that can predict and act on data, which is a subset of machine learning. Data science is an essential component of a number of fields because of the exponential growth of data. Python is a popular programming language for implementing machine learning models. The chapter discusses machine learning's role in data science, Python's role in this field, as well as how Python can be utilized. A breast cancer dataset is used as a data source for building machine learning models using Python libraries. Pandas, numpy, matplotlib, seaborn, scikit-learn, and tensorflow are some Python libraries discussed in this chapter, in addition to data preprocessing methods. A number of machine learning models for breast cancer treatment are discussed using this dataset and Python libraries. A discussion of machine learning's future in data science is provided at the conclusion of the chapter. Python libraries for machine learning are very useful for data scientists and researchers in general.

Chapter 2
Interdisciplinary Application of Machine Learning, Data Science, and Python
for Cricket Analytics 32
Haseeb Imdad, National Textile University, Pakistan
Haseeb Ahmad, National Textile University, Pakistan

The chapter explores the use of machine learning, data science, and Python in the context of cricket analytics. It highlights the importance of interdisciplinary collaboration and its potential to enhance the accuracy and speed of cricket analytics. It discusses the various data sources that can be used for cricket analytics and how machine learning algorithms can extract valuable insights. The chapter also provides an overview of various Python libraries commonly used in cricket analytics and explains how they can be used for data cleaning, feature engineering, and model building. Additionally, the chapter discusses the challenges and limitations of cricket analytics and provides suggestions for future research directions.

Chapter 3
Application of Machine Learning for Disabled Persons.....................................78
Rajeshri Shinkar, Sies (Nerul) College of ASC, Mumbai University, India

Communication with the disabled person who is deaf-mute person is very difficult. Even though sign language is crucial for deaf-mute persons to communicate with other people and with themselves, regular people still pay it little attention. Normal people often overlook the value of sign language unless they have family members who are deaf-mute. Using sign language interpreters is one way to communicate with those who are deaf-mute. However, hiring sign language interpreters can be expensive. A model that can automatically convert their motions into words can be used as a low-cost replacement for the interpreters. This chapter gives the description about the development of a model which helps automatic detection of actions with real time using the Mediapipe model and then with the help of sign language conversion model it translates into the textual format.

Chapter 4
Performing Facial Recognition Using Ensemble Learning 89
Layton Chetty, University of Wollongong in Dubai, UAE
Abshir Odowa, University of Wollongong in Dubai, UAE
Aeron Christler Avenido, University of Wollongong in Dubai, UAE
Ismail Hussein, University of Wollongong in Dubai, UAE
Yassin Elakkad, University of Wollongong in Dubai, UAE

Investment in facial recognition technologies has increased recently with the amount of venture capital invested in facial recognition startups dramatically increasing in 2021. Facial recognition uses AI and ML techniques to find human faces in the surrounding area. Facial recognition technology is used by the web application Automated Attendance System (AAS) which was developed by a group of students from the University of Wollongong in Dubai to automate attendance management in educational institutions. AAS is simple to use, quick to implement, and can be incorporated into current educational institutions. Deep convolutional neural networks, notably the VGG19 and EfficientNetB0 models, are the foundation of the system. These models were trained for high accuracy utilizing transfer learning and ensemble learning. The automation of attendance tracking reduces human error; increases efficiency, accuracy, and integrity; and does away with the need for manual methods of collecting attendance.

Chapter 5

Shiv Nath Chaudhri, Santhiram Engineering College, India
Ashutosh Mishra, Yonsei University, South Korea
Navin Singh Rajput, Indian Institute of Technology (BHU), India

Advanced data-driven approaches have transformed the development of intelligent systems, gaining recognition from researchers and industrialists. Data plays a critical role in shaping intelligent systems, including artificial olfaction systems (AOS). AOS has evolved from manual feature extraction to leveraging artificial neural networks (ANNs) and convolutional neural networks (CNNs) for automated feature extraction. This chapter comprehensively overviews the synergy between data-driven approaches and CNNs in intelligent AOS. CNNs have significantly improved the accuracy and efficiency of scent and odor detection in AOS by automating feature extraction. Exploiting abundant data and leveraging CNN capabilities can enhance AOS performance. However, challenges and opportunities remain, requiring further research and development for optimal utilization of data-driven approaches in intelligent AOS.

Chapter 6

Mohammed Furqanuddin Siddiqui, University of Wollongong in Dubai, UAE
Gaurav Gulshan Awatramani, University of Wollongong in Dubai, UAE
Cyril Kunjumon Daniel, University of Wollongong in Dubai, UAE
Rahul Manwani, University of Wollongong in Dubai, UAE
Shwetha Shaji, University of Wollongong in Dubai, UAE

One of the leading causes of early death nowadays is smoking. There are many applications available to assist individuals quit smoking, but many are inefficient as they require a lot of user involvement. These programs rely on the user to consistently track their smoking lapses and evaluate their success, which is quite unpleasant and demanding for the user. JustQuit is an application that has been developed for smokers who are motivated to quit. The application's goal is to assist users in effectively quitting smoking by automatically identifying their smoking behavior using a machine learning approach and lowering reliance on the user to monitor their progress. The application offers a novel approach to this issue by gathering data from wearable sensors and utilizing machine learning techniques to predict the user's smoking habit. The software will include elements like a points system, awards, and achievements based on the user's successes acting as a motivation factor.

Chapter 7
Zain Syed, University of Wollongong in Dubai, UAE
Omar Taher, University of Wollongong in Dubai, UAE

Email is one of the cheapest forms of communication that every internet user utilizes, from individuals to businesses. Because of its simplicity and wide availability, it is vulnerable to threats by perpetrators through spam with malicious intents, known to have resulted in huge financial losses and threatened the privacy of millions of individuals. Not all spam emails are malicious; however, they are a nuisance to users regardless. Because of these reasons, there is a dire need for good spam detection systems that are automatically able to identify emails as spam. This chapter aims to do exactly that by proposing a Naïve Bayes approach to create a spam detection system by using a combination of the Enron Email dataset and the 419 fraud dataset. The datasets are lemmatized in order to boost performance in terms of execution time and accuracy. Grid search is one technique adopted to maximize accuracy. Finally, the model is evaluated through various metrics and a comparative analysis is performed.

Chapter 8
Maryam Zia, University of Wollongong in Dubai, UAE
Hiba Gohar, University of Wollongong in Dubai, UAE

Brain tumors make up 85% to 90% of all primary central nervous system (CNS) malignancies. Over a thousand people are diagnosed with cancer each year, and brain tumors are one of those fatal illnesses. It is challenging to diagnose this because of the intricate anatomy of the brain. Medical image processing is expanding rapidly today as it aids in the diagnosis and treatment of illnesses. Initially, a limited dataset was utilized to develop a support vector machine (SVM) model for the classification of brain tumors. The tumors were classified as either present or absent. As the dataset was small, the SVM model achieved great accuracy. To increase the dataset's size, data augmentation, an image pre-processing technique was used. Due to the SVM's limitations in producing high accuracy over a large dataset, convolutional neural network (CNN) was used to produce a more accurate model. Using both SVM and CNN aided in drawing comparisons between deep learning techniques and conventional machine learning techniques. MRI scans were used for tumor classification using the mentioned models.

Chapter 9
Chaitali Choudhary, University of Petroleum and Energy Studies, India
Inder Singh, University of Petroleum and Energy Studies, India
Soly Mathew Biju, University of Wollongong in Dubai, UAE
Manoj Kumar, University of Wollongong in Dubai, UAE

Community detection in social network analysis is crucial for understanding network structure and organization. It helps identify cohesive groups of nodes, allowing for targeted analysis and interventions. Girvan-Newman, Walktrap, and Louvain are popular algorithms used for community detection. Girvan-Newman focuses on betweenness centrality, Walktrap uses random walks, and Louvain optimizes modularity. Experimental results show that the label propagation algorithm (LPA) is efficient in extracting community structures. LPA has linear time complexity and does not require prior specification of the number of communities. However, it focuses on characterizing the number of communities rather than labeling them. K-clique performs well when the number of communities is known in advance. Louvain excels in modularity and community identification. Overall, community detection algorithms are essential for understanding network structures and functional units.

Chapter 10
Python Libraries Implementation for Brain Tumor Detection Using MR
Eman Younis, Minia University, Egypt
Mahmoud N. Mahmoud, Minia University, Egypt
Ibrahim A. Ibrahim, Minia University, Egypt

Cancer is the major cause of death after cardiovascular infections. In comparison to other sorts of cancer, brain cancer has the lowest survival rate. Brain tumors have many types depending on their shape and location. Diagnosis of the tumor class empowers the specialist to decide the optimal treatment and can help save lives. Over the past years, researchers started investigating deep learning for medical disease diagnosis. A few of them are concentrated on optimizing deep neural networks for enhancing the performance of conventional neural networks. This involves incorporating different network architectures which are obtained by arranging their hyperparameters. The proposed idea of this chapter is concerned in providing implementation details of solutions for the problem of classifying brain tumors using classical and hybrid approaches combining convolutional neural networks CNN with classical machine learning. The authors assessed the proposed models using MRI brain tumor data set of three types of brain tumors (meningiomas, gliomas, and pituitary tumors).

Chapter 11

Mariana Marchenko, University of Wollongong in Dubai, UAE
Sandro Samaha, University of Wollongong in Dubai, UAE

Random forest regression is an ensemble, supervised learning algorithm capable of executing both classification and regression. Within this report, the use of the following algorithm will be implemented on an earthquake dataset which consists of all recorded occurrences of earthquakes from 1930 to 2018. Certain columns from the database will be used as target variables such as magnitude and depth to predict the following outcome based on trained data. Hyper parameter tuning will be performed to maximize the model's performance by increasing its accuracy, decreasing errors, and ensuring efficiency. The parameter in this model that contributed to the efficiency while performing hyper parameter tuning was number of estimators. Findings from the research report concluded that the model's accuracy levels were approximately 75%. Despite increasing the number of trees used, the model's accuracy did not significantly change and improve but rather significantly slowed down the run-time.

Preface

In this rapidly evolving age of information, the power of data has become undeniable. The ability to harness big data for gaining new insights and making informed decisions has transformed from a luxury to a necessity. As the demand for data-driven solutions continues to surge, the role of data analysts and data scientists has never been more critical. To meet the growing expectations and deliver quick and valuable results to clients, it is essential to have access to efficient and appropriate tools that facilitate cutting-edge data analysis.

This edited reference book, *Advanced Interdisciplinary Applications of Machine Learning Python Libraries for Data Science*, edited by Soly Mathew Biju, Ashutosh Mishra, and Manoj Kumar, fills a significant gap in the field of data science literature. It aims to provide aspiring and emerging data scientists with hands-on skills, combining real-world data with up-to-date Python code to address the challenges of the modern data landscape.

Comprehensive in its scope, this book covers all technical aspects, starting from the installation of necessary software to the importing of libraries and usage of the latest datasets. Its coverage spans a wide array of topics, including NumPy, Pandas, and matplotlib. The authors delve into various machine learning algorithms, such as Regression, Linear and Logical Regression, Classification, Support Vector Machine (SVM), Clustering, K-Nearest Neighbor, Market Basket Analysis, Apriori, K Means Clustering, and Visualization using Seaborn.

One of the distinguishing features of this book is its emphasis on practical implementation and Python code. Unlike existing resources in the field, it integrates essential algorithms with detailed examples and step-by-step Python implementations, along with references to the datasets used. Whether you are an academic researcher, an undergraduate or postgraduate student, an MBA or executive education participant, or a seasoned practitioner, this book serves as a comprehensive one-stop resource for mastering the foundations of data science.

With a focus on machine learning, model building, model evaluation, visualization, Python code for data science, and relevant datasets, this book equips readers with the necessary tools and knowledge to become proficient data scientists. It bridges the gap between theory and practice, guiding readers towards a deeper understanding of data analysis and its applications.

CHAPTER OVERVIEW

Chapter 1 explores the fundamental role of machine learning in data science and how Python plays a crucial role in this field. It emphasizes the importance of efficient Python libraries for data science, such as Pandas, NumPy, Matplotlib, Seaborn, scikit-learn, and TensorFlow. The focus is on building machine learning models using Python libraries with a specific dataset related to breast cancer. Readers will learn about various machine learning models utilized for breast cancer treatment, from data preprocessing to model evaluation. The chapter concludes with a glimpse into the future of machine learning in data science.

In Chapter 2, the editors explore the interdisciplinary collaboration of machine learning, data science, and Python in the context of cricket analytics. The chapter discusses the data sources available for cricket analytics and the application of machine learning algorithms to extract valuable insights. Readers will gain an understanding of the Python libraries commonly used in cricket analytics, enabling them to clean data, engineer features, and build models effectively. The challenges and future research directions in cricket analytics are also highlighted.

Chapter 3 focuses on addressing the difficulties faced in communicating with deaf-mute individuals. It introduces a model that automatically detects sign language gestures in real-time using the Mediapipe model and then translates them into textual format with the help of a sign language conversion model. This technology provides a low-cost alternative to sign language interpreters, making communication more accessible for the deaf-mute community.

Chapter 4 delves into the increasing investment in facial recognition technologies and their application in an Automated Attendance System (AAS). The chapter presents an innovative web application developed by students to automate attendance management in educational institutions. The system utilizes deep convolutional neural networks, particularly the VGG19 and EfficientNetB0 models, trained using transfer learning and ensemble learning. Readers will learn how facial recognition technology can improve attendance tracking efficiency, accuracy, and integrity, eliminating the need for manual methods.

Chapter 5 explores the synergy between data-driven approaches and Convolutional Neural Networks (CNNs) in intelligent Artificial Olfaction Systems (AOS). The editors emphasize how CNNs have significantly improved scent and odor detection in AOS by automating feature extraction. Abundant data and leveraging CNN capabilities enhance AOS performance, but challenges and opportunities remain, requiring further research and development.

Chapter 6 addresses the issue of smoking cessation and presents an application called JustQuit, aimed at assisting users in quitting smoking. The application utilizes wearable sensors and machine learning techniques to predict a user's smoking habit automatically. Through a points system, awards, and achievements, the application motivates users to quit smoking effectively.

Chapter 7 proposes a spam detection system using a Naïve Bayes approach that combines the Enron Email dataset and the 419 Fraud dataset. The chapter outlines the process of lemmatizing the datasets to boost performance and adopts Grid Search for maximizing accuracy. The model's performance is evaluated through various metrics, and a comparative analysis is conducted.

Chapter 8 focuses on brain tumor classification, utilizing Support Vector Machine (SVM) models initially and then incorporating Convolutional Neural Networks (CNNs) for improved accuracy. The editors discuss the challenges of diagnosing brain tumors due to the intricate anatomy of the brain. Readers will gain insights into how machine learning models can enhance brain tumor classification using MRI scans.

Chapter 9 explores the significance of community detection in social network analysis, helping identify cohesive groups of nodes for targeted analysis and interventions. The chapter discusses various algorithms used for community detection, including Girvan-Newman, Walktrap, Louvain, Label Propagation Algorithm (LPA), and K-clique, along with their respective strengths and limitations.

In Chapter 10, the editors present solutions for classifying brain tumors using a combination of Convolutional Neural Networks (CNN) and classical Machine Learning techniques. The chapter discusses the implementation details of the proposed models and evaluates their performance using MRI brain tumor datasets.

Chapter 11 explores the use of Random Forest Regression, an ensemble supervised learning algorithm, to predict outcomes in earthquake datasets. The chapter emphasizes hyperparameter tuning to optimize model performance in terms of accuracy and execution time. Readers will gain insights into how Random Forest Regression can be applied in the context of earthquake prediction.

These chapters collectively provide a comprehensive overview of the advanced interdisciplinary applications of machine learning Python libraries for data science, covering a wide range of real-world scenarios and cutting-edge techniques. It is our hope that this edited reference book serves as a valuable resource for data scientists, researchers, and practitioners in their pursuit of knowledge and excellence in the field of data science and machine learning.

As editors of this valuable resource, we are confident that it will serve as a reliable companion in your journey towards mastering the interdisciplinary applications of machine learning in data science. The knowledge contained within these pages is designed to empower you to take on the challenges of a data-driven world and drive meaningful insights to shape a better future.

Soly Mathew Biju
University of Wollongong in Dubai, UAE

Ashutosh Mishra
Yonsei University, South Korea

Manoj Kumar
University of Wollongong in Dubai, UAE

Chapter 1

An Exploration of Python Libraries in Machine Learning Models for Data Science

Jawahar Sundaram
 https://orcid.org/0000-0002-8101-8725
CHRIST University (Deemed), India

Sujith Jayaprakash
 https://orcid.org/0000-0003-1933-6922
BlueCrest University College, Ghana

K. Gowri
Sri Ramakrishna College of Arts and Science, India

Harishchander Anandaram
 https://orcid.org/0000-0003-2993-5304
Amrita Vishwa Vidyapeetham, India

S. Devaraju
 https://orcid.org/0000-0003-3116-4772
VIT Bhopal University, India

C. Manivasagan
Rathnavel Subramaniam College of Arts and Science, India

S. Gokuldev
 https://orcid.org/0000-0001-8393-4674
Rathinam College of Arts and Science, India

M. Thenmozhi
 https://orcid.org/0009-0002-0846-2325
Sri Eshwar College of Engineering, India

ABSTRACT

Python libraries are used in this chapter to create data science models. Data science is the construction of models that can predict and act on data, which is a subset of machine learning. Data science is an essential component of a number of fields because of the exponential growth of data. Python is a popular programming language for implementing machine learning models. The chapter discusses machine

DOI: 10.4018/978-1-6684-8696-2.ch001

learning's role in data science, Python's role in this field, as well as how Python can be utilized. A breast cancer dataset is used as a data source for building machine learning models using Python libraries. Pandas, numpy, matplotlib, seaborn, scikit-learn, and tensorflow are some Python libraries discussed in this chapter, in addition to data preprocessing methods. A number of machine learning models for breast cancer treatment are discussed using this dataset and Python libraries. A discussion of machine learning's future in data science is provided at the conclusion of the chapter. Python libraries for machine learning are very useful for data scientists and researchers in general.

1. INTRODUCTION

The process of data mining (DM) involves the preparation of data from different sources, such as databases, text files, streams, as well as the modeling of that data using a variety of techniques, depending on the goal that one is trying to achieve, such as classification, clustering, regression, association rule mining. The use of machine learning (ML) techniques in DM enables the discovery of new knowledge in the organization. Data preparation is a part of data analysis which includes preprocessing and manipulating the data as part of the analysis process. There are many aspects involved with data preprocessing, such as cleaning, integrating, transforming and reducing raw data to make it more suitable for analysis, and there are other aspects involved in data wrangling, which is a process of taking the preprocessed data and changing its format so that it can be easily modelled.

Machine learning has grown rapidly in the past few years, and today there are many types and subtypes of machine learning. In the field of machine learning, you are studying what makes computers capable of learning on their own without the need to be explicitly programmed. Using this method, it is possible to solve problems that cannot be solved numerically. Machine learning models can either be classified, grouped, or regressed depending on the purpose they are intended to serve. A linear regression model is used to understand the relationship between the inputs and the outputs of a project's numerical values.

There are many classification models that can be used to identify a particular post's sentiment. An individual's review can be classified as either positive or negative based on the words used in it. Using these models, it is possible to classify emails as spam or not based on their contents. Using a clustering model, we are able to find objects with characteristics that are similar to each other. ML algorithms in many different parts of the world are used in interesting and interesting ways.

Machine learning is a powerful tool for data scientists to analyze large amounts of data and to develop models to make predictions and decisions. It enables data scientists to automate the process of finding patterns and insights in data, which can be used to improve the efficiency and accuracy of decision-making. Machine learning can also be used to create new products and services. It can be used to automate tasks and improve customer experience. It can also be used to identify new opportunities and reduce costs. By using machine learning algorithms, data scientists can quickly process large amounts of data and find patterns and correlations that would otherwise be difficult to find. This enables them to make more informed decisions and create new products and services that are more tailored to customer needs. Additionally, machine learning can be used to automate mundane tasks, such as customer service, which can help improve customer experience and reduce costs.

The objective of the book chapter is 1. To provide basic understanding of python libraries used in data science for machine learning process, 2. How these libraries is used for analysing biological sequences and 3. To identify differentially expressed gene in the sequence for different predictions.

2. MACHINE LEARNING FRAMEWORK

A machine learning system is a software that is programmed to learn from past experience and improve itself based on what it has learned. In the following section, we will discuss how to apply machine learning to solve a problem using the architecture components that can be seen in figure. Figure 1 illustrates a graphic representation of the typical steps required to construct a machine learning model, which can be seen as a result of the example in the figure. With the use of this framework, one can develop predictive models that can be used in machine learning, data science, and other areas that require predictive modelling.

A training step in the learning process is when the algorithms are tuned based on the collected data that we have already collected. There are two types of data that we use when training our algorithm, the training set and the test data. A learning process is the process of constantly improving our software or machine by learning new things and improving its capabilities.

A data preparation library is a crucial element of data science since it is heavily reliant on data. A very popular library in the field of data science is Python's pandas library, which is among the best there is at the moment (McKinney, 2011). Besides excel and csv, Pandas supports many other formats for input and output data, including Python, HTML, and SQL as well as Excel, CSV, and Python.

Figure 1. Machine learning framework

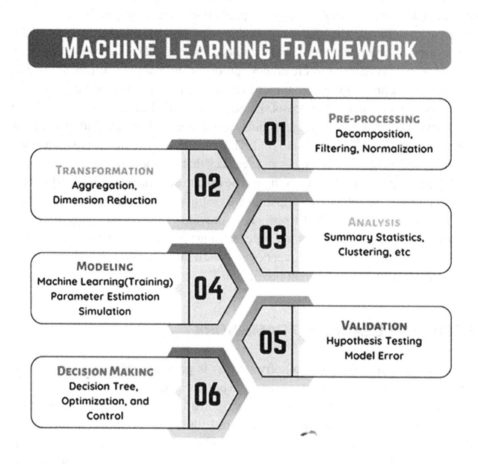

The Pandas package also offers powerful querying capabilities, statistical calculations, and basic visualization tools. It has a lot of documentation on it, but it is most notable for its sometimes-confusing syntax, which may be the most significant issue with this program.

3. PYTHON LIBRARIES OVERVIEW

An Python library is a collection of pre-written code that developers can use to perform a number of standard tasks as opposed to having to write them from scratch from scratch. In order to set up Python libraries, you will need to use a package manager, such as pip or conda (Vanderplas, 2016).

Table 1.

Library Name	Author(s)	Journal Title	Abstract Explanation	Year of Publication
NumPy	Travis Olliphant	Proceedings of the IEEE	NumPy is a fundamental library for scientific computing in Python. It provides powerful data structures and efficient functions for numerical operations, making it an essential tool for data analysis and machine learning tasks.	2006
Pandas	Wes McKinney	arXiv	Pandas is a popular library for data manipulation and analysis. It provides data structures like DataFrames, which allow easy handling of structured data. Pandas also offers a wide range of functions for data cleaning, transformation, and exploration, making it a valuable tool for data scientists.	2010
Scikit-learn	Fabian Pedregosa et al.	Journal of Machine Learning Research	Scikit-learn is a versatile machine learning library in Python. It provides a unified interface for various machine learning algorithms and tools for data preprocessing, model selection, and evaluation. With a large collection of algorithms and extensive documentation, Scikit-learn is widely used for building machine learning models.	2011
TensorFlow	Martin Abadi et al.	arXiv	TensorFlow is an open-source library developed by Google for numerical computation and machine learning. It offers a flexible framework for building and deploying deep learning models, with support for distributed computing and deployment on various platforms. TensorFlow has gained popularity for its scalability and extensive ecosystem of pre-trained models.	2015
Keras	François Chollet	Journal of Machine Learning Research	Keras is a high-level neural networks API written in Python. It provides a user-friendly interface for building and training deep learning models. Keras allows quick prototyping and experimentation with different architectures, making it a popular choice for both beginners and experienced deep learning practitioners.	2015
PyTorch	Adam Paszke et al.	Advances in Neural Information Processing Systems	PyTorch is a widely used deep learning library known for its dynamic computational graph and efficient GPU acceleration. It offers a seamless development experience with support for automatic differentiation and a flexible design that enables researchers to implement complex deep learning models with ease.	2019
XGBoost	Tianqi Chen et al.	Proceedings of the 22nd ACM SIGKDD International Conference on Knowledge Discovery and Data Mining	XGBoost is an optimized gradient boosting library that excels in solving structured data problems. It provides an implementation of the gradient boosting algorithm with enhanced performance and scalability. XGBoost has won numerous data science competitions and is widely used in various domains.	2016
LightGBM	Guolin Ke et al.	Neural Information Processing Systems	LightGBM is a gradient boosting framework that focuses on efficiency and accuracy. It employs a novel tree-based learning algorithm and offers faster training speeds compared to other gradient boosting implementations. LightGBM is particularly suitable for large-scale datasets and has gained popularity for its competitive performance.	2017

The Python library system can be classified into two different categories: built-in libraries and external libraries. Python is a language that includes built-in libraries, so these libraries do not need to be installed separately from Python. In contrast, third-party libraries are created by third-party developers and must be installed before they can be used (Abadi et al., 2016).

In Python scripts, import statements are used to include Python libraries, and these libraries are written as .py files, which are used to store them in Python scripts. Whenever a library is imported, its classes, functions, and variables are available to the script in order to make use of them (Chollet, 2017).

The Python programming language supports a variety of libraries that are useful for data analysis and visualization, web development, machine learning, and scientific computing. Some of the popular Python libraries are represented in Figure 2.

Figure 2. Different python libraries

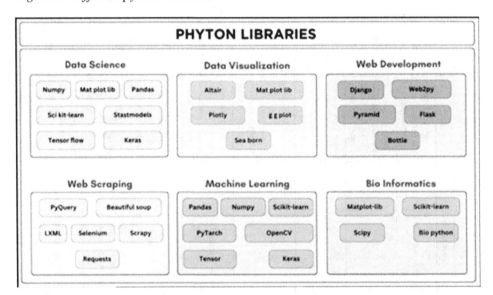

As shown in Figure 2, Python libraries are shown in a graphical representation that illustrates the different ways they can be used. There are many Python libraries available for use, but this figure shows a brief overview of some of the most common ones.

Table 2.

Library	Real-World Example
NumPy	Scientific computing, numerical operations
Pandas	Data manipulation, analysis, and cleaning
Matplotlib	Data visualization, plotting
TensorFlow	Machine learning, deep learning
Keras	Neural network models, deep learning
Scikit-learn	Machine learning algorithms, model training
NLTK	Natural language processing, text mining
BeautifulSoup	Web scraping, parsing HTML and XML
Django	Web development framework, building web applications
OpenCV	Computer vision, image and video processing
PyTorch	Deep learning, neural networks
PySpark	Distributed computing, big data processing

4. DIFFERENT PYTHON LIBRARIES

A Python programming language is one of the most powerful programming languages available nowadays, and it is used for a wide range of tasks, such as web development, data analysis, and machine learning (Pedregosa et al., 2011). The Python community has developed a broad range of libraries over the years, as a result of which the Python language can perform a wide range of functions much more easily and is more capable than it has ever been.

4.1 Python Libraries Used for Data Science

The Python programming language is one of the most popular languages for data science, and there are many libraries available that can be used for performing machine learning, doing data analysis, and doing other tasks as well. Here are some of the most commonly used libraries for data science in Python:

NumPy

Python's NumPy library is one of the most popular libraries for scientific computations. It is possible to perform mathematical operations on arrays and matrices by using functions available in the library.

Example Code:

```
import numpy as np
# Create a NumPy array of integers
a = np.array([1, 2, 3, 4, 5])
# Create a NumPy array of floating-point numbers
b = np.array([0.1, 0.2, 0.3, 0.4, 0.5])
# Perform some numerical operations on the arrays
c = a + b
d = a * b
e = np.sqrt(a)
# Print the arrays and the results of the operations
print('a:', a)
```

Pandas

Pandas is a Python library that can be used to manipulate and analyze data in a variety of ways. A similar concept can be applied to data structures such as data frames and series, in addition to the functions for cleaning, transforming, and analyzing data that are provided.

Example Code:

```
import pandas as pd
# Create a Pandas DataFrame
df = pd.DataFrame({
    'Name': ['Alice', 'Bob', 'Charlie', 'David'],
    'Age': [25, 32, 18, 47],
    'Gender': ['F', 'M', 'M', 'M'] })
# Print the DataFrame
print(df)
# Filter the DataFrame to only show rows where Age is greater
than 30
df_filtered = df[df['Age'] > 30]
# Print the filtered DataFrame
print(df_filtered)
# Group the DataFrame by Gender and calculate the mean Age for
each group
df_grouped = df.groupby('Gender').agg({'Age': 'mean'})
# Print the grouped DataFrame
print(df_grouped)
```

Matplotlib

The Matplotlib Python library is used to create static visualizations, animated visualizations, and interactive visualizations using Python. It has a wide range of chart types that can be customized, and it supports many formats.

Example Code:

```
import matplotlib.pyplot as plt
# Create some sample data
x = [1, 2, 3, 4, 5]
y = [2, 4, 6, 8, 10]
# Create a line chart
plt.plot(x, y)
# Add some labels and a title
plt.xlabel('X axis')
plt.ylabel('Y axis')
plt.title('Sample line chart')
# Display the chart
plt.show()
```

Scikit-learn

In Python, there is a machine-learning library called scikit-learn, which is part of the scikit-learn library. It supports machine learning algorithms such as classification, regression, and clustering, as well as tools for selecting and evaluating models, as well as tools for selecting and evaluating models.

Example Code:

```
from sklearn.datasets import load_iris
from sklearn.model_selection import train_test_split
from sklearn.tree import DecisionTreeClassifier
# Load the iris dataset
iris = load_iris()
# Split the data into training and testing sets
X_train, X_test, y_train, y_test = train_test_split(iris.data,
iris.target, test_size=0.2)
# Train a decision tree classifier on the training data
clf = DecisionTreeClassifier()
clf.fit(X_train, y_train)
# Test the classifier on the testing data
```

```
accuracy = clf.score(X_test, y_test)
print(f"Accuracy: {accuracy}")
```

TensorFlow

In Python, TensorFlow provides support for a variety of machine learning and deep learning algorithms. A number of tools are included in the program, including tools for evaluating and deploying models, as well as tools for creating and training neural networks.

Example Code:

```
import tensorflow as tf
from tensorflow.keras.datasets import mnist
# Load the MNIST dataset
(x_train, y_train), (x_test, y_test) = mnist.load_data()
# Normalize the data
x_train = x_train / 255.0
x_test = x_test / 255.0
# Create a simple neural network model
model = tf.keras.models.Sequential([
    tf.keras.layers.Flatten(input_shape=(28, 28)),
    tf.keras.layers.Dense(128, activation='relu'),
    tf.keras.layers.Dense(10)])
# Compile the model
model.compile(optimizer='adam',
              loss=tf.keras.losses.SparseCategoricalCrossentrop
y(from_logits=True),
              metrics=['accuracy'])
# Train the model
model.fit(x_train, y_train, epochs=5)
# Evaluate the model on the testing data
test_loss, test_acc = model.evaluate(x_test, y_test, verbose=2)
print(f"Test accuracy: {test_acc}")
```

Keras

Keras is a Python-based high-level neural network library that is used on TensorFlow, Theano, and CNTK platforms to build powerful neural networks. It has an easy-to-use interface that makes the process of building deep learning models a breeze.

Example Code:

```
import numpy as np
import keras
from keras.models import Sequential
from keras.layers import Dense
# Create a toy dataset
X = np.array([[0, 0], [0, 1], [1, 0], [1, 1]])
y = np.array([[0], [1], [1], [0]])
# Create a simple neural network model
model = Sequential()
model.add(Dense(8, input_dim=2, activation='relu'))
model.add(Dense(1, activation='sigmoid'))
# Compile the model
model.compile(loss='binary_crossentropy', optimizer='adam',
metrics=['accuracy'])
# Train the model
model.fit(X, y, epochs=1000, verbose=0)
# Evaluate the model on the training data
scores = model.evaluate(X, y)
print(f"{model.metrics_names[1]}: {scores[1]*100}")
```

Statsmodels

In order to perform statistical modeling and analysis, Statsmodels is a Python library that can be used. Data exploration and visualization tools are included in the package, as well as support for a variety of statistical tests and models that can be used to examine the data.

Example Code:

```
import numpy as np
import statsmodels.api as sm
# Create a toy dataset
x = np.array([0, 1, 2, 3, 4, 5])
y = np.array([1, 3, 2, 5, 7, 8])
# Add a constant to the data for the intercept term
x = sm.add_constant(x)
# Fit a simple linear regression model
model = sm.OLS(y, x).fit()
```

```
# Print the model summary
print(model.summary())
```

There are a number of Python libraries that are available that can be used for data science in Python. As with all libraries, there are strengths and weaknesses, so you should decide which one is best suited to your specific needs based on their strengths and weaknesses (Hunter, 2007).

Table 3.

Library	Description	Key Features
NumPy	Numerical computing libraries such as this one support multi-dimensional arrays and matrix operations in all their forms.	Arrays, mathematical operations, the generation of random numbers, linear algebra, and Fourier analysis are just some of the skills one can acquire through learning and practicing them.
Pandas	A library for data manipulation and analysis. The DataFrame data structure is one of the most flexible and powerful data structures available for handling tabular data very easily.	A number of data processing tasks are involved: preprocessing and cleaning data, exploring and analyzing data, indexing and selecting data, and merging and combining data sets.
Matplotlib	The library provides a wide variety of plots and charts including line plots, scatter plots, bar plots, and histogram plots, as well as the ability to define your own plots and charts.	Plots can be customized in a variety of ways including 3D plots, subplots, animations, and interactive plots, as well as customizable plots and subplots.
Scikit-learn	The machine learning library provides algorithms for supervised learning as well as unsupervised learning.	An array of preprocessing, clustering, classification, regression, dimension reduction, and model selection procedures are included.
TensorFlow	Machine learning models can be built and trained using the Google Machine Learning Platform, which is an open-source platform.	Multi-language support, advanced APIs for developing models at the highest level of abstraction, and automatic differentiation.
Keras	A TensorFlow-based neural network API that can be used to build and train deep learning models at a high level.	Models that have already been trained, easy-to-use APIs, and support for convolutional, recurrent, and dense networks are all included.
Statsmodels	A collection of tests and models for statistical modeling that can be used in a variety of applications.	Modeling linear and generalized linear systems, mixed-effects models, time series analysis, and survival analyses are among the techniques we use.

4.2 Python Libraries Used for Machine Learning

A number of Python libraries are available for machine learning, and Python is a popular programming language for machine learning. Here are some of the most commonly used libraries for machine learning in Python:

Table 4.

Library	Description	Main Use Cases	Programming Language
Scikit-learn	Machine learning library for traditional models	Classification, regression, clustering, etc.	Python
TensorFlow	Deep learning framework	Neural networks, natural language processing	Python, C++, Java
Keras	High-level API for deep learning	Rapid prototyping, easy model building	Python
PyTorch	Deep learning framework	Neural networks, natural language processing	Python
OpenCV	Computer vision library	Image and video processing	C++, Python, Java

4.3 Python Libraries Used for Web Development

Python's extensive ecosystem of libraries and frameworks make it an easy and enjoyable experience to develop websites with Python. Some of the most popular ones are:

Django

In the world of high-level web frameworks, model-view-controller (MVC) is a pattern of architecture that is widely used (Waskom, 2021). The Django framework includes a database access system called ORM that allows you to work with databases, along with a built-in editor that you can use to manage the contents of the site. As one of the most important characteristics of this system, it is fast, secure, and scalable.

Example Code:

```
from django.http import HttpResponse
def index(request):
    return HttpResponse("Hello, world!")
```

Flask

Developers can build web applications quickly using the Flask programming language, since it is flexible and allows them to write code quickly. The framework is designed to be lightweight and easy to use, which makes it a good choice for beginners. Even though it lacks some built-in features, it offers a wide range of extensions that can be installed to customize the interface to meet your own needs.

Example Code:

```
from flask import Flask
app = Flask(__name__)
@app.route('/')
def index():
    return 'Hello, world!'
if __name__ == '__main__':
    app.run()
```

Pyramid

An open source framework that supports a wide range of web applications ranging from small to large in size. This Pyramid is highly customizable, and it adheres to the "Don't Repeat Yourself" (DRY) principle, which means it is extremely flexible. There are a number of features included on the site, such as URL routing, templating, and security.

Example Code:

```
from pyramid.response import Response
from pyramid.view import view_config
@view_config(route_name='home')
def home(request):
    return Response('Hello, world!')
```

Bottle

Using this micro web framework is very simple and easy to do. Using a Bottle application will save you a lot of time and money because it is lightweight, fast, and provides a set of basic features like routing, templating, and data integration that are extremely useful.

Example Code:

```
from bottle import route, run
@route('/')
def index():
    return 'Hello, world!'
if __name__ == '__main__':
    run()
```

Web2py

The framework includes many built-in features, such as an ORM, an admin interface, and a web-based development environment, all of which make it much easier to use. Web2py is a framework based on the MVC architectural pattern, and it is designed to be both scalable and secure.

Example Code:

```
def index():
    return 'Hello, world!'
def user():
return 'User page'
```

The Python language offers a wide variety of libraries and frameworks for web development which are available for free. A different library or framework may be necessary in order to meet the specific requirements of your project.

Table 5.

Framework	Pros	Cons
Django	Powerful built-in features, such as authentication, URL routing, and object-relational mapping (ORM), extensive documentation, and a large community of developers.	Can be overkill for smaller projects, can be difficult to customize, and can have a steep learning curve for beginners.
Flask	Easy to set up and get started, minimal boilerplate code, and a large ecosystem of extensions and plugins.	Limited built-in features, which can lead to more code and setup for larger projects, and requires more manual configuration.
Pyramid	Offers a balance between simplicity and flexibility, provides a wide range of built-in features, and has excellent documentation.	Can be less intuitive to use than other frameworks, and requires more manual configuration for certain tasks.
Bottle	Simple and easy to get started with, requires minimal setup and configuration, and has a small footprint.	Limited built-in features, which can lead to more code for larger projects, and a smaller community of developers.
Web2py	Offers a comprehensive set of built-in features, such as authentication, database abstraction, and web-based IDE, has a simple and intuitive syntax, and is designed to be easy to learn and use.	Can be less flexible than other frameworks, and can have performance issues with large-scale applications.

4.4 Data Visualization

Several libraries for the visualization of data are available in the Python programming language that are popular with data scientists and analysts (Reback & McKinney, 2020; Satyanarayan et al., 2017; Wickham, 2009).

Matplotlib

Data visualization libraries such as Matplotlib allow easy visualization of data with their ease of use and high level of customization. There is a wide range of charts you can create using this library, including line, bar, scatter, and histogram charts, to showcase your data.

Example Code:

```
import matplotlib.pyplot as plt
# Sample data
x = [1, 2, 3, 4, 5]
y = [2, 4, 6, 8, 10]
# Create a plot
plt.plot(x, y)
# Add labels and title
plt.xlabel('X-axis')
plt.ylabel('Y-axis')
plt.title('Sample plot')
# Show the plot
plt.show()
```

Seaborn

Based on the Matplotlib library, Seaborn provides an interface for creating more advanced visualizations of data based on the Seaborn data visualization library. There are a variety of ways to use it, including creating heatmaps, violin plots, data regression plots, and other methods, with which it can be used for exploratory data analysis.

Example Code:

```
import seaborn as sns
import matplotlib.pyplot as plt
# Load the iris dataset
iris = sns.load_dataset("iris")
```

```
# Create a scatter plot of the iris data
sns.scatterplot(data=iris, x="sepal_length", y="sepal_width",
hue="species")
# Show the plot
plt.show()
```

Plotly

Plotly provides a data visualization library that allows you to create online interactive charts and graphs in minutes. It is possible to create scatter plots, line charts, bar charts, as well as visualizations of data in three dimensions, using the program.

Example Code:

```
import plotly.graph_objs as go
# Sample data
x = [1, 2, 3, 4, 5]
y = [2, 4, 6, 8, 10]
# Create a plotly figure
fig = go.Figure(data=go.Scatter(x=x, y=y, mode='markers'))
# Add labels and title
fig.update_layout(title='Sample plot', xaxis_title='X-axis',
yaxis_title='Y-axis')
# Show the plot
fig.show()
```

ggplot

It is a Python implementation of ggplot2 which is one of the most popular R libraries. A data visualization can be created using this program by using a grammar of graphics interfaces, and it is particularly useful for plots that have multiple layers and aspects, and it is also very easy to use.

Example Code:

```
from plotnine import ggplot, aes, geom_point
# Sample data
x = [1, 2, 3, 4, 5]
y = [2, 4, 6, 8, 10]
# Create a plotnine plot
plot = ggplot() + aes(x=x, y=y) + geom_point()
# Add labels and title
```

```
plot += ggplot() + labs(title='Sample plot', x='X-axis', y='Y-
axis')
# Show the plot
plot.draw()
```

Altair

Using Altair's declarative visualization library, you can create an interactive visualization of your data by using its declarative visualization. A wide variety of chart types can be used, such as scatter plots, lines, and heatmaps, and they can all be used in conjunction with a variety of data visualizations to provide dynamic and engaging information.

   Example Code:

```
import altair as alt
from vega_datasets import data
# Load the iris dataset
iris = data.iris()
# Create a scatter plot of the iris data
scatter_plot = alt.Chart(iris).mark_point().encode(
    x='sepalLength',
    y='sepalWidth',
    color='species')
# Show the plot
scatter_plot.show()
```

Table 6.

Library	Popular Charts
Matplotlib	Line charts, bar charts, scatter plots, histograms
Seaborn	Violin plots, box plots, count plots
Plotly	Interactive line charts, scatter plots, bar charts
ggplot	Line charts, bar charts, scatter plots, histograms
Altair	Line charts, bar charts, scatter plots, histograms

4.5 Python Libraries Used for Web Scraping

Python is a programming language that supports several libraries that can be used to retrieve data from websites, which is called web scraping in Python (Cock et al., 2009; Jarvis et al., 2006). Here are some of the most commonly used ones:

Beautiful Soup

Python is used in the Beautiful Soup library to extract information from HTML or XML documents. There is a simple and intuitive interface that makes it easy for users to parse HTML and extract data from its contents.

Example Code:

```
import requests
from bs4 import BeautifulSoup
# Make a request to a web page
page = requests.get('https://en.wikipedia.org/wiki/Python_
(programming_language)')
# Create a Beautiful Soup object
soup = BeautifulSoup(page.content, 'html.parser')
# Find the page title
title = soup.title.string
# Find all the paragraph tags on the page
paragraphs = soup.find_all('p')
# Print the page title and the first paragraph
print(title)
print(paragraphs[0])
```

Scrapy

Scrapy is a Python framework that provides users with a comprehensive set of tools for scraping the web. It is often used for large-scale web scraping projects, in addition to URL management, data extraction, and spider middleware, and is widely used for URL management.

Example Code:

```
import scrapy
class MySpider(scrapy.Spider):
    name = 'myspider'
    start_urls = ['https://en.wikipedia.org/wiki/Python_
```

```
(programming_language)']
    def parse(self, response):
        # Find the page title
        title = response.css('title::text').get()
        # Find all the paragraph tags on the page
        paragraphs = response.css('p::text').getall()
        # Print the page title and the first paragraph
        print(title)
        print(paragraphs[0])
```

Selenium

In Python's Selenium library, web browsers are automatically tested using automated processes. By automating interactions with web pages, such as clicking buttons and completing forms, it can be used for web scraping.

Example Code:

```
from selenium import webdriver
# Create a new Chrome browser instance
browser = webdriver.Chrome('/path/to/chromedriver')
# Navigate to a web page
browser.get('https://en.wikipedia.org/wiki/Python_(programming_
language)')
# Find the page title
title = browser.title
# Find all the paragraph tags on the page
paragraphs = [elem.text for elem in browser.find_elements_by_
tag_name('p')]
# Print the page title and the first paragraph
print(title)
print(paragraphs[0])
# Close the browser
browser.quit()
```

Requests

Requests is a Python library that can be used to make HTTP requests using the Python language. The scraping of websites is accomplished by sending HTTP requests to a site and parsing the HTML or JSON response that is returned.

Example Code:

```
import requests
# Make a GET request to a web page
response = requests.get('https://en.wikipedia.org/wiki/Python_
(programming_language)')
# Print the response status code
print(response.status_code)
# Print the response content
print(response.content)
```

PyQuery

PyQuery is a Python library that is similar to jQuery in many ways. The interface makes it easy to parse and extract data from HTML and XML documents thanks to its simple and intuitive design.

Example Code:

```
from pyquery import PyQuery as pq
# Parse an HTML string
html = '''
<html>
    <head>
        <title>PyQuery Example</title>
    </head>
    <body>
        <h1>PyQuery Example</h1>
        <ul>
            <li>Item 1</li>
            <li>Item 2</li>
            <li>Item 3</li>
        </ul>
    </body>
</html>
'''
doc = pq(html)
# Find the page title
title = doc('title').text()
# Find all•the list items on the page
items = [elem.text for elem in doc('li')]
```

```
# Print the page title and the list items
print(title)
print(items)
```

LXML

Parsing XML and HTML documents is performed using a Python library called LXML, which is written in Python. This library provides many features that can help you work with XML and HTML data in a variety of ways.

Example Code:

```
from lxml import etree
# Parse an XML string
xml = ''
<root>
    <title>LXML Example</title>
    <items>
        <item>Item 1</item>
        <item>Item 2</item>
        <item>Item 3</item>
    </items>
</root>
''
doc = etree.fromstring(xml)
# Find the page title
title = doc.find('title').text
# Find all the list items on the page
items = [elem.text for elem in doc.findall('.//item')]
# Print the page title and the list items
print(title)
print(items)
```

Table 7.

Library	Popular Use Cases
Beautiful Soup	Scraping HTML and XML documents
Selenium	Scraping dynamic web pages, testing web applications
Requests	Scraping JSON and XML APIs
PyQuery	Scraping HTML and XML documents
LXML	Scraping HTML and XML documents

4.6 Python Libraries Used for Bioinformatics

Biopython

Biopython is a library for Python that provides an extensive set of tools for doing bioinformatics tasks. It can be used for a variety of bioinformatics tasks, including the analysis of sequences, the analysis of protein structures, as well as parsing of most common file formats.

SciPy

The SciPy library is one of the Python libraries that can be used for scientific computations. There are various bioinformatics tasks that can be carried out with it, including statistical analysis, optimization, and signal processing.

Table 8.

Library	Popular Use Cases
Biopython	DNA and protein sequence analysis, structure prediction and analysis, phylogenetics
SciPy	Statistical analysis, machine learning, data visualization
scikit-learn	Predictive modeling, data analysis, pattern recognition
Matplotlib	Data visualization, publication-quality figures

5. CANCER DNA SEQUENCE USING PYTHON LIBRARIES

Machine learning models are used to analyze large datasets to identify patterns and trends in the data that can be used to make predictions about the risk of breast cancer. The models are trained on the data to recognize characteristics associated with the disease. These predictions can help doctors make more accurate diagnoses and improve treatment decisions. Additionally, machine learning models can identify risk factors that may not have been previously known. Machine learning models can also be used to monitor a patient's condition over time, allowing doctors to detect changes that may indicate a worsening of the disease. This can be used to adjust treatment plans accordingly and improve patient outcomes (McKinney, 2012; Reback et al., 2020; Rossant, 2014).

As we will be implementing this sequence in Jupyter Notebook, we will first import the necessary libraries in order to create the sequence using the dataset in order to create the breast cancer sequence. The Breast Cancer Wisconsin (Diagnostic) Data Set will be used with Scikit-Learn as it makes use of the Scikit-Learn library.

Comparative analysis of python libraries including other sources:

Table 9.

Library	Pros	Cons
NumPy	Efficient numerical operations, multi-dimensional arrays, broadcasting capabilities	Steeper learning curve for beginners, limited support for string manipulation
pandas	Powerful data manipulation and analysis, easy integration with other libraries	Memory-intensive for large datasets, slower performance compared to NumPy for numerical computations
Matplotlib	Flexible data visualization options, extensive customization capabilities	Complex syntax for certain plot types, limited interactivity compared to other libraries
seaborn	Simplified syntax for statistical visualization, aesthetically pleasing default styles	Limited customization options, may require additional libraries for advanced plotting features
scikit-learn	Comprehensive machine learning algorithms and tools, well-documented API	Limited support for deep learning, may require additional libraries for advanced techniques
TensorFlow	Powerful deep learning framework, support for neural networks, distributed computing	Steeper learning curve, verbosity in certain operations, limited support for non-neural network models
Keras	User-friendly deep learning library, easy model prototyping, seamless integration with TensorFlow	Less flexibility for complex model architectures, slower performance compared to TensorFlow
PyTorch	Dynamic computational graph, support for neural networks, strong community support	Limited deployment options compared to TensorFlow, slower performance on certain tasks
SQLAlchemy	Database abstraction layer, supports multiple database systems, ORM capabilities	Steeper learning curve for complex queries, some performance overhead compared to raw SQL
Django	Full-featured web framework, built-in authentication and admin interface, scalable	Relatively heavy, may not be suitable for smaller projects or microservices

Code to import the necessary libraries and load the dataset:

```
import pandas as pd
import numpy as np
import matplotlib.pyplot as plt
```

```
import seaborn as sns
from sklearn.datasets import load_breast_cancer
cancer = load_breast_cancer()
df_cancer = pd.DataFrame(np.c_[cancer['data'],
cancer['target']],
                          columns = np.append(cancer['feature_
names'],'target']))
df_cancer.shape
sns.countplot(df_cancer['target'])
```

Figure 3.

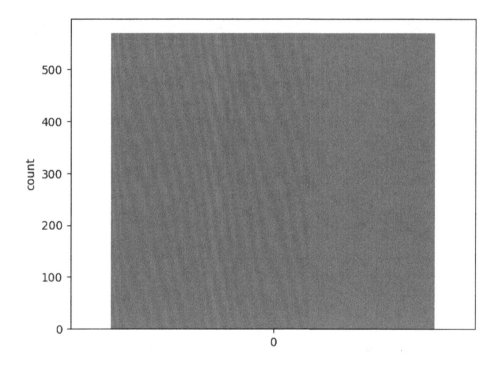

```
plt.figure(figsize=(20,10))
sns.heatmap(df_cancer.corr(), annot=True)
```

Figure 4.

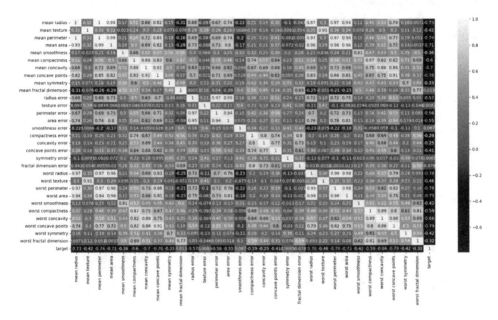

```
from sklearn.model_selection import train_test_split
from sklearn.svm import SVC
X = df_cancer.drop(['target'], axis = 1)
y = df_cancer['target']
X_train, X_test, y_train, y_test = train_test_split(X, y, test_
size = 0.2, random_state = 5)
svc_model = SVC()
svc_model.fit(X_train, y_train)
from sklearn.metrics import classification_report, confusion_
matrix
y_predict = svc_model.predict(X_test)
cm = confusion_matrix(y_test, y_predict)
sns.heatmap(cm, annot=True)
```

Figure 5.

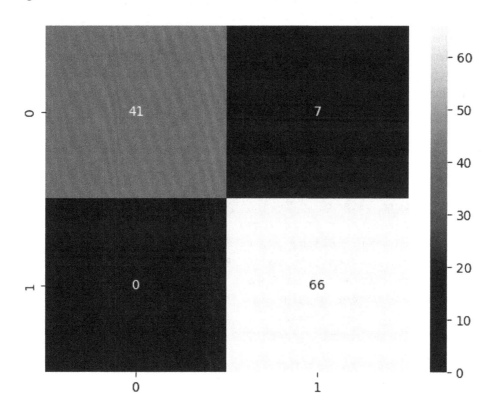

```
print(classification_report(y_test, y_predict))
```

Table 6.

	Precision	Recall	F1-Score	Support
0.0	1.00	0.85	0.92	48
1.0	0.90	1.00	0.95	66
accuracy			0.94	114
macro avg	0.95	0.93	0.94	114
weighted avg	0.94	0.94	0.94	114

breast cancer dataset differential gene analysis:

In this code, we first load the breast cancer dataset and normalize the data using the StandardScaler function from scikit-learn. We then perform principal component analysis (PCA) to reduce the dimensionality of the data to 2, and filter for differentially expressed genes using the mean and quantile functions from pandas. Finally, we perform clustering analysis using the KMeans function from scikit-learn and visualize the results using seaborn.

```python
# Import libraries
import pandas as pd
import numpy as np
import matplotlib.pyplot as plt
import seaborn as sns
from sklearn.datasets import load_breast_cancer
from sklearn.preprocessing import StandardScaler
from sklearn.decomposition import PCA
from sklearn.cluster import KMeans
# Load breast cancer dataset
cancer = load_breast_cancer()
df = pd.DataFrame(cancer['data'], columns=cancer['feature_
names'])
# Normalize data
scaler = StandardScaler()
scaled_data = scaler.fit_transform(df)
# Perform PCA to reduce dimensions
pca = PCA(n_components=2)
pca_data = pca.fit_transform(scaled_data)
# Filter for differentially expressed genes
diff_exp_genes = df.columns[df.mean() > df.mean().
quantile(0.75)]
# Perform clustering analysis
kmeans = KMeans(n_clusters=2)
kmeans.fit(pca_data)
# Visualize results
plt.figure(figsize=(10, 5))
plt.subplot(1, 2, 1)
sns.scatterplot(x=pca_data[:, 0], y=pca_data[:, 1],
hue=cancer['target'], palette='coolwarm')
plt.title('Actual Labels')
plt.subplot(1, 2, 2)
sns.scatterplot(x=pca_data[:, 0], y=pca_data[:, 1], hue=kmeans.
```

```
labels_, palette='coolwarm')
plt.title('K-Means Clustering')
plt.show()
```

Figure 6.

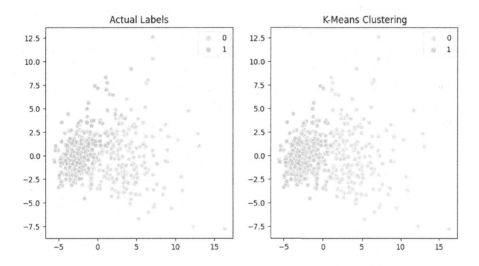

The challenges and limitations of using Python libraries in machine learning models:

Scalability: When it comes to the scaling of machine learning applications, Python's Global Interpreter Lock (GIL) can be one of the biggest limitations. A GIL ensures that only one thread can execute Python bytecode at a time. This can hamper parallel execution and limit the use of multi-core processors because the GIL ensures that only one thread can execute Python bytecode at a time. Thus, Python may not be the most efficient choice for highly parallelizable tasks, although there are workarounds such as using multiprocessing and offloading intensive computations to a lower-level language in cases where this is possible.

Hardware acceleration support is limited: Python libraries like TensorFlow, PyTorch, and scikit-learn provide interfaces for utilizing hardware acceleration frameworks such as CUDA for GPUs, as well as Python libraries like TensorFlow, PyTorch, and scikit-learn. Certain operations or custom models may, however, not have GPU optimizations, resulting in a reduced performance on GPU-accelerated systems when running certain operations or custom models. There are also libraries for specialized hardware accelerators like TPUs that might have limited or experimental support in Python.

6. CONCLUSION AND FUTURE WORK

As a conclusion, the exploration of Python libraries in the context of machine learning models for data science has illustrated how many tools are available for data scientists to build and analyze models using them. In order to efficiently and effectively solve complex data science problems, researchers use libraries such as NumPy, Pandas, and Scikit-Learn to manipulate data, TensorFlow and Matplotlib to apply machine learning to the data, and Seaborn and Matplotlib to visualize the data. Furthermore, the authors also point out that a number of other libraries and algorithms are available which can be investigated in future work in addition to the one we described in this research paper. Scikit-learn and TensorFlow are two machine learning libraries that can be compared to PyTorch and OpenCV in terms of their capabilities. Plotly and Altair can also be compared with Matplotlib and Seaborn, which are also visualization libraries. The field of data science and machine learning continues to provide new algorithms and libraries to be developed and released every day, thanks to Python libraries, which are used for these purposes. Future exploration and experimentation with these tools will likely benefit both researchers and practitioners in the field in the future.

REFERENCES

Abadi, M., Barham, P., Chen, J., Chen, Z., Davis, A., Dean, J. M., Devin, M., Ghemawat, S., Irving, G., Isard, M., Kudlur, M., Levenberg, J., Monga, R., Moore, S., Murray, D. G., Steiner, B., Tucker, P. A., Vasudevan, V., Warden, P., . . . Zheng, X. (2016). TensorFlow: A system for large-scale machine learning. *Operating Systems Design and Implementation*, 265–283. https://doi.org/ doi:10.5555/3026877.3026899

Chollet, F. (2017). *Deep Learning with Python*. http://cds.cern.ch/record/2301910

Cock, P. J. A., Antao, T., Chang, J. T., Chapman, B., Cox, C. J., Dalke, A., Friedberg, I., Hamelryck, T., Kauff, F., Wilczyński, B., & De Hoon, M. (2009). Biopython: Freely available Python tools for computational molecular biology and bioinformatics. *Bioinformatics (Oxford, England)*, 25(11), 1422–1423. doi:10.1093/bioinformatics/ btp163 PMID:19304878

Hunter, J. (2007). MatPlotLib: A 2D Graphics environment. *Computing in Science & Engineering*, 9(3), 90–95. doi:10.1109/MCSE.2007.55

Jarvis, R. M., Broadhurst, D., Johnson, H. E., O'Boyle, N. M., & Goodacre, R. (2006). PYCHEM: A multivariate analysis package for python. *Bioinformatics (Oxford, England)*, 22(20), 2565–2566. doi:10.1093/bioinformatics/btl416 PMID:16882648

McKinney, W. (2010). Data structures for statistical computing in Python. *Proceedings of the Python in Science Conferences*. 10.25080/Majora-92bf1922-00a

McKinney, W. (2011). Pandas: A Foundational Python Library for Data Analysis and Statistics. *Python High Performance Science Computer*. https://www.dlr.de/sc/en/Portaldata/15/Resources/dokumente/pyhpc2011/submissions/pyhpc2011_submission_9.pdf

McKinney, W. (2012). *Python for data analysis*. O'Reilly Media, Inc. eBooks. http://ci.nii.ac.jp/ncid/BB11531826

Pedregosa, F., Varoquaux, G., Gramfort, A., Michel, V., Thirion, B., Grisel, O., Blondel, M., Prettenhofer, P., Weiss, R., Dubourg, V., Vanderplas, J., Passos, A., Cournapeau, D., Brucher, M., Perrot, M., & Duchesnay, E. (2011). SciKit-Learn: Machine Learning in Python. *HAL (Le Centre Pour La Communication Scientifique Directe)*. https://hal.inria.fr/hal-00650905

Reback, J., & McKinney, W. (2020). pandas-dev/pandas: Pandas 1.0.5. Zenodo. doi:10.5281/zenodo.3898987

Reback J. McKinney W. Van Den Bossche J. Augspurger T. Cloud P. Klein A. Seabold S. (2020). pandas-dev/pandas: Pandas 1.0. 5. Zenodo.

Rossant, C. (2014). *IPython Interactive Computing and Visualization Cookbook*. https://scholarvox.library.inseec-u.com/catalog/book/docid/88851238?_locale=fr

Satyanarayan, A., Moritz, D., Wongsuphasawat, K., & Heer, J. (2017). Vega-Lite: A grammar of interactive Graphics. *IEEE Transactions on Visualization and Computer Graphics*, *23*(1), 341–350. doi:10.1109/TVCG.2016.2599030 PMID:27875150

Vanderplas, J. (2016). *Python Data Science Handbook: Essential Tools for Working with Data*. http://cds.cern.ch/record/2276771

Waskom, M. (2021). seaborn: Statistical data visualization. *Journal of Open Source Software*, *6*(60), 3021. doi:10.21105/joss.03021

Wickham, H. (2009). *ggplot2: Elegant Graphics for Data Analysis*. http://ndl.ethernet.edu.et/bitstream/123456789/60263/1/107.pdf

Chapter 2
Interdisciplinary Application of Machine Learning, Data Science, and Python for Cricket Analytics

Haseeb Imdad
National Textile University, Pakistan

Haseeb Ahmad
National Textile University, Pakistan

ABSTRACT

The chapter explores the use of machine learning, data science, and Python in the context of cricket analytics. It highlights the importance of interdisciplinary collaboration and its potential to enhance the accuracy and speed of cricket analytics. It discusses the various data sources that can be used for cricket analytics and how machine learning algorithms can extract valuable insights. The chapter also provides an overview of various Python libraries commonly used in cricket analytics and explains how they can be used for data cleaning, feature engineering, and model building. Additionally, the chapter discusses the challenges and limitations of cricket analytics and provides suggestions for future research directions.

DOI: 10.4018/978-1-6684-8696-2.ch002

INTRODUCTION

Cricket is a bat-ball team sport started in England in the 16th century. It has gained fame quickly and become the second most popular game in the world with a global following. This sport is known for its strategic complexity and dynamic gameplay, thus, making it a favorite among players and fans. According to the International Cricket Council (ICC), cricket is played in 106 countries worldwide and has 1.5 billion fans worldwide. Most global interest and finance are focused on the 10 entire ICC member nations, mainly the 'big three' of England, Australia, and India.

One Day International (ODI) cricket, Twenty20 (T20) cricket, and Test matches are the three main formats of cricket. T20 cricket has many fans due to its short and fascinating format compared to others. Indian Premier League (IPL) is also a T20 cricket league famous worldwide. It was started in 2008 and has conducted many successful sessions. Because of the large fan base, team spirit, and financial stakes, the outcomes of these matches are essential. It depends upon several factors, including pitch conditions, tosses winning, players combination, and many other environmental factors like records of your players help determine a match's outcome.

Machine learning, data science, and Python have revolutionized how we analyze and make predictions about complex systems. Machine learning is a subset of artificial intelligence that solves real-world engineering problems. Unlike traditional programming, it focuses on learning from data rather than being exclusively programmed. On the other hand, data science involves using various techniques and algorithms to extract insights and knowledge from data. Python is a high-level programming language that has become the preferred choice for data science and machine learning due to its ease of use, extensive libraries, and vast community support. The combination of machine learning, data science, and Python has the potential to provide powerful and accurate predictions and insights for data-driven decisions in various domains.

This chapter will explore the application of machine learning, data science, and Python for cricket analytics, focusing on appropriate tools and libraries for data processing and predictive modeling. We will analyze IPL data from 2008-2022 using the Jupyter Notebook data analysis tool and leverage visualization techniques to gain valuable insights and facilitate a deeper understanding of the data. The chapter will also highlight the successful applications of these techniques in cricket, including player performance analysis, match prediction, and team selection. Machine learning, data science, and Python can revolutionize how cricket is played and analyzed, leading to better decision-making by players, coaches, and teams.

BACKGROUND

In recent years, there has been a surge of interest in applying machine learning and data science techniques to cricket analytics, encompassing player performance analysis, match outcome prediction, and team selection. Researchers have employed various algorithms and approaches to extract insights from cricket data.

Player performance analysis has been a prominent focus, utilizing machine learning algorithms to identify key performance indicators. For instance, Mittal et al. (Mittal et al., 2021) developed a predictive model that considered batting average, strike rate, and bowling economy to assess player performance and predict match results. Vestly et al. (Vestly et al., 2023) utilized data science techniques to analyze batting techniques and uncover patterns correlated with successful innings.

Match prediction has also garnered attention, with researchers employing machine learning algorithms to forecast match outcomes based on historical data. Priya et al. (Priya et al., 2022) utilized logistic regression, random forest, k-Nearest neighbor, support vector machine, and decision tree algorithms to predict winners in T20 cricket matches. Anuraj et al. (Anuraj et al., 2023) explored sports data mining approaches, considering factors such as venue conditions, team rankings, and past performance, to develop predictive models for T20 International World Cup matches.

Similarly, various studies have focused on predicting cricket match outcomes and specific player-related factors using techniques like KNN, SVM, Logistic regression, Naïve Bayes, and Bayesian Classifier. Ahmed and Nazir (Ahmed, 2015), Shah and Khan (Khan & Shah, 2015), Kaluarachchi and Amal (Kaluarachchi & Aparna, 2010), Prakash and Patwardhan et al. (Prakash et al., 2016), Mago and Rasheed et al. (Vistro et al., 2019), and Ahmad and Asif et al. (Ahmad et al., 2021) have contributed to this field with their respective prediction models.

Team selection has been enhanced through the application of machine learning and data science approaches. Gunawardhana (Gunawardhana, 2022) optimized team selection in One Day Internationals by considering players' overall performance, consistency, venue, opposition, and recent form. Das et al. (Das et al., 2023) employed clustering techniques to group players and facilitate team formation, providing selectors with a reliable method based on player similarities and compatibility.

In conclusion, the growing interest in applying machine learning and data science to cricket analytics is evident in the diverse research on player performance analysis, match outcome prediction, and team selection. By harnessing advanced algorithms and utilizing Python as a versatile programming language, researchers can unlock valuable insights within cricket data, revolutionizing the analysis and understanding of the sport.

MAIN FOCUS OF THE CHAPTER

1. Issues

a. Lack of Domain Knowledge

One of the critical issues in cricket analytics is the need for more domain knowledge among technical experts and sports analytics ability among domain experts. Cricket domain experts may need to learn about data science and machine learning, while technical experts may need an interest in sports analytics. This lack of knowledge and expertise can hinder the progress and development of cricket analytics.

b. Data Quality

Cricket data quality issues such as missing data, outliers, and errors may need to be better understood by cricket experts. In contrast, data analysis experts may need more familiarity with cricket data to identify and correct these issues. Therefore, understanding cricket data and data quality issues must ensure accurate analysis. Proper data cleaning and preparation techniques should address data quality issues and prevent misleading conclusions. Additionally, collaboration between cricket experts and data analysis experts can help to bridge the knowledge gap and improve data quality.

c. Interpretability

Cricket experts may need a good understanding of how they work to interpret the results of machine learning models and data analysis techniques. In contrast, data analysis experts may need help interpreting the results in the context of cricket.

d. Implementation

Cricket experts may need to learn how to integrate the results of machine learning models and data analysis techniques into their decision-making processes. In contrast, data analysis experts may need help communicating their findings to cricket experts in an actionable way.

e. Biasness

Data analysis experts should be conscious of the potential for bias in the data and their models. At the same time, cricket experts must understand how to incorporate the possibility of bias into their decision-making processes. Awareness of the presence and effects of bias in cricket data and analyses can help prevent incorrect conclusions and improve decision-making accuracy. Collaboration between experts in both fields can further enhance understanding and mitigate the impact of bias in cricket data analysis.

f. Data Integration

Cricket experts often require data integration from various sources, including weather data and player injury reports, to enhance their analysis. This integration can present challenges for data analysis experts, who must ensure the accuracy and compatibility of the different data sources. Collaboration between the two groups can facilitate the integration process, allowing for more comprehensive and accurate analyses. Proper data integration techniques and tools can also help to simplify the process and improve data quality.

g. Context

In cricket analysis, some variables, such as pitch conditions or player fatigue, may need to be adequately captured by data analysis techniques. Therefore, cricket experts must provide context around these variables to enhance the accuracy and relevance of the analysis. Data analysis experts must understand the significance of such variables and incorporate them into their models to achieve a comprehensive analysis. Collaborative efforts between cricket and data analysis experts can enable the incorporation of relevant contextual variables, leading to more accurate and useful analyses.

2. Controversies

a. Objective vs. Subjective Analysis

The use of data analysis in cricket has often been a topic of debate among experts, with some favoring traditional, subjective analysis based on personal experience and observation. In contrast, others prefer objective analysis based on statistical models and algorithms. The challenge lies in finding a balance between these two approaches, as both can provide valuable insights.

b. Traditional vs. Modern Analysis

Like the above, cricket experts may prefer traditional analysis methods like scorecards or averages, while data analysis experts may prefer modern techniques like machine learning or predictive modeling. The challenge is determining which approach best suits a given situation and ensuring the analysis is accurate and reliable.

c. Theory vs. Practice

Cricket experts may have theories about how the game should be played or how players should perform, while data analysis experts may focus on empirical evidence and data-driven insights. The challenge is to incorporate both the theory and practice in the analysis and t the analysis is relevant and applicable to real-world scenarios.

d. Explaining vs. Predicting

Cricket experts may be more interested in explaining past events or patterns, while data analysis experts may be more interested in predicting future outcomes. The challenge is to balance these two approaches and ensure that the analysis is informative and useful for decision-making.

e. Causation vs. Correlation

Cricket experts may want to identify causal relationships between variables, such as training techniques and player performance, while data analysis experts may focus more on identifying correlations and patterns. The challenge is understanding the limitations of data analysis in establishing causal relationships and ensuring that the analysis is interpreted correctly.

3. Problems

Cricket domain experts may face these issues by applying machine learning, data science, and python for cricket analytics.

a. Data Acquisition

Collecting high-quality data for cricket analytics can be a significant challenge. The various data sources, including live matches, player performance, and historical data, must be curated and integrated to provide a complete picture of cricket analytics.

b. Data Preprocessing

Raw data often requires significant cleaning and preprocessing to be helpful in machine learning models. This process can be time-consuming and resource-intensive for cricket domain experts.

c. Model Selection

Various machine learning models are available to analyze cricket data, and selecting the most appropriate model for a specific problem can be daunting for cricket domain experts.

d. Feature Engineering

Feature engineering involves selecting and transforming relevant features from raw data to improve model accuracy. This process can be challenging for cricket domain experts who may need more statistical or computational skills.

e. Lack of Expertise

Cricket domain experts may need the technical skills to apply machine learning and data science techniques effectively. This lack of expertise can hinder the progress of cricket analytics projects.

f. Lack of Standardization

One of the challenges in cricket analytics is the need for more standardization in data collection and analysis. Different teams and organizations may use different data collection and analysis methods, making comparing and combining data from different sources difficult.

These are some of the issues that data analysis experts may face in cricket analytics.

a. Cleaning and Pre-Processing

Cleaning and pre-processing data: Data analysts often spend significant time cleaning and pre-processing data before they can begin their analysis. This can be a time-consuming and tedious process.

b. Choosing the Suitable Algorithm

Various machine learning algorithms are available, and choosing the right one for a particular problem can be challenging. Data analysts need to understand the algorithms and their strengths and weaknesses deeply.

c. Underfitting or Overfitting

Overfitting and underfitting are common problems in machine learning that can affect the performance of models. Overfitting occurs when the model is trained too well on the training data, causing it to perform poorly on new data. On the other hand, underfitting occurs when the model needs to be more complex and capture the complexity of the data. Data analysts must be able to identify and avoid overfitting and underfitting to ensure accurate and reliable models.

d. Data Visualization

Data visualization: Communicating the analysis results to stakeholders is critical, and data visualization can be a powerful tool. However, creating effective visualizations that accurately convey insights can be challenging.

SOLUTIONS AND RECOMMENDATIONS

A beginner in data science may find this chapter helps to understand the types of models, graphs, and python libraries used in data science and machine learning for interdisciplinary applications. The practical implication will facilitate understanding, including importing data, pre-processing, training models, predicting results, and visualizing information.

Figure 1 depicts the chapter sections divided into five main components: IDEs, Data Repositories, Libraries, Models, Evaluation Metrics, and Visualization. First, Python-supported IDEs for Data Science and Machine will be detailed. Subsequently, data sources will be discussed, consisting of massive data from the cricket domain. The next module will categorize Python libraries into three further sub-categories. This section will discuss the implementation of different libraries for different applied purposes. The following section will briefly about the training of some supervised and unsupervised machine learning models for solving real-world problems. Subsequently, evaluation metrics for the evaluation of models will be discussed. In the final section, different data visualization tools will be discussed.

Figure 1. Python for machine learning and data science

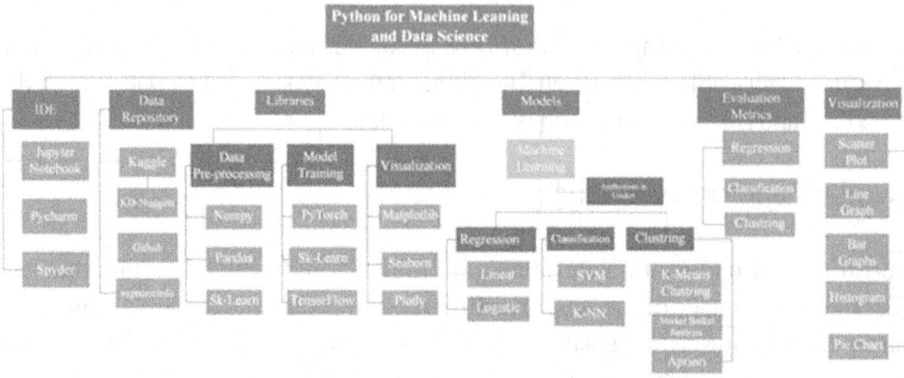

Moreover, a case study from the cricket domain will be presented to highlight the practical implications of data science and machine learning for interdisciplinary domains. Overall, this chapter intends to answer the question, "How could data science and machine learning potentially be used for revealing cricket analytics?"

1. INTEGRATED DEVELOPMENT ENVIRONMENTS (IDEs)

The three most used IDEs for Python data science and machine learning are:

a.   Jupyter Notebook:

Jupyter Notebook is a web-based interactive computing platform that allows users to create and share documents that contain live code, equations, visualizations, and narrative text. It is widely used for data analysis, scientific computing, and visualization. Jupyter Notebook is popular among data scientists and machine learning practitioners because it combines code, output, and visualizations in one place, making it easier to understand and interpret results.

b.   PyCharm:

PyCharm is a Python-integrated development environment (IDE) developed by JetBrains. It provides a range of features to support professional Python development, including code navigation, code completion, error highlighting, and debugging. PyCharm is well-suited for data science and machine learning projects, as it supports popular data science libraries such as Pandas, NumPy, and Matplotlib.

c.   Spyder:

Spyder is an open-source Python IDE explicitly designed for data science and scientific computing. It has a user-friendly interface and various features to support data analysis, including a variable explorer, interactive console, and data visualization capabilities. Spyder integrates well with popular data science libraries, making it a popular choice among data scientists and machine learning practitioners.

Installing Anaconda

Anaconda (Wang, 2012) is open-source software that contains Jupyter notebook, Spyder, PyCharm etc. To begin with Anaconda, first, you need to install it.

2. DATA REPOSITORIES

These are the top free data repositories for a data scientist:

a.   Kaggle:

Kaggle (Goldbloom, 2010) is a platform for data science competitions and hosts several cricket-related datasets.

These datasets include information about cricket matches, player statistics, and ball-by-ball commentary. Users can download and use the datasets to build predictive models, explore trends and patterns, and develop visualizations. In addition to the datasets, Kaggle hosts several cricket-related competitions, such as the Indian Premier League (IPL) competition, where data scientists can compete to develop the most accurate models for predicting match outcomes.

b.   KDnuggets:

KDnuggets (Piatetsky-Shapiro, 2013) is a website that covers various data science and analytics topics, including cricket. The website features articles and tutorials on cricket analytics, discussing topics such as player performance analysis, match outcome prediction, and fan engagement. The articles and tutorials are written by experts in the field and can be a valuable resource for cricket domain experts and data analytics experts alike.

c.   GitHub:

GitHub (Dakhel et al., 2023) is a popular platform for hosting code repositories, and several cricket-related repositories are available on the forum. These repositories contain code for various tasks, such as scraping cricket data from websites, cleaning and preprocessing data, and building predictive models. Some of these repositories also have data visualizations and dashboards that can be used to explore cricket-related data. GitHub can be a helpful resource for cricket domain and data analytics experts, as it provides access to code and tools to help with data analysis and visualization.

d.   ESPNcricinfo:

ESPNcricinfo (Rasmussen, 2010) is a popular website for cricket news and analysis, and it also provides access to various cricket-related statistics and data. The website features a stats section that contains information about players, teams, and matches. Users can access statistics such as batting and bowling averages, match results, and player rankings. ESPNcricinfo can be a helpful resource for cricket domain experts looking to access and analyze cricket statistics and data analytics experts looking for a source of cricket data to build predictive models or perform data analysis.

3. LIBRARIES

Python libraries play a crucial role in data science and machine learning. Numerous libraries are available in Python, each with unique features and capabilities. By dividing the libraries into three sub-categories, Data-Preprocessing, Model Training, and Visualization, it becomes easier to understand the role of each library and how they can be used in the data science and machine learning workflow. Before moving ahead, first, we need to understand an important concept.

Exploratory Data Analysis

Exploratory data analysis (EDA) analyzes data to summarize its main characteristics and gain insights into its underlying patterns, trends, and relationships. It involves various techniques and tools for summarizing, visualizing, and understanding the data to identify interesting patterns or anomalies that can be further investigated.
These are the main components of EDA:

- **Data Collection:** The first step in EDA is to collect the data from various sources such as databases, CSV files, or APIs.

- **Data Cleaning:** The collected data may contain errors, missing values, or outliers. Data cleaning involves identifying and correcting these issues to ensure the data is suitable for analysis.
- **Data Visualization:** The next step in EDA is to visualize the data using various graphical and statistical techniques such as histograms, scatter plots, and box plots. This helps in understanding the distribution and relationships between variables.
- **Data Analysis:** Once the data has been cleaned and visualized, data analysis can be performed to identify patterns, trends, and relationships between variables.
- **Hypothesis Testing:** Hypothesis testing tests the significance of the patterns and relationships identified during data analysis. It helps determine if the observed results are due to chance or are statistically significant.

EDA aims to understand the data by analyzing and summarizing its main characteristics. It is a crucial step in data analysis. It allows data analysts to detect patterns, anomalies, relationships, and outliers in the data. It helps to identify the key features identify the data's key features and is tested with more advanced statistical techniques.

EDA also helps to identify errors and inconsistencies in the data and to determine the quality of the data. By performing it, data analysts can ensure that the data is clean, relevant, and suitable for the intended analysis. EDA is an iterative process that can help data analysts refine their research questions, develop appropriate analysis methods, and explore the data in a structured and systematic way. Pandas, NumPy, Matplotlib, Seaborn, and Plotly are the libraries that can be used individually or in combination to perform EDA in Python.

Importing the data file named 'IPL Matches 2008-2020.csv' with the help of the **pandas** library and showing the top 5 records from data using the **head**() function.

The **info**() method is a built-in Python function that can gather information about the columns in a given dataset.

The **describe**() method is a built-in Python function that can generate statistical summaries for a given dataset. It provides descriptive statistics, such as count, mean, standard deviation, minimum, and maximum values, for each numerical column in the DataFrame.

The **isnull**() is a built-in method in the panda's library of Python, which detects the missing or null values in a DataFrame. It returns a DataFrame or a Boolean value that indicates whether a particular value in the DataFrame is null or not. This method can help identify missing or null values in a DataFrame and can be followed by other methods like **sum**() to count the number of null values in each column or row of the DataFrame.

Figure 2. Importing data and showing the top 5 records

```
import pandas as pd
df = pd.read_csv("IPL Matches 2008-2020.csv")

df.head()
```

	id	city	date	player_of_match	venue	neutral_venue	team1	team2	toss_winner	toss_decision	winner	result	result_ma
0	335982	Bangalore	2008-04-18	BB McCullum	M Chinnaswamy Stadium	0	Royal Challengers Bangalore	Kolkata Knight Riders	Royal Challengers Bangalore	field	Kolkata Knight Riders	runs	1
1	335983	Chandigarh	2008-04-19	MEK Hussey	Punjab Cricket Association Stadium, Mohali	0	Kings XI Punjab	Chennai Super Kings	Chennai Super Kings	bat	Chennai Super Kings	runs	
2	335984	Delhi	2008-04-19	MF Maharoof	Feroz Shah Kotla	0	Delhi Daredevils	Rajasthan Royals	Rajasthan Royals	bat	Delhi Daredevils	wickets	
3	335985	Mumbai	2008-04-20	MV Boucher	Wankhede Stadium	0	Mumbai Indians	Royal Challengers Bangalore	Mumbai Indians	bat	Royal Challengers Bangalore	wickets	
4	335986	Kolkata	2008-04-20	DJ Hussey	Eden Gardens	0	Kolkata Knight Riders	Deccan Chargers	Deccan Chargers	bat	Kolkata Knight Riders	wickets	

Figure 3. Displaying all columns information

```
In [8]: df.info()

        <class 'pandas.core.frame.DataFrame'>
        RangeIndex: 816 entries, 0 to 815
        Data columns (total 17 columns):
         #   Column           Non-Null Count   Dtype
        ---  ------           --------------   -----
         0   id               816 non-null     int64
         1   city             803 non-null     object
         2   date             816 non-null     object
         3   player_of_match  812 non-null     object
         4   venue            816 non-null     object
         5   neutral_venue    816 non-null     int64
         6   team1            816 non-null     object
         7   team2            816 non-null     object
         8   toss_winner      816 non-null     object
         9   toss_decision    816 non-null     object
         10  winner           812 non-null     object
         11  result           812 non-null     object
         12  result_margin    799 non-null     float64
         13  eliminator       812 non-null     object
         14  method           19 non-null      object
         15  umpire1          816 non-null     object
         16  umpire2          816 non-null     object
        dtypes: float64(1), int64(2), object(14)
        memory usage: 108.5+ KB
```

Figure 4. Getting statistical summary

```
df.describe()
```

	id	neutral_venue	result_margin
count	8.160000e+02	816.000000	799.000000
mean	7.563496e+05	0.094363	17.321652
std	3.058943e+05	0.292512	22.068427
min	3.359820e+05	0.000000	1.000000
25%	5.012278e+05	0.000000	6.000000
50%	7.292980e+05	0.000000	8.000000
75%	1.082626e+06	0.000000	19.500000
max	1.237181e+06	1.000000	146.000000

The **fillna()** method can be used to fill missing or null values in any column of a pandas DataFrame.

```
df["result_margin"].fillna(0).
```

This operation replaces all the missing or null values in the 'result_margin' column with a 0 and returns a new pandas Series object, after removing all null values from the dataset.

The complete implementation of EDA is given here.

a.   Data Preprocessing

Data-Preprocessing is a method for preparing the raw data and making it suitable for a machine learning model, and python-built libraries are used for this purpose. Some libraries include Pandas, NumPy, and SciPy. These libraries provide functions and methods for data cleaning, missing data imputation, data normalization, and more.

Figure 5. Counting null values in every column

```
df.isnull().sum()

id                   0
city                13
date                 0
player_of_match      4
venue                0
neutral_venue        0
team1                0
team2                0
toss_winner          0
toss_decision        0
winner               4
result               4
result_margin       17
eliminator           4
method             797
umpire1              0
umpire2              0
dtype: int64
```

i.   *NumPy*

NumPy is a popular library in Python for numerical computing and is widely used in data pre-processing. It provides functions for performing array operations, including element-wise operations, reshaping, and broadcasting. NumPy arrays are a flexible and efficient way to store and manipulate large datasets, making them an ideal choice for pre-processing.

Figure 6. After removing all null values from dataset

```
df.isnull().sum()

id                  0
city                0
date                0
player_of_match     0
venue               0
neutral_venue       0
team1               0
team2               0
toss_winner         0
toss_decision       0
winner              0
result              0
result_margin       0
eliminator          0
method              0
umpire1             0
umpire2             0
Year                0
Month               0
Day                 0
dtype: int64
```

ii.   *Pandas*

Pandas is a highly efficient and flexible data analysis and manipulation tool that is open-source and built in Python. It is mainly used for data cleaning and analysis purposes. It provides easy-to-use data structures and functions for processing large and complex datasets, making it ideal for handling real-world data challenges.

iii.   *Scikit-learn*

Pandas is a highly efficient and flexible data analysis and manipulation tool that is open-source and built in Python. It is mainly used for data cleaning and analysis purposes. It provides easy-to-use data structures and functions for processing large and complex datasets, making it ideal for handling real-world data challenges.

The complete implementation of libraries, as mentioned above, is given here.

b.   Model Training

Model training is teaching a machine learning model to make accurate predictions on new, unseen data. It is a crucial step in building predictive models, enabling the model to learn from historical data and generalize to new data. Model training involves selecting the suitable algorithm, optimizing its parameters, and evaluating its performance on a validation set. By training a model, you can make data-driven decisions and solve complex problems more effectively. There are famous libraries used for model training.

i.   Scikit-learn:

Scikit-learn is a popular machine-learning library in Python that offers a wide range of data analysis, modeling, and visualization tools. It includes algorithms for classification, regression, clustering, and more and provides an easy-to-use API for beginners and advanced users.

ii.   TensorFlow:

TensorFlow is a powerful machine-learning library in Python that provides a platform for building and deploying machine-learning models at scale. It includes a range of high-level APIs for building and training neural networks and is widely used in deep learning applications.

iii.   PyTorch:

PyTorch is a popular machine-learning library in Python that offers a dynamic and efficient framework for building and training neural networks. It provides a range of high-level APIs for building and training deep learning models and is particularly popular in the research community.

c.   Visualization

Data visualization is representing data in a graphical or pictorial format. It is used to explore, analyze, and communicate insights from data. Data visualization can help identify patterns and trends, discover outliers and anomalies, and communicate complex ideas and results clearly and intuitively. It is a critical tool for anyone working with data, including data analysts, data scientists, and business professionals.

i.   Matplotlib:

Matplotlib is a popular data visualization library in Python that provides a wide range of tools for creating static, animated, and interactive visualizations. It is highly customizable and can be used to create a variety of plots, charts, and diagrams, including line plots, scatter plots, bar plots, and more.

Figure 7. Visualization using matplotlib library with plot function

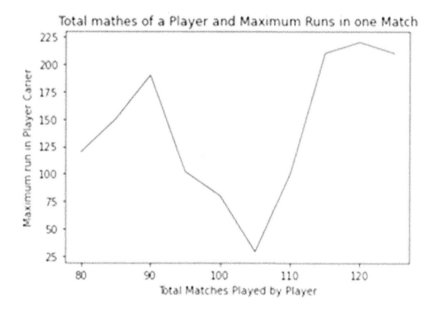

ii.   Seaborn:

Seaborn is a data visualization library built on Matplotlib that provides a high-level interface for creating statistical graphics. It includes various tools for visualizing distributions, regression models, and categorical data and is particularly useful for exploring and analyzing large datasets.

Figure 8. Visualization using seaborn library with lmplot function

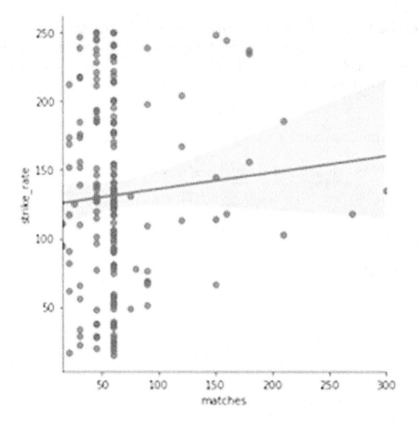

iii.   Plotly:

Plotly is a web-based data visualization library that provides various interactive tools for creating dynamic and engaging visualizations in Python and other programming languages. It includes a range of chart types, including scatter plots, line plots, bar charts, 3D visualizations, and animated graphics. Plotly also provides an online platform for sharing and collaborating on visualizations with others.

The complete implementation of libraries, as mentioned above, is given here.

Figure 9. Visualization using plotly library with scatter function

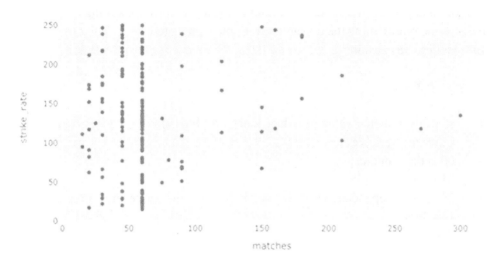

4. MODELS

Machine learning involves using algorithms and statistical models to enable computers to learn from data and improve performance without explicit programming. Models represent patterns known from data and can make predictions or identify similarities and differences between data points. Techniques like supervised, unsupervised, and reinforcement learning can be used to train models for tasks like image recognition and prediction. This section further classifies models into three subcategories: Regression, Classification, and Clustering.

a. Regression

Regression is a statistical method to model the relationship between a dependent variable and one or more independent variables. It finds the best-fit line or curve to explain the variables' relationship and can predict the dependent variable's value based on the independent variables' values. Regression models, such as linear, logistic, and polynomial regression, are used in diverse fields, including economics, social sciences, engineering, and biology, to make predictions and understand variable relationships. Linear and logistic regression is explained below.

i. Linear Regression

Linear regression models the relationship between a dependent variable and one or more independent variables, assuming a linear relationship, aiming to find the best-fit line representing the dependent variable's predicted value. The formula for simple linear regression:

$$y = \beta_0 + \beta_1 X + \epsilon$$

- y is the predicted value of a dependent variable (y) for any given value of x (response variable)
- $\beta 0$ is the y-intercept
- $\beta 1$ is the slop of line
- X is an independent variable that influences the value of y (explanatory variable)
- ϵ is the difference between actual and observed value. It is also called an error or residual

On the other hand, multiple linear regression is used when there are two or more independent variables. It involves fitting a linear equation to the data that best describes the relationship between the dependent and independent variables. The linear equation takes the form:

$$y = \beta_0 + \beta_1 x_1 + \beta_2 x_2 + \beta_3 x_3 \ldots \ldots, + \beta_n x_n + \epsilon$$

Where y is the dependent variable, x1, x2, ..., xn are the independent variables, $\beta 1$, $\beta 2$, ..., βn are the slopes of the lines for each independent variable, a is the intercept, and e is the error term. Each slope ($\beta 1$, $\beta 2$, ..., βn) represents the change in y for a one-unit increase in the corresponding independent variable, while holding all other independent variables constant.

Multiple linear regression can be helpful when numerous factors may influence the dependent variable, and we want to understand how each element contributes to the outcome. It can also help to identify which independent variables have the strongest association with the dependent variable.

Linear regression is a useful statistical technique for modeling the relationship between a continuous dependent variable and one or more independent variables. However, it is unsuitable for modeling binary outcomes because the predicted values of a linear regression model can exceed the range of 0 to 1, which is required for binary outcomes. In addition, the assumptions of linear regression, such as normality and constant variance of errors, may not hold for binary outcomes, leading to biased or unreliable results.

ii. Logistic Regression

Logistic regression is a statistical method used to model the relationship between a binary (two-class) dependent variable and one or more independent variables, also known as predictors or features. Logistic regression aims to predict the probability of an event occurring (i.e., the chance of the binary outcome) given a set of independent variables.

For example:

- To predict whether an email is spam or not
- Whether the patient has covid or not
- Predicting whether a tumor is malignant or not

Logistic regression is particularly useful when the outcome variable is binary, and there is a need to predict the probability of the outcome rather than the magnitude. Logistic regression can handle continuous and categorical independent variables and nonlinear model relationships between independent variables and outcomes. In addition, logistic regression provides interpretable coefficients that can help explain the relationship between the independent variables and the outcome.

The equation of logistic regression is given below:

$$p = \frac{1}{1 + e^{-z}}$$

Where:
- p is the predicted probability of the binary outcome, which ranges from 0 to 1.
- e is the base of the natural logarithm, which is approximately equal to 2.71828.
- z is the linear combination of the independent variables and their coefficients.

The linear combination of the independent variables and their coefficients (z) is given by:

$$z = \beta_0 + \beta_1 x_1 + \beta_2 x_2 + \beta_3 x_3 \ldots\ldots + \beta_k x_k$$

Where:

- β_0 is the intercept, representing the expected log odds of the binary outcome when all independent variables equal zero.
- $\beta_1, \beta_2, ..., \beta_k$ are the coefficients, which represent the change in the log odds of the binary outcome for a one-unit increase in the corresponding independent variable.
- $x_1, x_2, ..., x_k$ are the independent variables, which can be continuous or categorical.

In logistic regression, the model estimates the coefficients $(\beta_1, \beta_2, ..., \beta_k)$ that maximize the likelihood of the observed binary outcomes given the independent variables. The estimated coefficients can then be used to predict the probability of the binary output for new observations.

b. Classification

Classification in machine learning is a supervised learning task where an algorithm predicts a categorical label for an input based on the patterns and relationships in the input data, mapping input features to a categorical output variable, such as 'yes' or 'no', 'spam' or 'ham', 'dog' or 'cat', etc.

i. Support Vector Machine (SVM)

SVM is a popular classification algorithm in machine learning, which aims to find the best hyperplane that separates the data into different classes. The hyperplane is chosen to maximize the margin, which is the distance between the hyperplane and the nearest points of each class. SVM effectively handles high-dimensional and complex datasets and is widely used in many applications, such as image recognition, text classification, and bioinformatics.

The following examples show where SVM is widely used:

- **Image classification:** SVM is used in image classification tasks to recognize objects, such as detecting whether an image contains a dog or a cat.
- **Text classification:** In natural language processing tasks, such as categorizing emails as spam, to classify text documents.
- **Bioinformatics:** In various applications, such as gene expression analysis, protein structure prediction, and cancer diagnosis.
- **Face detection:** SVM is used to identify faces in images and videos.

- **Fraud detection:** SVM is also used in financial fraud detection systems to identify potentially fraudulent transactions based on patterns and anomalies in the data.

These are the following cases when we prefer SVM over other algorithms.

- When the dataset has a clear margin of separation between classes, SVM is an effective choice.
- SVM can easily handle high-dimensional data, making it ideal for tasks involving many features.
- SVM is relatively insensitive to overfitting and can generalize well to new data, which is useful when the dataset is limited.
- SVM can work with both linear and non-linear data, thanks to kernel functions.
- SVM is a popular choice for tasks such as image and text classification, where the goal is to classify data into one of several categories.

Every algorithm has some limitations. Similarly, these are the following cases when SVM is prohibited from using.

- SVM is computationally expensive when dealing with large datasets, making it impractical for some tasks.
- When the dataset has a lot of noise or overlapping classes, SVM may not perform well.
- Tuning the hyperparameters of an SVM model can be challenging, and it may require extensive experimentation to find the best configuration.
- SVM does not provide a probability estimate for its predictions, which can be problematic for specific applications.
- SVM can be sensitive to the choice of the kernel function, and selecting the appropriate kernel can be difficult in some cases.

ii. K-Nearest Neighbors (K-NN)

K-Nearest Neighbors (K-NN) is a machine learning algorithm for classification and regression tasks. It is a type of instance-based learning where the algorithm makes predictions based on the k-nearest neighbors of a given data point. In K-NN, the nearest neighbors are identified based on a distance metric, usually Euclidean distance. The majority class or the mean of the k-nearest neighbors is used as the prediction for the data point.

The value of k is a hyperparameter that can be set according to the complexity of the problem. If k=1, then the algorithm will predict the class of a given data point based on the class of its nearest neighbor. If k=3, then the algorithm will consider the three closest neighbors and predict the class that occurs most frequently among them.

How does K-NN work?

The K-NN works based on the following algorithm:

- Select the value of K (number of neighbors for comparison
- Calculate the distance between the selected neighbors (using Euclidian, Manhattan, or any distance formula)
- Take the formula that calculates neighbors
- Among these neighbors, count the number of data points in each category
- Assign the class to a new data point, which contains the maximum number of neighbors

What should be the value of K? How to select the value of K? Is there any fixed value we use in every case? When choosing the value of K in the K-NN algorithm, keep the following points in mind:

- There is no definitive method to determine the best value for K, so it is necessary to experiment with different values to find the optimal one. Typically, K=5 is a commonly preferred value.
- Choosing a very low value of K, such as K=1 or K=2, may lead to noise and be sensitive to outliers in the data.
- Although larger values of K may be beneficial in some cases, they may also pose difficulties in accurately classifying the data.

Euclidean Distance Formula

The Euclidean distance formula is a way to calculate the distance between two points in Euclidean space. Machine learning algorithms, such as K-NN, often use it to measure the distance between data points. The formula for calculating the Euclidean distance between two points, (x1, y1) and (x2, y2), in a two-dimensional space is:

$$d = \sqrt{\left(x_1 - x_2\right)^2 + \left(y_1 - y_2\right)^2}$$

Where d is the distance between the two points, in higher-dimensional spaces, the formula is extended as:

$$d = \sqrt{\left(x_1 - x_2\right)^2 + \left(y_1 - y_2\right)^2 + \left(z_1 - z_2\right)^2 + \ldots + \left(n_k - n_{k-1}\right)^2}$$

Where n is the number of dimensions. In general, the Euclidean distance can be calculated between any two points in n-dimensional space, and the formula gives it:

$$d = \sqrt{\Sigma(x_i - x_i)^2}$$

Where x_i and y_i are the coordinates of the two points in the n-dimensional space. The Euclidean distance is always positive, and it satisfies the triangle inequality, which means that the distance between any two points is always less than or equal to the sum of the distances between intermediate points.

c. Clustering

Clustering is a technique used in unsupervised learning to group similar data points based on their characteristics. Clustering aims to find patterns in the data, identify relationships among data points, and gain insights from the data. It is often used in exploratory data analysis (discussed in the next section), data mining, and pattern recognition. Clustering can be used for a variety of purposes, such as:

- **Customer segmentation:** Clustering can help identify customers with similar characteristics, such as buying behavior, demographics, or preferences.
- **Image and signal processing:** It can segment images or signals into regions with common properties or features.
- **Anomaly detection:** It can also help identify unusual or anomalous data points that do not fit into known clusters.
- **Bioinformatics:** Clustering can group genes, proteins, or cells based on their characteristics.

Why do we need to use clustering if we already have seen the abovementioned techniques for classification? While K-NN is a classification algorithm that assigns a new data point to a pre-existing class based on the majority class of the k-nearest neighbors, clustering is used to group similar data points without any pre-existing classes. K-NN is a supervised learning technique, whereas clustering is an unsupervised learning technique. Furthermore, clustering can also be used to find the optimal value of K in the K-NN algorithm by examining the cluster formation and choosing the value of K that provides the best classification accuracy. Many clustering algorithms are used, such as K-means, Market basket analysis, Apriori, mean shift, and Gaussian mixture model.

i. K-Means Clustering

K-means clustering is a popular unsupervised machine learning algorithm for clustering or grouping similar data points based on their similarity or distance. In K-means clustering, the data is divided into K clusters, each representing a group of similar data points. The algorithm iteratively assigns each data point to its nearest cluster center and then updates the cluster centers based on the new assignments until the clusters stabilize.

K-means clustering is used in various applications, such as image segmentation, customer segmentation, anomaly detection, and more. It helps discover patterns in data, identify groups of similar data points, and reduce the dimensionality of high-dimensional data.

K-means clustering algorithm works as follows:

- **Initialization:** Choose the number of clusters K and randomly select K data points from the dataset as the initial cluster centers.
- **Assignment:** For each data point in the dataset, calculate its distance from each K cluster center and assign it to the nearest cluster.
- **Update:** After all the data points have been assigned to clusters, update the cluster centers by calculating the mean of all the data points assigned to each cluster.
- **Repeat:** Repeat steps 2 and 3 until the cluster assignments no longer change or a maximum number of iterations is reached.

The goal of the K-means algorithm is to minimize the sum of the squared distances between each data point and its assigned cluster center. This is known as the within-cluster sum of squares (WCSS) and can be used to measure the clustering quality. In the end, the K-means algorithm outputs the final cluster centers and the cluster assignments for each data point in the dataset.

It's important to note that the K-means algorithm may converge to a local minimum, which means that the resulting clusters may depend on the initial choice of cluster centers. To mitigate this issue, the algorithm is often run multiple times with different initializations, and the best clustering is chosen based on the lowest WCSS.

ii. Market Basket Analysis

Market Basket Analysis is a technique used to uncover the association between the items by determining the retail purchase pattern. It analysis the combination of the products that are bought together. Association rules are widely used to analyze transactional data to look for the relationships of the objects that "go together." It helps the retailers know about people's interest in the products they buy together to keep those items available in their inventory.

It is based on Association rule mining, if { }, then { }. For example, if a customer buys a laptop, he will likely buy a charger. The association rules as {laptop} -> {charger}. The items on the right side will probably be purchased along with those on the left.

These are the two essential terms to understand in this concept Antecedent and Consequent.

- **Antecedent:** Antecedents are the set of items found within the data. It is the if component in the association rule. A laptop will be the antecedent in the above example.
- **Consequent:** It includes the item or set of items found in combination with the antecedent. It is on the right-hand side of the rule. In the above example, the charger is consequent.

With the help of the Apriori algorithm, we can further classify and simplify the item sets bought together.

iii. Apriori Algorithm

Apriori is an algorithm used for Market Basket Analysis, a data mining technique that analyzes customer transaction data to identify patterns and associations among items purchased together. The Apriori algorithm helps to identify frequent itemset and association rules in large transactional datasets.

The Apriori algorithm generates a set of candidate item sets and prunes them based on their frequency of occurrence in the dataset. The process is repeated iteratively, generating longer and longer item sets until no more frequent item sets can be found.

Support, confidence, and lift are measures used in association rule mining to evaluate the strength of the association between two or more items. Here's what they mean:

Support

Support measures the frequency of occurrence of an item set in the dataset. It is calculated as the number of transactions containing the itemset divided by the total number of transactions.

$$Support\ (x \rightarrow y) = \frac{Transaction\ containing\ both\ X\ and\ Y}{Total\ Number\ of\ Transactions}$$

For example, if there are 100 transactions in a dataset, and the itemset {apple, banana} occurs in 20 transactions, then the support of the itemset is $20/100 = 0.2$.

Confidence

Confidence measures the likelihood of item Y being purchased when item X is purchased. It is calculated as the number of transactions containing item X and item Y divided by the number of transactions containing item X.

$$Confidence\ (x \rightarrow y) = \frac{Transactions\ containing\ both\ X\ and\ Y}{Transactions\ containing\ X}$$

For example, if the itemset {apple, banana} has a confidence of 0.5 for {apple}, 50% of the transactions containing apples also contain bananas.

Lift

Lift measures the strength of the association between two items, independent of their support. It is calculated as the ratio of the observed support of the itemset {X, Y} to the expected support if X and Y were independent. A lift value greater than 1 indicates a positive association between the items, while a value less than 1 indicates a negative association.

$$Lift\ (x \rightarrow y) =$$
$$\frac{(Transactions\ containing\ both\ X\ and\ Y)/(Transactions\ contain\ X)}{Fraction\ of\ Transactions\ containing\ Y}$$

Market Basket Analysis is a concept or technique used to identify item associations. At the same time, Apriori Algorithm implements this technique that uses a specific algorithm to identify frequent item sets and association rules.

Common Cricket Analytics Techniques

These are some specific techniques used in cricket analytics, several machine learning algorithms and techniques are commonly used to gain insights and make predictions. Here are the top 3-4 algorithms frequently employed in cricket analytics:

- **Random Forest:** Random Forest is a popular ensemble learning algorithm that combines multiple decision trees to make predictions. It is widely used in cricket analytics to predict match outcomes, player performance, and team selection. Random Forest can handle large datasets with numerous features and provides feature importance rankings, making it valuable for identifying key factors in cricket analytics.
- **Support Vector Machines (SVM):** SVM is a supervised learning algorithm that is often used for classification tasks in cricket analytics. It works by finding an optimal hyperplane that separates data points of different classes. SVM has been utilized in cricket analytics to predict match results, player performance, and team rankings. It is particularly useful when dealing with datasets with clear class boundaries.
- **K-Nearest Neighbors (KNN):** KNN is a simple, yet effective algorithm used in cricket analytics for both classification and regression tasks. It classifies new data points based on the majority class of their nearest neighbors. In cricket analytics, KNN has been applied to predict match outcomes, player rankings, and team performance. It is known for its simplicity and intuitive decision-making process.
- **Gradient Boosting:** Gradient Boosting is a machine learning technique that combines multiple weak models, typically decision trees, to create a strong predictive model. It sequentially builds models, where each subsequent model corrects the errors made by the previous models. Gradient Boosting is widely used in cricket analytics for tasks such as match prediction, player performance analysis, and team selection. It provides high accuracy and can handle complex relationships in the data.

These are some of the frequently used machine learning algorithms in cricket analytics. However, it's important to note that the choice of algorithm depends on the specific task and the nature of the data being analyzed. Other algorithms such as Logistic Regression, Decision Trees, and Neural Networks may also be employed depending on the requirements of the analysis.

d. Application of Machine Learning in Cricket Analytics

Machine learning and data science techniques have been successfully applied in various aspects of cricket analytics, providing valuable insights and practical benefits. Here are some specific examples of successful applications:

i. Player Performance Analysis

Machine learning algorithms have been used to analyze player performance and identify key factors that contribute to success. For example, predictive models have been developed to assess a player's batting average, bowling economy, or fielding efficiency based on historical data. These models consider various features such as batting strike rate, bowling average, and fielding statistics to provide a comprehensive assessment of a player's performance.

ii. Match Outcome Prediction

Predicting the outcome of cricket matches is a challenging task due to the dynamic nature of the game. However, machine learning models have shown promising results in this area. By analyzing historical match data, including factors such as team composition, past performance, pitch conditions, and weather, predictive models can provide insights into the likely outcome of future matches. This information can assist teams in making strategic decisions and help fans in making informed predictions.

iii. Team Selection and Strategy Optimization

Data science techniques have been employed to optimize team selection and strategize for matches. By considering player performance data, opposition analysis, and other relevant factors, models can recommend the most effective team composition and batting/bowling order. This helps teams in maximizing their chances of success by making data-driven decisions and identifying optimal strategies for different game situations.

iv. Fan Engagement and Experience

Machine learning algorithms have been utilized to enhance fan engagement and provide a personalized experience. By analyzing fan behavior, preferences, and social media interactions, models can generate targeted recommendations, customized content, and match predictions tailored to individual fans. This enhances fan involvement, increases viewership, and improves overall fan experience.

These examples demonstrate the practical benefits of using machine learning and data science in cricket analytics. By leveraging historical data, extracting meaningful patterns, and applying advanced algorithms, these methodologies offer valuable insights to players, coaches, teams, and fans, leading to improved decision-making and an enhanced cricketing experience.

5. EVALUATION METRICS

Evaluation metrics are quantitative measures that are used to assess the performance of a machine learning model. These metrics help us understand how well the model performs in terms of its prediction capabilities.

Regression, classification, and clustering are distinct types of machine learning tasks, and as such, they are evaluated using different sets of metrics. The evaluation metrics used for each of these tasks are specific to the problem they are solving and the nature of the data being analyzed. The evaluation criteria for every class is give below:

Table 1. Evaluation metrics according to technique

Technique	Evaluation Metrics
Regression	• Mean Squared Error (MSE) • Root Mean Squared Error (RMSE) • Mean Absolute Error (MAE) • R-squared (R^2) coefficient of determination
Classification	• Accuracy • Precision • Recall (Sensitivity) • F1 Score • Confusion Matrix
Association	• Support • Confidence • Lift

a. Confusion Matrix

A confusion matrix is a table used to evaluate the model's performance. It compares the predicted classes against the actual classes in the data. The confusion matrix has four cells: true positives (TP), false positives (FP), false negatives (FN), and true negatives (TN). TP represents the number of positive cases correctly identified by the model, while FP represents the number of negative cases incorrectly classified as positive. FN represents the number of positive cases that were incorrectly classified as negative, and TN represents the number of negative cases that the model correctly identified.

b. Accuracy

Accuracy is the most used metric for evaluating classification models. It measures the proportion of correctly classified instances out of the total number of instances. It is calculated as the sum of TP and TN divided by the sum of TP, TN, FP, and FN.

$$Accuracy = \frac{TP + TN}{TP + TN + FP + FN}$$

c. F1 Score

F1 score is another commonly used metric for evaluating classification models. It is the harmonic mean of precision and recall, where precision is the proportion of true positives out of all the instances classified as positive, and recall is the proportion of true positives out of all the actual positive instances. F1 score provides a balanced measure of precision and recall, and it is often used when the classes are imbalanced, i.e., when the number of instances in one class is much larger than the number of instances in the other class.

$$Precision = \frac{TP}{TP + FP}$$

$$Recall = \frac{TP}{TP + FN}$$

$$F1 = \frac{2 \times precision \times recall}{precision + recall}$$

d. Mean Squared Error (MSE)

Mean Squared Error (MSE) is a standard metric used to evaluate the performance of regression models. It measures the average of the squared differences between the predicted and actual values of the target variable. The formula for calculating MSE is as follows:

$$MSE = \frac{1}{n} * \sum_{i=1}^{n} (y_i - \bar{y})^2$$

Where:

- n: the number of data points
- y_i: the actual value of the target variable for the i-th data point
- $\bar{y}$: the mean value of the target variable across all data points

In simple terms, MSE measures how far the predicted values are from the actual values. The smaller the MSE value, the better the model's performance. MSE is used as an evaluation metric for regression models because it gives more weight to more significant errors than smaller ones, as the errors are squared before averaging.

e. Root Mean Squared Error (RMSE)

RMSE is another commonly used evaluation metric for regression models that is similar to MSE but provides a more interpretable score as it is expressed in the same units as the target variable. RMSE is calculated as the square root of the average of the squared differences between the predicted and actual values of the target variable. The formula for RMSE is:

$$RMSE = \sqrt{\frac{1}{n} * \sum_{i=1}^{n} (y_i - \bar{y})^2}$$

- n: the number of data points
- y_i: the actual value of the target variable for the i-th data point
- $\bar{y}$: the mean value of the target variable across all data points

f. Mean Absolute Error (MAE)

MAE is another commonly used evaluation metric for regression models that is simpler than RMSE as it doesn't involve squaring the errors. MAE is calculated as the average of the absolute differences between the predicted and actual values of the target variable. The formula for MAE is:

$$MAE = \frac{1}{n} * \sum_{i=1}^{n} |y_i - \bar{y})|$$

Where:
- n: the number of data points
- y_i: the actual value of the target variable for the i-th data point
- $\hat{y}_i$: the predicted value of the target variable for the i-th data point

g. R-Squared (R²)

R-squared is a metric that measures how well the regression model fits the data by explaining the proportion of the variance in the target variable defined by the model's independent variables. R-squared takes values between 0 and 1, with higher values indicating a better fit of the model to the data. The formula for R-squared is:

$$R^2 = \frac{SSres}{SStot}$$

Where:
- **SSres:** the sum of squared residuals, i.e., the sum of the squared differences between the predicted and actual values of the target variable
- **SStot:** the total sum of squares, i.e., the sum of the squared differences between the actual values of the target variable and their mean value

h. Within-Cluster Sum of Squares (WCSS)

WCSS is a measure of how much variance exists within the clusters that are formed by a clustering algorithm. It is calculated as the sum of the squared distances between each data point and the centroid of the cluster to which it belongs. The formula for WCSS is:

$$WCSS = \sum (x - c)^2$$

Where:
- x: a data point
- c: the centroid of the cluster to which x belongs

The goal of clustering algorithms is to minimize WCSS, as this indicates that the clusters are compact and well-separated.

6. VISUALIZATION

Visualization is an essential aspect of Machine Learning that involves creating visual representations of data and patterns to help gain insights and understanding from complex data sets. It can help identify patterns, correlations, and outliers in the data and can be used to communicate the findings to others clearly and concisely. There are some examples of graphs used for visualization.

a. Line Graph

A line graph shows a variable's trend over time or another continuous dimension. Line graphs can help identify patterns and trends over time or for comparing multiple variables simultaneously.

Figure 10. Line graph between total matches played in year

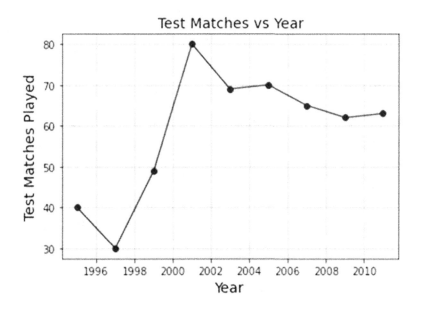

b. Scatter Plot

A scatter plot is used to visualize the relationship between two variables. It is a 2D graph in which each data point is represented as a dot, with one variable on the x-axis and the other on the y-axis. Scatter plots help identify patterns, trends, and correlations between variables.

Figure 11. Scatter plot between players runs vs contribution in match-winning

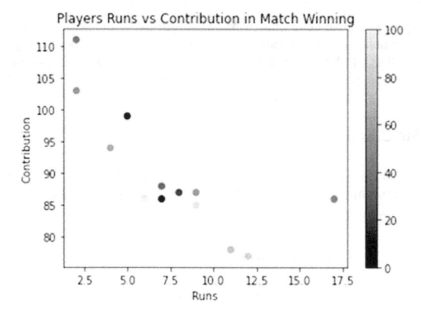

c. Bar Chart

A bar graph is used to compare different categories of data. It is a 2D graph in which the x-axis represents the categories, and the y-axis represents the values. Bar graphs help visualize categorical data and identify trends and comparisons between categories.

Figure 12. Bar chart between the number of matches played by respective players

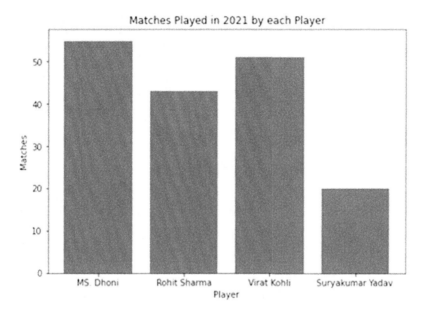

d. Histogram

A histogram is used to visualize the distribution of a single variable. It is a 1D graph in which the x-axis represents the range of values for the variable, and the y-axis represents the frequency of occurrence. Histograms help identify the shape of the distribution of the variable, including whether it is skewed, bimodal, or normal.

e. Pie Chart

A pie chart shows the distribution of a categorical variable as a percentage of the whole. It is a circular graph in which each category is represented as a slice of the pie, with the size of each slice corresponding to the proportion of the data it represents. Pie charts can help visualize the relative proportions of different categories in a data set.

In summary, the choice of visualization depends on the type of data being analyzed and the questions being asked. Scatter plots, line graphs, and bar graphs are commonly used for analyzing numerical data, while histograms and pie charts are more appropriate for categorical data.

Figure 13. Histogram between the total matches played and players who participated

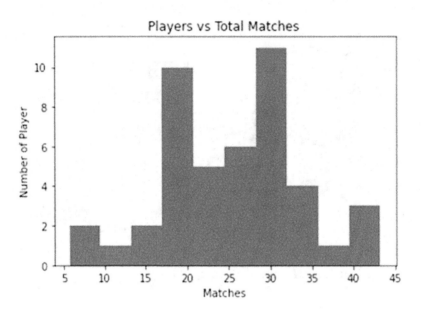

Figure 14. Pie chart between the percentage of every player's contribution to match winning

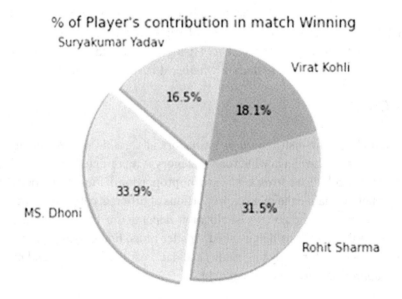

CASE STUDIES

1. Pakistan Super League (PSL) Win Prediction

This case study involves building a machine-learning model to predict the outcome of cricket matches in the Pakistan Super League (PSL). The model will use data about the number of wickets taken by each team, the number of balls left to be bowled, and the number of runs remaining to be scored by the team batting second to make its prediction. Based on these factors, the goal is to build a model that accurately predicts whether a team will win or lose a match. The model will be trained on a subset of the available data and tested on another subset to ensure accuracy. The ultimate goal of the study is to create a tool that cricket enthusiasts and analysts can use to predict the outcomes of future PSL matches with the help of the following models:

- Random Forest Classifier
- XGBoost Classifier
- SVM
- Logistic Regression

The complete implementation of the above case study is given here.

2. Player Performance Prediction

One potential case study could involve using machine learning and data science to predict the performance of individual players in cricket. This could include collecting data on various factors, such as past performance, age, bowling average, and batting average, and using that data to build predictive models to forecast how well players are likely to perform in future matches.

FUTURE RESEARCH DIRECTIONS

Future research in cricket data analysis can explore interdisciplinary collaborations with experts in sports science, biomechanics, computer vision, natural language processing, economics, psychology, and geography. This can lead to advancements in player performance analysis, injury prevention, real-time monitoring, fan sentiment analysis, economic impact assessment, and psychological factors influencing player motivation. Additionally, researchers should address implementation challenges, consider new data sources, develop advanced statistical models, and conduct comparative analyses of teams and players for improved cricket analytics.

- **Sports Science and Biomechanics:** Collaborating with experts in sports science and biomechanics can provide insights into player performance and injury prevention through the analysis of biomechanical data, such as body movements, muscle activity, and kinematics.
- **Internet of Things (IoT):** Leveraging IoT technology can enable real-time monitoring of player performance and health metrics, such as heart rate, body temperature, and fatigue levels, which can enhance performance analysis and inform training strategies.
- **Computer Vision and Image Analysis:** Applying computer vision techniques to cricket can involve ball tracking, player tracking, and object detection for performance analysis, umpire decision support systems, and player safety monitoring.
- **Natural Language Processing (NLP):** Utilizing NLP techniques can involve sentiment analysis of cricket fans' social media data, extracting insights from textual data, and analyzing commentary to understand public sentiment and engagement with the game.
- **Economics:** Incorporating economic analysis can provide insights into the financial aspects of cricket, such as analyzing the economic impact of tournaments, sponsorship valuation, ticket pricing, and revenue generation.
- **Psychology:** Collaborating with psychologists can contribute to understanding the psychological factors influencing player performance, mental health support systems, and strategies for enhancing player motivation and focus.
- **Advancements in machine learning and AI:** With the growth of big data, machine learning and AI can help cricket experts make sense of vast amounts of data generated during games. Future research could explore how machine learning algorithms can be applied to cricket data analysis to gain new insights into player performance, team dynamics, and fan engagement.
- **Integration of multiple data sources:** Integrating multiple data sources, such as wearables, social media, and streaming data, can provide a comprehensive understanding of the game of cricket. Future research could focus on effectively integrating these data sources into existing models for player analysis and team strategies.
- **New methods for injury prevention:** Player injuries are a significant concern in cricket, and there is a need for new methods to prevent them. Future research could explore how data analysis can help identify injury risks, optimize player training, and prevent injuries.
- **Cultural and linguistic barriers:** Cultural and linguistic barriers may make implementing new data analysis programs or models in cricket challenging. Future research could explore ways to overcome these challenges, such as

developing training programs or collaborations between cricket and data analysis experts.

- **Comparative analysis of different teams or players:** Comparative analysis of different teams or players can provide valuable insights into what factors contribute to winning performances in cricket. Future research could explore new methods for comparative analysis, such as network analysis or social network analysis, to better understand the game.

CONCLUSION

In conclusion, this chapter has provided a comprehensive exploration of the interdisciplinary application of machine learning, data science, and Python in cricket analytics. The analysis of diverse data types in cricket games and the associated challenges and opportunities were examined. By utilizing machine learning algorithms and Python, this chapter showcased the potential of these methodologies in gaining valuable insights into player performance, team strategies, and fan engagement. Emphasizing the importance of interdisciplinary collaboration, the chapter highlighted the significant role of machine learning, data science, and Python in enhancing cricket analytics. Aspiring to inspire further research and innovation in this dynamic field, this chapter serves as a valuable resource for individuals interested in the exciting realm of cricket analytics.

REFERENCES

Ahmad, H., Ahmad, S., Asif, M., Rehman, M., Alharbi, A., & Ullah, Z. (2021). Evolution-based performance prediction of star cricketers. *Computers, Materials & Continua, 69*(1), 1215–1232. doi:10.32604/cmc.2021.016659

Ahmed, W. (2015). *A Multivariate Data Mining Approach to Predict Match Outcome in One-Day International Cricket* [Doctoral dissertation]. Karachi Institute of Economics and Technology.

Anuraj, A., Boparai, G. S., Leung, C. K., Madill, E. W., Pandhi, D. A., Patel, A. D., & Vyas, R. K. (2023, March). Sports data mining for cricket match prediction. In *International Conference on Advanced Information Networking and Applications* (pp. 668-680). Cham: Springer International Publishing. 10.1007/978-3-031-28694-0_63

Dakhel, A. M., Majdinasab, V., Nikanjam, A., Khomh, F., Desmarais, M. C., & Jiang, Z. M. J. (2023). Github copilot ai pair programmer: Asset or liability? *Journal of Systems and Software*, *203*, 111734. doi:10.1016/j.jss.2023.111734

Das, N. R., Mukherjee, I., Patel, A. D., & Paul, G. (2023). An intelligent clustering framework for substitute recommendation and player selection. *The Journal of Supercomputing*, 1–33. doi:10.100711227-023-05314-z PMID:37359323

Goldbloom, A. (2010, October 1). *Kaggle*. Kaggle. Retrieved February 27, 2023, from https://www.kaggle.com/

Gunawardhana, L. G. U. P. (2022). *Optimising Cricket Team Selection for One Day International Series Based on Match Conditions* [Doctoral dissertation].

Kaluarachchi, A., & Aparna, S. V. (2010, December). CricAI: A classification based tool to predict the outcome in ODI cricket. In *2010 Fifth International Conference on Information and Automation for Sustainability* (pp. 250-255). IEEE. 10.1109/ICIAFS.2010.5715668

Khan, M., & Shah, R. (2015). Role of external factors on outcome of a One Day International cricket (ODI) match and predictive analysis. *International Journal of Advanced Research in Computer and Communication Engineering*, *4*(6), 192–197.

Mittal, H., Rikhari, D., Kumar, J., & Singh, A. K. (2021). *A study on machine learning approaches for player performance and match results prediction*. arXiv preprint arXiv:2108.10125.

Piatetsky-Shapiro, G. (2013). *KDnuggets*. Data Science and AI Consulting.

Prakash, C. D., Patvardhan, C., & Lakshmi, C. V. (2016). Data analytics based deep mayo predictor for IPL-9. *International Journal of Computer Applications*, *152*(6), 6–10. doi:10.5120/ijca2016911080

Priya, S., Gupta, A. K., Dwivedi, A., & Prabhakar, A. (2022, April). Analysis and Winning Prediction in T20 Cricket using Machine Learning. In *2022 Second International Conference on Advances in Electrical, Computing, Communication and Sustainable Technologies (ICAECT)* (pp. 1-4). IEEE. 10.1109/ICAECT54875.2022.9807929

Rasmussen, B. (2010, October 1). *ESPNcricinfo*. ESPNcricinfo. Retrieved February 27, 2023, from https://www.espncricinfo.com/

Vestly, D. J., Hariharan, S., Kukreja, V., Prasad, A. B., Swaraj, K., & Gopichand, D. (2023, May). Parametric Analysis of a Cricketer's Performance using Machine Learning Approach. In *2023 7th International Conference on Intelligent Computing and Control Systems (ICICCS)* (pp. 344-348). IEEE. 10.1109/ICICCS56967.2023.10142664

Vistro, D. M., Rasheed, F., & David, L. G. (2019). The cricket winner prediction with application of machine learning and data analytics. *International Journal of Scientific & Technology Research*, 8(09).

Wang, P. (2012, July 17). *Download and Install Anaconda*. Anaconda. Retrieved February 27, 2023, from https://www.anaconda.com/

ADDITIONAL READING

Anshuman, A. (2022). Cricket geographies: Towards a spatial analysis of cricket in the maidans in India. *GeoJournal*, *87*(6), 4915–4930. doi:10.100710708-021-10536-w

Awan, M. J., Gilani, S. A. H., Ramzan, H., Nobanee, H., Yasin, A., Zain, A. M., & Javed, R. (2021). Cricket match analytics using the big data approach. *Electronics (Basel)*, *10*(19), 2350. doi:10.3390/electronics10192350

Biswas, M., Niamat Ullah Akhund, T. M., Mahbub, M. K., Saiful Islam, S. M., Sorna, S., & Shamim Kaiser, M. (2022). A survey on predicting player's performance and team recommendation in game of cricket using machine learning. In Information and Communication Technology for Competitive Strategies (ICTCS 2020) ICT: Applications and Social Interfaces (pp. 223-230). Springer Singapore. doi:10.1007/978-981-16-0739-4_22

Chitra, R., Jayapreetha, N., Swetha, S., & Swetha, D. (2022, March). Runout detection in cricket using IOT. In *2022 International Conference on Communication, Computing and Internet of Things (IC3IoT)* (pp. 1-5). IEEE.

Constable, M., Wundersitz, D., Bini, R., & Kingsley, M. (2021). Quantification of the demands of cricket bowling and the relationship to injury risk: A systematic review. *BMC Sports Science, Medicine and Rehabilitation*, *13*(1), 1–12. doi:10.118613102-021-00335-8 PMID:34507613

Foysal, M. F. A., Islam, M. S., Karim, A., & Neehal, N. (2019). Shot-Net: A convolutional neural network for classifying different cricket shots. In *Recent Trends in Image Processing and Pattern Recognition: Second International Conference, RTIP2R 2018, Solapur, India, December 21–22, 2018, Revised Selected Papers, Part I 2* (pp. 111-120). Springer Singapore. 10.1007/978-981-13-9181-1_10

Glazier, P. S., & Wheat, J. S. (2014). An integrated approach to the biomechanics and motor control of cricket fast bowling techniques. *Sports Medicine (Auckland, N.Z.), 44*(1), 25–36. doi:10.100740279-013-0098-x PMID:24065337

Han, J., Kamber, M., & Pei, J. (2011). *Data Mining Concepts and Techniques.* Morgan Kaufmann.

Millar, R., Plumley, D., Wilson, R., & Dickson, G. (2023). Federated networks in England and Australia cricket: A model of economic dependency and financial insecurity. *Sport, Business and Management, 13*(2), 161–180. doi:10.1108/SBM-09-2021-0100

Mustafa, R. U., Nawaz, M. S., Lali, M. I. U., Zia, T., & Mehmood, W. (2017). Predicting the cricket match outcome using crowd opinions on social networks: A comparative study of machine learning methods. *Malaysian Journal of Computer Science, 30*(1), 63–76. doi:10.22452/mjcs.vol30no1.5

Omuya, E. O., Okeyo, G., & Kimwele, M. (2023). Sentiment analysis on social media tweets using dimensionality reduction and natural language processing. *Engineering Reports, 5*(3), e12579. doi:10.1002/eng2.12579

Passi, K., & Pandey, N. (2017). *Predicting players' performance in one day international cricket matches using machine learning. Computer Science & Information Technology.*

Prakash, C. D., Patvardhan, C., & Singh, S. (2016). A new machine learning based deep performance index for ranking IPL T20 cricketers. *International Journal of Computer Applications, 137*(10), 42–49. doi:10.5120/ijca2016908903

Swartz, T. B. (2017). Research directions in cricket. In *Handbook of statistical methods and analyses in sports* (pp. 461–476). Chapman and Hall/CRC.

Wickramasinghe, I. (2022). Applications of Machine Learning in cricket: A systematic review. *Machine Learning with Applications, 10*, 100435. doi:10.1016/j.mlwa.2022.100435

Yedurkar, D. P., Metkar, S., Al-Turjman, F., Yardi, N., & Stephan, T. (2023). An IoT Based Novel Hybrid Seizure Detection Approach for Epileptic Monitoring. *IEEE Transactions on Industrial Informatics*, 1–13. doi:10.1109/TII.2023.3274913

KEY TERMS AND DEFINITIONS

Analytics: Collecting, processing, and analyzing data to obtain insights and make informed decisions.

Data Science: A multidisciplinary field that uses statistical and computational methods to extract knowledge and insights from data.

Machine Learning: A subfield of artificial intelligence that involves the development of algorithms and models that enable computers to learn and improve from experience.

Predictive Modeling: Using statistical algorithms and machine learning techniques to build models that can predict future outcomes.

Python: An open-source programming language widely used in data science and machine learning.

Regression Analysis: A statistical technique used to model the relationship between a dependent variable and one or more independent variables.

Supervised Learning: A type of machine learning where the algorithm is trained on labeled data, meaning that the desired output is known beforehand, and the algorithm learns to map the input to the output.

Visual Analytics: The use of visual representations, such as graphs and charts, to facilitate data exploration and analysis.

Chapter 3
Application of Machine Learning for Disabled Persons

Rajeshri Shinkar
Sies (Nerul) College of ASC, Mumbai University, India

ABSTRACT

Communication with the disabled person who is deaf-mute person is very difficult. Even though sign language is crucial for deaf-mute persons to communicate with other people and with themselves, regular people still pay it little attention. Normal people often overlook the value of sign language unless they have family members who are deaf-mute. Using sign language interpreters is one way to communicate with those who are deaf-mute. However, hiring sign language interpreters can be expensive. A model that can automatically convert their motions into words can be used as a low-cost replacement for the interpreters. This chapter gives the description about the development of a model which helps automatic detection of actions with real time using the Mediapipe model and then with the help of sign language conversion model it translates into the textual format.

INTRODUCTION

Deafness is a handicap that affects hearing and renders a person mute, whereas muteness is a disability that affects speaking and renders a person speechless. Both can still perform many other things because their hearing and/or speaking is the only thing that is impaired. Communication is the only thing separating them from average people. The deaf-mute people can live easily as a regular person if there is a mechanism for normal people and deaf-mute people to communicate. And sign language is the only means of communication for them. The visual means

DOI: 10.4018/978-1-6684-8696-2.ch003

of communication used in sign language to communicate meaning include facial expressions, hand gestures, and body movements. The use of sign language is very beneficial for those who have hearing loss (Mandeep Kaur Ahuja, 2015).

Therefore, translating sign language into words using an algorithm or model can aid in closing the communication gap between those who have hearing or speech disability and the rest of society (Supriya A.K., 2009) .Computer vision and machine learning researchers are now conducting intensive research in the area of image-based hand gesture identification. With the aim of making human computer interaction (HCI) simpler and more natural without the use of additional devices, it is an area where many researchers are researching. Therefore, the main objective of research on gesture recognition is to develop systems that can recognise certain human gestures and use them, for instance, to convey information. Vision-based hand gesture interfaces need quick and incredibly reliable hand detection for that (Sunitha K.A, 2016).

OBJECTIVES

- A real-time vision-based system called the Sign Language Recognition model is used to identify the Universal Sign Language.
- The model's goal was to evaluate the viability of a vision-based approach to sign language recognition while also testing and selecting body features (key points) that could be used with machine learning algorithms to enable their use in real-time sign language recognition systems.
- Once fully implemented, this technology will be able to automate translation instead of relying on human translators, which will save time and resources.

METHODOLOGY AND STEPS

The system is a vision-based approach. All the signs are represented with bare hands and so it eliminates the problem of using any artificial devices for interaction.

Following is the FlowChart of steps involved in building the proposed system.

Import and Install Dependencies
⇓
Keypoints using MP Holistic
⇓
Extract Keypoint Values
⇓

Setup Folders for Collection

Collect Keypoint Values for Training and Testing(Dataset Generation)

Preprocess Data and Create Labels and Features

Build and Train LSTM Neural Network

Make Predictions

Save Weights
⇓
Evaluation using Confusion Matrix and Accuracy
⇓
Testing in Real Time

Import and Install Dependencies

Tensorflow, OpenCV and Mediapipe are the primary libraries used here. Apart from these, Sklearn, Matplotlib, Numpy, OS and Time are some other libraries that are imported and used while building this system (Nakul Nagpal, 2017).

Keypoints Using MP Holistic and Extract Keypoint Values

Mediapipe is a cross-platform library developed by Google that provides amazing ready-to-use ML solutions for computer vision tasks.

MediaPipe Holistic utilizes the pose, face and hand landmark models in MediaPipe Pose, MediaPipe Face Mesh and MediaPipe Hands respectively to generate a total of 543 landmarks (33 pose landmarks, 468 face landmarks, and 21 hand landmarks per hand).

The MediaPipe perception pipeline is called a Graph. Let us take the example of the first solution, Hands. We feed a stream of images as input which comes out with hand landmarks rendered on the images.

The flowchart below represents the MP hand solution graph.

Figure 1. Hand landmarks

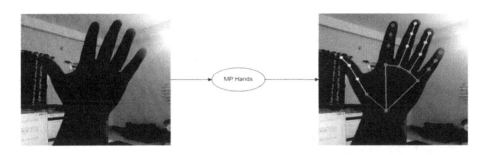

Figure 2. Hand solution flowchart

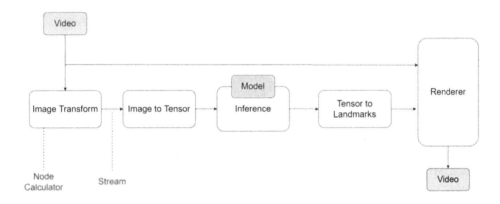

Figure 3. Pose landmarks key points

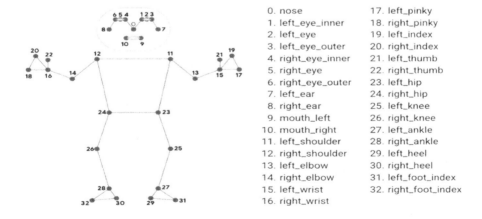

0. nose	17. left_pinky
1. left_eye_inner	18. right_pinky
2. left_eye	19. left_index
3. left_eye_outer	20. right_index
4. right_eye_inner	21. left_thumb
5. right_eye	22. right_thumb
6. right_eye_outer	23. left_hip
7. left_ear	24. right_hip
8. right_ear	25. left_knee
9. mouth_left	26. right_knee
10. mouth_right	27. left_ankle
11. left_shoulder	28. right_ankle
12. right_shoulder	29. left_heel
13. left_elbow	30. right_heel
14. right_elbow	31. left_foot_index
15. left_wrist	32. right_foot_index
16. right_wrist	

Figure 4. Pose landmarks key points visualization

Setup Folders for Collection

As a part of storing our data, we need a folder to hold our input values. A folder named MP_Data has been created with 3 sub folders within it that will hold our actions(3 actions here) and this may depend on the number of actions that we need to use. Each folder here will contain 30 values(frames) i.e 30 frames for each action.

Collect Keypoint Values for Training and Testing (Dataset Generation)

The main device used as an input process in Sign Language Recognition (SLR) is the camera. The SLR input data is in the form of gesture (action) that can be easily captured by camera using OpenCV. We have captured 30 frames per second real-time video, which was then analyzed for dynamic gestures frame by frame.

Preprocess Data and Create Labels and Features

After the data collection process we now need to name the collected input values w.r.t their actions and this is done by labelling. By using Label_map we label the actions generated with their respective names.

Build and Train LSTM Neural Network

Sequential models have been used along with LSTM and Dense layers in the model building part. Relu activation function has been used in the hidden layers and in the output layer softmax has been applied.

Make Predictions

Using the "model.predict" function we can manually predict how the system is working once the model is trained.

Save Weights

We can even save our trained model weights so that we can skip the training part everytime we run this system by using the"model.save" function that saves the weights in h5 format. "Model.load_weights" is used to reload the saved weights while re-running the system.

Evaluation using Confusion Matrix and Accuracy

A confusion matrix is a table that is used to define the performance of a classification algorithm. A confusion matrix visualizes and summarizes the performance of a classification algorithm and Accuracy score is the most intuitive performance measure of the system. An Accuracy score of 80% and above has been achieved in this system.

Testing in Real Time

This is the final phase where you check the working of the model. The system will now predict the sign language action based on the training provided and display the respective labels or outputs. Once the model is successfully built you can see the outputs along with their respective probability bar and occurrence at the top which helps in a better visualization. (Banerji, 1928)

Figure 5. Confusion matrix representation

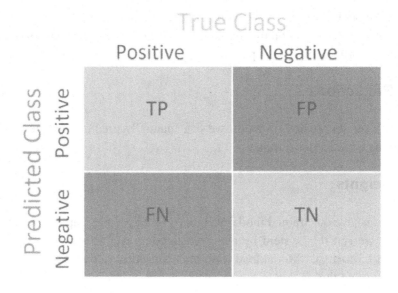

Figure 6. Detected action for YOUR

Figure 7. Detected action for NAME

Figure 8. Detected action for PLEASE

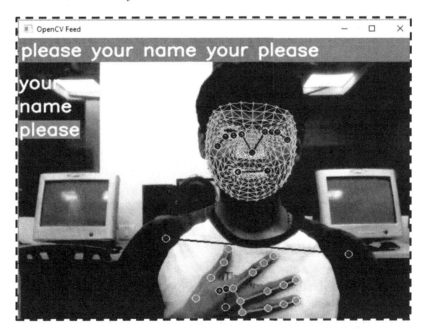

Network Diagram

Figure 9.

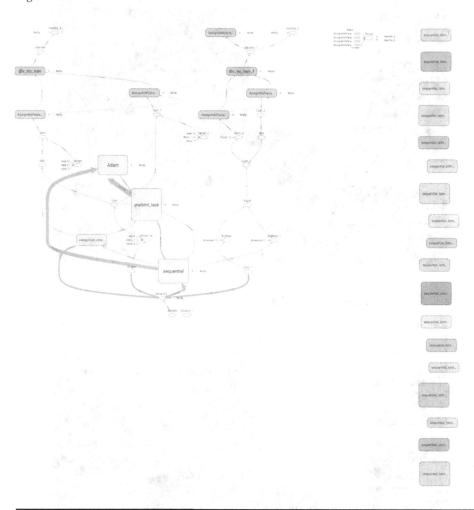

RESULTS AND CONCLUSION

In this report, a functional real time action recognition for sign language for Deaf and Mute people has been developed for some common actions and words. We achieved a final accuracy of around 80.00%+ on our dataset. The model is accurately predicting the actions and is displaying the respective labelled results that have been fed during the training. As shown in Figures 5-7 the model has accurately predicted

3 actions performed which were "YOUR", "NAME" and "PLEASE" that actually points to the formation of the sentence "YOUR NAME PLEASE". Keypoints are also displayed along with the video feed so that the user can adjust the body part that is being displayed on the screen for generating better results. This system when integrated with existing SL models with advanced vision detection functionalities can be a game changer to detect real time actions and generate their labels accordingly in no time making is much easier to hold a strong conversation with Deaf and Mute people and will definitely act as a language bridge to overcome the existing communication gap among normal people and the deaf-mute.

LIMITATIONS

The methods used in developing Sign Language Recognition are varied between the developers. Each method has its own strengths and limitations compared to other methods. There always is a scope of improvement in any system; and following are the drawbacks of the built model:

1. The implemented solution uses only one camera(laptop), and is based on a set of actions that we have trained and are, hereby defined.
2. The user must be within a defined perimeter area, in front of the camera.
3. The user must be within a defined distance range, due to camera limitations.
4. Limited actions/dataset.
5. A system with good speed, memory and GPU/TPU is required for the development of such models that have a large amount of dataset that has to be trained and tested.

FUTURE SCOPE

The system generated here can be termed as a small-scale model due to the system and processing limitations. If computed and processed on a large scale with state-of-the-art technologies this system can do wonders. It can be implemented in any location where there's a need to interpret and communicate with deaf-mute people. The system can be used in public places, schools, hospitals, and various institutes where there's a need for such translations due to the lack of human interpreters. Television broadcasting systems can also use this model to generate real time news and will in turn save time. There are many other places as well where such a system is required for SL translation. May it be any place, this system will never go out of use because there always is a need for some service that has to be used as a communication bridge between the deaf-mute and normal people.

REFERENCES

Ahuja, M. K., & Singh, A. (2015, July). Hand Gesture Recognition Using PCA. *International Journal of Computer Science and Engineering Technology, 5*(7), 267–27.

Banerji, J. N. (1928). *India International Reports of Schools for the Deaf. Washington City.* Volta Bureau.

Brill, R. (1986). *The Conference of Educational Administrators Serving the Deaf: A History.* Gallaudet University Press.

Munib, Q., Habeeb, M., Takruri, B., & Al-Malik, H. A. (2007). American Sign Language (ASL) recognition based on Hough transform and neural networks. *Expert Systems with Applications, 32*(1), 24–37. doi:10.1016/j.eswa.2005.11.018

Nagpal, Mitra, & Agrawal. (n.d.). Design Issue and Proposed Implementation of Communication Aid for Deaf & Dumb People. *International Journal on Recent and Innovation Trends in Computing and Communication, 3*(5), 147-149.

Sunitha, K. A. (2016). Deaf Mute Communication Interpreter-A Review. *International Journal of Applied Engineering Research, 11*, 290–296.

Suryapriya, A. K., Sumam, S., & Idicula, M. (2009). Design and Development of a Frame based MT System for English to ISL. *World Congress on Nature and Biologically Inspired Computing*, 1382-1387.

Chapter 4
Performing Facial Recognition Using Ensemble Learning

Layton Chetty
University of Wollongong in Dubai, UAE

Abshir Odowa
University of Wollongong in Dubai, UAE

Aeron Christler Avenido
University of Wollongong in Dubai, UAE

Ismail Hussein
University of Wollongong in Dubai, UAE

Yassin Elakkad
University of Wollongong in Dubai, UAE

ABSTRACT

Investment in facial recognition technologies has increased recently with the amount of venture capital invested in facial recognition startups dramatically increasing in 2021. Facial recognition uses AI and ML techniques to find human faces in the surrounding area. Facial recognition technology is used by the web application Automated Attendance System (AAS) which was developed by a group of students from the University of Wollongong in Dubai to automate attendance management in educational institutions. AAS is simple to use, quick to implement, and can be incorporated into current educational institutions. Deep convolutional neural networks, notably the VGG19 and EfficientNetB0 models, are the foundation of the system. These models were trained for high accuracy utilizing transfer learning and ensemble learning. The automation of attendance tracking reduces human error; increases efficiency, accuracy, and integrity; and does away with the need for manual methods of collecting attendance.

DOI: 10.4018/978-1-6684-8696-2.ch004

INTRODUCTION

The most important factor to recognize a person is their face. Facial recognition can be used to distinguish between people's faces using the technologies of the modern day with applications such as an unlock system for a phone and airport boarding and checks. The automated attendance system allows a student's attendance to be recorded on a particular day. The student needs to go through facial recognition to mark the attendance. Once facial recognition is done, the details of ID number, date and in-time are saved in the database. The information will be stored in a cloud that forms a connection with the system and server through the internet. The system will consist of a GUI where additional information about the student will be present.

The automated attendance system is made for students at universities and can be applied to students at schools to record their attendance and in-time to be stored in a database. The system involves two AI models, namely, VGG19 and EfficientNet to gather information and differentiate between students by utilizing transfer learning and ensemble learning and a GUI to verify the attendance of those students. The GUI will present information such as the details of the student, the date and how many absences they have.

Pre-Requisites

Before starting the project, research about facial recognition, how it is done, and how to increase its accuracy in different environments is necessary. Since the project involves artificial intelligence, choosing which language to use is important and understanding the libraries which can be used for image processing and machine learning itself. Determining what hardware is needed for the project is also something which is considered.

BACKGROUND

Facial recognition is a cutting-edge topic with enormous implications for security, surveillance, and human-computer interaction. It allows machines to recognize and authenticate people based on their distinctive facial traits. Researchers, technologists, and society at large have all become fascinated by the capacity to automatically detect and distinguish faces. This technology has a lot of potential because it provides accurate and dependable identification solutions across a wide range of industries. AI and ML algorithms are used in facial recognition to identify human faces in the environment. Usually, the algorithm looks for human eyes first, then for eyebrows, nose, mouth, nostrils, and iris (Suneratech, 2021). Intelligent software powered by

AI can instantly search face databases and match them to one or more faces found in an environment. Incredibly accurate findings can be received instantly; typically, systems provide 99.5% accuracy rates on open standard data sets. Each AI facial recognition system requires extensive face picture training. AI models need to be trained on facial photos that differ in terms of age, ethnicity, lighting, angles, and other elements (Recfaces, 2021). As mentioned by Mohanakrishnan (2021), a facial recognition software goes through three steps:

Detection

An image of a face is discerned and extracted digitally. A 'faceprint', a special code used to identify the assigned person, is formed by marking a wide variety of facial traits (including eye distance, nose shape, race and demographic information, and even facial emotions).

Matching

The database uses multiple layers of technology to verify this faceprint against other templates that are already saved on the system. The algorithms have been trained to recognize subtleties and take into account variations in lighting, angle, and human emotion.

Identification

Whether face recognition software is being utilized for surveillance or authentication will determine this phase. In an ideal scenario, the technology should provide a one-to-one match for the subject, working through numerous intricate layers to whittle down the available alternatives. Some software developers, for instance, analyze skin texture in addition to facial recognition algorithms in order to improve accuracy.

Adjabi et al. (2020) stated that facial recognition technology has evolved significantly over the years. In 1964, American researchers developed a semi-automatic method that required operators to enter twenty measures for facial recognition such as eyes or mouth size. Subsequent improvements in 1977 added additional markers, and in 1988, artificial intelligence and mathematics were introduced to interpret and manipulate images without relying on human markers. In 1991, the Eigenfaces method demonstrated successful facial recognition using statistical Principal Component Analysis (PCA). DARPA's FERET program in 1998 and the FRGC competition in 2005 further advanced facial recognition research. Deep learning, based on artificial neural networks, gained momentum in 2011, with Facebook's Deepface algorithm achieving near-human accuracy in 2014. Presently, facial recognition technology finds applications in various sectors, including Apple's implementation in retail and banking, Mastercard's Selfie Pay for online transactions, and the use of live facial recognition by Chinese police for surveillance and identification purposes.

The amount of money invested in facial recognition technology has surged recently. In 2021, venture funding for facial recognition start-ups has significantly increased. There are various industries that have integrated AI in face recognition in the form of new use cases and business models in the areas of marketing, healthcare, security, proctoring, airports, etc. will emerge as a result of technological improvements (Suneratech, 2021).

LITERATURE REVIEW

According to Pintelas and Livieris (2020), an ensemble-based semi-supervised learning method was developed by Livieris et al. to classify lung abnormalities from chest X-rays. The suggested technique makes use of a new weighted voting system that gives each ensemble member learner a vector of weights based on how accurately it can identify each class. The Pneumonia chest X-rays dataset from Guangzhou Women and Children's Medical Center, the Tuberculosis dataset from Shenzhen Hospital, and the Cancer CT-medical imaging dataset were used as the primary benchmarks for the proposed algorithm's thorough evaluation. Their numerical results demonstrated the effectiveness of the suggested ensemble methodology in comparison to the simple voting method and other conventional semi-supervised methods.

Pintelas and Livieris (2020) mentioned that Papageorgiou et al. proposed an original ensemble time-series forecasting model to forecast the demand for gas in Greece. The model is built on an ensemble learning method that uses time-series prediction capabilities of evolutionary Fuzzy Cognitive Maps (FCMs), Artificial Neural Networks (ANNs), and their hybrid structure, known as FCM-ANN. On three time-series datasets involving information from distribution sites that make up the natural gas grid of a Greek region, the prediction performance of the suggested model was contrasted with that of the Long Short-Term Memory (LSTM) model. The results provide empirical proof that the suggested method could be successfully applied to forecast consumption of gas needs.

Karlos et al. (2020) introduced an ensemble-based co-training technique for binary classification issues. The foundation of the suggested methodology is the co-training framework's imposition of an ensemble classifier as a base learner. A static ensemble selection method from a pool of potential students determines its structure. Their experimental findings in a variety of traditional benchmarks, along with the statistical analysis they published, demonstrated the effectiveness and efficiency of their methodology.

Zvarevashe and Olugbara (2020) put up the use of "Ensemble Learning of Hybrid Acoustic Features for Speech Emotion Recognition" by looking into the issue that many categorization algorithms did not effectively and accurately distinguish the emotion of dread in comparison to other emotions. They developed an elegant methodology, based on an intriguing feature extraction technique, to improve the accuracy of fear along with other emotions' recognition from speech signals in order to solve this issue. A novel set of hybrid acoustic features is created by agglutinating highly discriminating speech emotion representations of features from several sources. Using several cutting-edge ensemble classifiers, the researchers ran a number of experiments on two publicly accessible databases. The investigation that was presented, which evaluated the effectiveness of their methodology, showed that using the new features improved the generalization capacity of all ensemble classifiers.

Haralabopoulos et al. (2020) constructed a multilabel ensemble model for classifying emotions that makes use of a brand-new weighted voting scheme based on differential evolution. The suggested model also made use of deep learning learners, which included layers for convolutional and pooling functions as well as (LSTM) layers specifically designed for classification challenges. They conducted a performance test of their model versus cutting-edge single models and ensemble models made up of the same basic learners on two significant and commonly used datasets to demonstrate its efficacy. The observed numerical experiments demonstrated that the proposed model outperformed cutting-edge comparative models in terms of enhanced classification performance.

Methodology

There are a few main problems regarding attendance and its integrity amongst university students. Depending on the university and their classroom requirements, these problems can vary in their impact on the attendance system.

- **Time consuming:** Some classrooms can hold 100 or more students which would require excess amounts of time to record the students' attendance manually. Any time taken away from the students can potentially hinder their learning and schedule.
- **Integrity:** Without an attendance system, students could deliberately fabricate the attendance of another student by either including the student's details on a paper or sending the QR code to the absent student to record their attendance depending on the adoption of the teacher.

- • **Inaccurate information:** The teacher could mishear or enter a typo when recording the students' attendance manually.

The aim of this chapter is to provide an understanding of how to create a powerful facial recognition system that overcomes the constraints and difficulties presented by the available technology using various other technologies. The current facial recognition systems frequently struggle with problems like low accuracy, trouble identifying faces in various lighting situations, position fluctuations, occlusions, and a lack of training data. The system's effectiveness is hampered by these flaws, which can result in misidentification, false positives and negatives, and compromised security. Therefore, it is necessary to develop and deploy a sophisticated facial recognition system that can distinguish faces properly and dependably under a variety of lighting, stance, and occlusion conditions. Modern deep learning methods, a variety of training datasets, and cutting-edge algorithms should all be used by the system to enhance face detection, feature extraction, and matching.

The automated attendance system (AAS) can be used as a solution to solve the problem stated above. The focus being on efficiency, integrity, and precision. The process of this solution involves taking multiple pictures of the students at different angles and distances and then using RetinaFace to extract the faces from those pictures which then makes up the dataset that will be used for this study. Two models, VGG19 and EfficientNet that are initially pre-trained on the ImageNet dataset will be created and fine-tuned on the dataset before training. The two models are then used to make predictions in real time on the detected faces of the students which gets carried out by using the MTCNN face detector followed by computing the average of those predictions through ensemble learning to make more accurate predictions on the detected faces. This makes it so that learning is efficient for the students and teaching is immediately started by the professor instead of wasting time marking attendance manually. The integrity of attendance will be improved considering the use of paper, QR code or any other manual process will no longer be required because this can be easily fabricated by the students. Having an automated attendance system will reduce the possibility of human error by the teacher when recording students' attendance considering that the system does not require any involvement from the teacher.

DISCUSSION

The automated attendance system can address these problems by reducing the time taken to record students' attendance since that process would only involve the students standing in front of the camera located at the entrance of the classroom.

The integrity of attendance will be improved considering the use of paper, QR code or any other manual process will no longer be required. Having an automated attendance system will reduce the possibility of human error by the teacher when recording students' attendance considering that the system does not require any involvement from the teacher.

Although, the implementation explained in this chapter will not provide 100% accuracy. There are many parameters to the technologies used and aspects to facial recognition that contribute towards an efficient evaluation. The implementation of facial recognition in this chapter was achieved with respect to the computing power available. With more computing power, the implementation can be enhanced for a better evaluation.

Technologies Used

Image Processing Tools

OpenCV: OpenCV is an open-source library that is predominantly used image processing in addition to computer vision and machine learning in real-time operations. The library is utilized to perform real time operations such as identifying faces, objects, etc. In addition, OpenCV provides capabilities that allow systems to utilize GPU acceleration for better refined real-time operations (YoungWonks, 2021). OpenCV can be used to build a facial recognition pipeline by applying deep learning methods. This is done in two steps:

Face detection where model understands and detects presence of a face in an image or a video.

Obtaining the 128-d feature embedding that characterizes faces in images or videos.

Keras: is a popular open-source deep learning framework that provides a high-level API for building and training neural networks. Keras is often used for image processing tasks, such as image classification, object detection, and image segmentation (Simplilearn, 2021).

In Keras, the image processing model typically consists of several layers of neural networks, which are designed to extract meaningful features from the input images. These layers can include convolutional layers, pooling layers, and fully connected layers (Simplilearn, 2021).

Convolutional layers are the key building blocks of a (CNN), which is a type of neural network that is widely used for image processing tasks. These layers perform convolution operations on the input image, which involve sliding a small filter or kernel over the image and computing the dot product between the filter and the image at each location. This process helps to extract important features from the image, such as edges, textures, and shapes (Simplilearn, 2021).

Machine Learning Tools

<u>TensorFlow:</u> TensorFlow is an open-source library that is used to increase efficiency of machine learning and development of neural networks. In addition, it provides users with wide range of pre-trained models that can be used for testing and much more (Serdar, 2022).

<u>Keras:</u> The open-source Keras neural network library was created in Python and may be used with TensorFlow, CNTK, or Theano. It is renowned for its user-friendliness, flexibility, and extensibility since it is intended to facilitate quick experimentation with deep neural networks (Simplilearn, 2021).

There are several pre-built models in Keras that may be utilized for facial recognition jobs. The FaceNet model, a deep convolutional neural network that learns to provide a compact embedding of face traits, is one example of such a model. The model can identify faces with a high degree of accuracy because it was trained on a sizable collection of facial images (Simplilearn, 2021).

In order to guarantee that facial features are appropriately positioned and aligned, Keras also incorporates pre-processing capabilities for facial recognition tasks like face alignment. Moreover, Keras has several techniques for data augmentation that can assist facial recognition models perform better by enlarging and diversifying the training dataset (Simplilearn, 2021).

All things considered, Keras is a strong and adaptable tool for creating and refining deep learning models, including those for face recognition applications. For academics and developers working on deep learning projects, it is a popular option because to its simplicity of use and extensive library of pre-built models (Simplilearn, 2021).

<u>FaceNet:</u> It is a deep neural network that can be used for image processing purposes as well as face detection utilizing a person's different facial features such as: right and left eye; right and left side of the nose; right and left side of the mouth. For each face image, the model creates a high-dimensional embedding using a neural network that can be used to compare and identify faces accurately (Luka, 2019).

Multi-Task Cascaded Network (MTCNN): A neural network called a convolutional neural network can recognize faces and other facial landmarks in photos. Three neural networks are coupled in a cascade using this system (Luka, 2019).

RetinaFace: RetinaFace was utilized to find faces in the photos in the dataset. To do this, each picture is run through the RetinaFace model to get the bounding boxes for the faces that were recognized. Using these bounding boundaries, the next step is to extract the identified faces from the photos (Serengil, 2023).

The extracted faces were then saved as separate pictures with file names that match to the original photos in order to create another dataset that only contained the identified faces (Serengil, 2023).

VGG19

Researchers from the Visual Geometry Group (VGG) at the University of Oxford introduced the deep convolutional neural network (CNN) known as the VGG19 model in 2014 (Simonyan & Zisserman, 2014). Due to its superior performance and relatively straightforward architecture, it is one of the CNN models that is most frequently used for image recognition tasks. The VGG19 model uses max pooling and ReLU activation functions and has 19 layers, including 16 convolutional layers and 3 fully connected layers. On the ImageNet Large Scale Visual Recognition Challenge (IMAGENET, 2014) in 2014, the model demonstrated state-of-the-art performance (Simonyan & Zisserman, 2014). Since then, it has served as the foundation model for numerous computer vision applications of transfer learning.

EfficientNet

A series of convolutional neural network (CNN) designs known as the EfficientNet model has completely changed the area of computer vision. EfficientNet, created by Google researchers, tackles the problem of striking a balance between model size, accuracy, and processing efficiency (Tan & Le, 2019). EfficientNet uses a compound scaling method to automatically scale the depth, breadth, and resolution of the model, in contrast to previous approaches that manually create network designs. By scaling, EfficientNet is able to perform at the cutting edge on a variety of computer vision tasks while utilizing less input parameters and processing resources.

The EfficientNet model can be used effectively for facial recognition applications thanks to its effective and strong design. Identification or verification of people based on their facial traits is known as facial recognition. Due to EfficientNet's deep learning capabilities, it can recognize faces in images with high accuracy and efficiency by learning and extracting relevant facial features from them. EfficientNet can accurately capture each person's distinctive face features by being trained on extensive facial datasets.

The trained EfficientNet model may take input photos with faces, extract pertinent characteristics, and compare them to a database of recognized faces during inference to identify or verify the faces. EfficientNetB0 is especially well suited for real-time or resource-constrained applications because of its small size and great computational efficiency, while more demanding situations can make use of bigger variations like EfficientNetB1 or higher (Tan & Le, 2019).

TRAINING MODELS

VGG19 Model

Figure 1.
Note: The following codes were executed using Python version 3.10.0.

```
import matplotlib.pyplot as plt
import tensorflow as tf
import pickle
from keras import regularizers
from tensorflow.python.keras.layers import Dense, Flatten, Dropout
from keras.models import Sequential
from keras.optimizers import RMSprop
from datetime import datetime
```

Import the libraries for training and evaluating the model.

Figure 2.

```
# Preparing data
num_classes=5                   # Value is the number of folders in the dataset folder

img_height,img_width=224,224
batch_size=64                   # Number of samples processed before the model is updated
```

Prepare data with respect to how many students/people are in the dataset by specifying num_classes and specify the image dimensions and number of samples to be processed before updating the model.

Figure 3.

```
# Loading data from directories
train_ds=tf.keras.preprocessing.image_dataset_from_directory(
  'student dataset',
  validation_split=0.15,
  subset="training",
  seed 123,
  shuffle=True,        # shuffle order of data during training to prevent memorization and learn general patterns in data better
  image_size=(img_height, img_width),
  batch_size=batch_size,
  )

val_ds=tf.keras.preprocessing.image_dataset_from_directory(
  'student dataset',
  validation_split=0.15,
  subset="validation",
  seed=123,
  shuffle=False,
  image_size=(img_height, img_width),
  batch_size=batch_size,
  )

test_ds=tf.keras.preprocessing.image_dataset_from_directory(
  'student_dataset',
  validation_split=0.15,
  subset="validation",
  seed=123,
  shuffle=False,
  image_size=(img_height, img_width),
  batch_size=batch_size,
  )
```

Load and split the dataset into train, validation and test datasets.

Figure 4.

```
# Creating model
vgg19_model=Sequential(name='VGG19_Model')

# Creating a pre-trained VGG19 model on the imagenet dataset
pretrained_model=tf.keras.applications.VGG19(include_top=False,
                 input_shape=(224,224,3),
                 pooling='avg',classes=num_classes,
                 weights='imagenet')

# Freeze the weights of the pre-trained layers
for layer in pretrained_model.layers:
        layer.trainable=False

# Define the VGG19 model architecture
vgg19_model.add(pretrained_model)
vgg19_model.add(Flatten())
vgg19_model.add(Dropout(0.5)) # Add dropout layer with a rate to prevent overfitting
  # Can add more Dense layers if adding more data to model
vgg19_model.add(Dense(512, activation='relu', kernel_regularizer=regularizers.l2(0.01)))  # Add l2 regularization to prevent overfitting
vgg19_model.add(Dropout(0.5))
vgg19_model.add(Dense(num_classes, activation='softmax', kernel_regularizer=regularizers.l2(0.01)))

vgg19_model.summary()
```

Create and define VGG19 model architecture.

Figure 5.

```
# Compiling model
vgg19_model.compile(optimizer=RMSprop(learning_rate=0.001),loss='sparse_categorical_crossentropy',metrics=['accuracy'])
```

Compile model with the RMSprop optimizer for improving the accuracy along with specifying the learning_rate which for this case is 0.001.

Figure 6.

```
# Training model
start = datetime.now()

epochs=40              # Number of iterations through the dataset
history = vgg19_model.fit(
    train_ds,
    validation_data=val_ds,
    epochs=epochs
)

# Save model
vgg19_model.save("models/vgg19_model")
```

Train model by specifying how many iterations to have through the dataset and call the fit function on the training and validation data along with the number of iterations through the dataset and then save model.

Evaluate model, outputs two graphs, "fig1" and "fig2" with data about the model accuracy and model loss respectively.

Test model using the test dataset and output its test accuracy.

Figure 7.

```python
# Evaluating model
fig1 = plt.gcf()
plt.plot(history.history['accuracy'])
plt.plot(history.history['val_accuracy'])
plt.axis(ymin=0.4, ymax=1)
plt.grid()
plt.title('Model accuracy')
plt.ylabel('Accuracy')
plt.xlabel('Epoch')
plt.legend(['Train', 'Val'], loc='upper left')
plt.savefig('VGG19_model_accuracy.png')
plt.show()

fig2 = plt.gcf()
plt.plot(history.history['loss'])
plt.plot(history.history['val_loss'])
plt.axis(ymin=0, ymax=3)
plt.grid()
plt.title('Model loss')
plt.ylabel('Loss')
plt.xlabel('Epoch')
plt.legend(['Train', 'Val'], loc='upper right')
plt.savefig('VGG19_model_loss.png')
plt.show()
```

Figure 8.

```python
# Testing model
test_loss, test_acc = vgg19_model.evaluate(test_ds, verbose=2)
print('\nTest accuracy:', test_acc)
```

VGG19 Model Results

Figure 9.

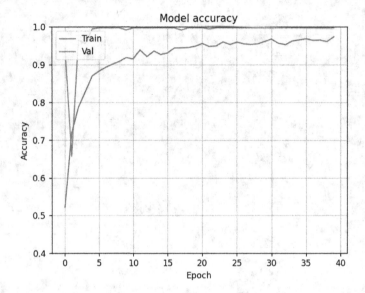

Model accuracy graph, shows the trend in training and validation accuracy from the beginning of training the model until training is done. As the number of iterations through the dataset increased, the training accuracy increased whilst validation accuracy remained stable from 5 epochs onwards.

Model loss graph, shows the trend in training and validation loss from the beginning of training the model until training is done. As the number of iterations through the dataset increased, the training loss decreased whilst validation loss remained stable from 5 epochs onwards.

Test accuracy of the model is evaluated at 99%.

Figure 10.

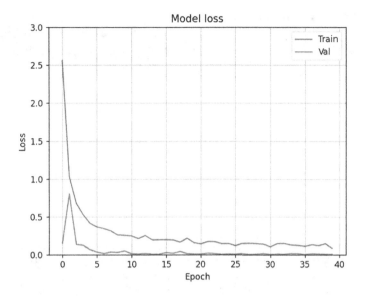

Figure 11.

```
Training completed in time:  3:06:59.692862
6/6 - 35s - loss: 0.0070 - accuracy: 0.9971 - 35s/epoch - 6s/step

Test accuracy: 0.9970501661300659
```

EfficientNetB0 Model

Figure 12.

```
import matplotlib.pyplot as plt
import pickle
import tensorflow as tf
from keras import regularizers
from tensorflow.python.keras.layers import Dense, Flatten, Dropout
from keras.models import Sequential
from keras.optimizers import RMSprop
from datetime import datetime
```

Import the libraries for training and evaluating the model.

Figure 13.

```
# Preparing data
num_classes=5                    # Value is the number of folders in the dataset folder

img_height,img_width=224,224
batch_size=64                    # Number of samples processed before the model is updated
```

Prepare data with respect to how many students/people are in the dataset by specifying num_classes and specify the image dimensions and number of samples to be processed before updating the model.

Figure 14.

```
# Loading data from directories
train_ds = tf.keras.preprocessing.image.ImageDataGenerator(
    validation_split=0.3,
).flow_from_directory(
    'student_dataset',
    target_size=(img_height, img_width),
    batch_size=batch_size,
    class_mode='sparse',
    subset='training',
    shuffle=True,         # shuffle order of data during training to prevent memorization and learn general patterns in data better
    seed=123
)

val_ds = tf.keras.preprocessing.image.ImageDataGenerator(
    validation_split=0.15,
).flow_from_directory(
    'student_dataset',
    target_size=(img_height, img_width),
    batch_size=batch_size,
    class_mode='sparse',
    subset='validation',
    shuffle=False,
    seed=123
)

test_ds = tf.keras.preprocessing.image.ImageDataGenerator(
    validation_split=0.15,
).flow_from_directory(
    'student_dataset',
    target_size=(img_height, img_width),
    batch_size=batch_size,
    class_mode='sparse',
    subset='validation',
    shuffle=False,
    seed=123
)
```

Load and split the dataset into train, validation and test datasets.

Figure 15.

```
# Creating model
efficientnet_model = Sequential(name='EfficientNetB0_Model')

# Creating a pre-trained EfficientNetB0 model on the imagenet dataset
pretrained_model = tf.keras.applications.EfficientNetB0(include_top=False,
                   input_shape=(224, 224, 3),
                   pooling='avg', classes=num_classes,
                   weights='imagenet')

# Freeze the weights of the pre-trained layers
for layer in pretrained_model.layers:
    layer.trainable = False

# Define the EfficientNetB0 model architecture
efficientnet_model.add(pretrained_model)
efficientnet_model.add(Flatten())
efficientnet_model.add(Dropout(0.5))  # Add dropout layer with a rate to prevent overfitting
# Can add more Dense layers if adding more data to model
# Add L2 regularization to prevent overfitting
efficientnet_model.add(Dense(512, activation='relu', kernel_regularizer=regularizers.l2(0.01)))
efficientnet_model.add(Dropout(0.5))
efficientnet_model.add(Dense(num_classes, activation='softmax', kernel_regularizer=regularizers.l2(0.01)))

efficientnet_model.summary()
```

Create and define EfficientNetB0 model architecture.

Figure 16.

```
# Compiling model
efficientnet_model.compile(optimizer=RMSprop(learning_rate=0.001),
                           loss='sparse_categorical_crossentropy',
                           metrics=['accuracy'])
```

Compile model with the RMSprop optimizer for improving the accuracy along with specifying the learning_rate which for this case is 0.001.

Figure 17.

```
# Training model
start = datetime.now()

epochs = 30                # Number of iterations through the dataset
history = efficientnet_model.fit(
    train_ds,
    validation_data=val_ds,
    epochs=epochs
)

# Save model
tf.saved_model.save(efficientnet_model, 'models/efficientnetb0_model')
```

Figure 18.

```
# Evaluating model
fig1 = plt.gcf()
plt.plot(history.history['accuracy'])
plt.plot(history.history['val_accuracy'])
plt.axis(ymin=0.4, ymax=1)
plt.grid()
plt.title('Model accuracy')
plt.ylabel('Accuracy')
plt.xlabel('Epoch')
plt.legend(['Train', 'Val'], loc='upper left')
plt.savefig('EfficientNetB0_model_accuracy.png')
plt.show()

fig2 = plt.gcf()
plt.plot(history.history['loss'])
plt.plot(history.history['val_loss'])
plt.axis(ymin=0, ymax=3)
plt.grid()
plt.title('Model loss')
plt.ylabel('Loss')
plt.xlabel('Epoch')
plt.legend(['Train', 'Val'], loc='upper right')
plt.savefig('EfficientNetB0_model_loss.png')
plt.show()
```

Train model by specifying how many iterations to have through the dataset and call the fit function on the training and validation data along with the number of iterations through the dataset and then save model.

Evaluate model, outputs two graphs, "fig1" and "fig2" with data about the model accuracy and model loss respectively.

Figure 19.

```
# Testing model
test_loss, test_acc = efficientnet_model.evaluate(test_ds, verbose=2)
print('\nTest accuracy:', test_acc)
```

Test model using the test dataset and output its test accuracy.

EfficientNetB0 Model Results

Figure 20.

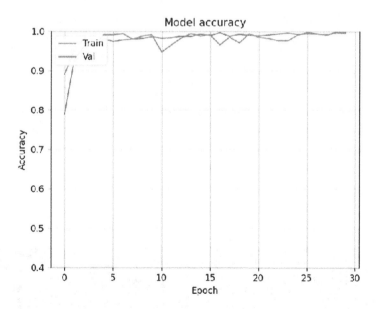

Model accuracy graph, shows the trend in training and validation accuracy from the beginning of training the model until training is done. As the number of iterations through the dataset increased, the training accuracy increased whilst validation accuracy fluctuated before stabilizing.

Figure 21.

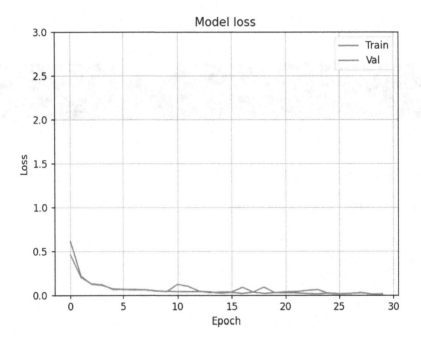

Model loss graph, shows the trend in training and validation loss from the beginning of training the model until training is done. As the number of iterations through the dataset increased, the training loss decreased whilst validation loss remained fairly stable from 5 epochs onwards.

Figure 22.

```
Training completed in time:  0:22:55.204388
6/6 - 8s - loss: 0.0113 - accuracy: 0.9970 - 8s/epoch - 1s/step

Test accuracy: 0.9970414042472839
```

Test accuracy of the model is evaluated at 99%.

With all these machine learning tools, transfer learning and ensemble learning techniques were explored and implemented to train the two models in facial recognition in this project.

Transfer learning is a machine learning approach that enables a model that has already been trained on one task to be used as the basis for training a new model on a separate but related task. In transfer learning, the quantity of data and computing power needed to train a new model from scratch is reduced by applying the knowledge the model learned during the training process of one task to the training of another task. This is accomplished by tweaking the previously trained model to the new task, where the model parameters are changed to better match the fresh data (Brownlee, 2017).

A machine learning approach called ensemble learning combines numerous models to increase the precision and effectiveness of a single model. Ensemble learning may be used in the context of facial recognition by training many models with various features or architectures on the same dataset. Each individual model may be compared to a "weak learner" who occasionally misclassifies or makes mistakes. The predictions of several weak learners may be combined, however, to create a "strong learner" that is more resilient to outliers and noise in the data and has increased accuracy (Lutins, 2017).

Limitations

Firstly, poor image quality: Image quality influences how well facial recognition systems work. The scanned video's quality pales in comparison to that of a digital camera. Even high-resolution videos, which can be as high as 1080p, is commonly 720p. The corresponding amounts are roughly 2MP and 0.9MP, while a cheap digital camera may be able to capture 15MP (Chowdhury, 2022). In the case of AAS, if a student is at the very back of the classroom and the cameras will only be in the front area of the classroom, the image quality that the camera will capture will be poor, therefore making it hard for the software to detect the face and might mark that student as absent because of this. Furthermore, bad lighting or a dark room can hinder the system when trying to detect a student, this can also lead to poor-image quality which can result in once again marking a student as absent in the attendance.

Secondly, data processing and storage: despite having a resolution much lower than that of digital camera images, the high-definition video uses quite a lot of disc space. Processing every single frame of video would be a laborious task, thus only about 10% to 25% of videos are normally exposed to a recognition system (Chowdhury, 2022). Which in this case if a class has over 100 students' storage for all the images, frames and videos will be a problem even if only 10% to 25% is being exposed to the recognition system. Therefore, processing all that data will require a lot of processing power and storage to store all the data. In addition, when a student is at the very back of the class it might be hard for the camera to capture that student in focus and then the outcome could be blurry which in turn will make a student un-recognizable.

WORK BREAKDOWN STRUCTURE

High-Level System Architecture

Figure 23.

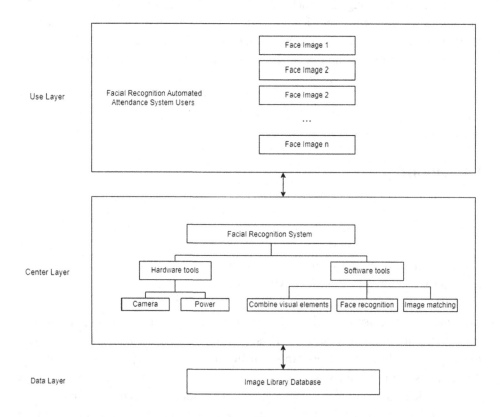

High-Level System Operation

Flow of System: The system starts by utilizing external hardware cameras to capture face images from varying angles. These captured images are then sent to the facial recognition system. The facial recognition system utilizes software tools to correctly mark attendance of a captured face. By combining visual elements, the system eradicates movements for ease of processing. It is then followed by image processing in which the images are either setup for enhancements or used to extract useful features. After the images are processed, they are put through an image matching process in which the system identifies a captured face by comparing it to images stored in an Image Library Database. Lastly, the data about attendance record, percentages and overall information is presented through a UI that populates from the database.

Face Images: Face Images are fed to the system by utilizing external cameras.

Facial Recognition: Process by which system correctly identifies a face in a captured image.

Image Processing: Processing images by enhancing them or/and extracting useful features.

Image Matching: Process by which facial images captured by hardware tools is compared to existing ones to correctly identify the given face image.

Combining Visual Elements: Consists of tackling and eradicating movement from images that are supposed to be processed.

Image Library Database: Image Library database contains all the facial images of the students in the system.

Activity Diagram

The user which is the "Professor" in this case, would need to activate the attendance system by entering their details for the system to know which classes and timings to mark attendance for. Then the system will confirm the connection to the camera for the camera to start scanning. The professor would then select the class and time which they would like to start marking attendance for. The camera would then start scanning the room for faces for 20 minutes. Throughout the 20 minutes, if the camera detects a face in the class and the system recognizes it, the system will mark the student whose face was detected present, but if the camera detects a face that is unfamiliar or in a different class, the system will ignore that person. The professor has the option to start the attendance again for 20 minutes or conclude the scanning by deactivating the system. Every student in that particular class who was not marked present would be marked as absent.

Figure 24.

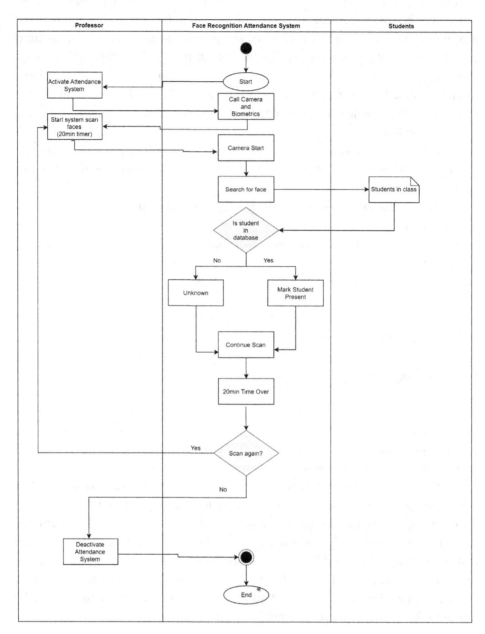

System Architecture

Figure 25.

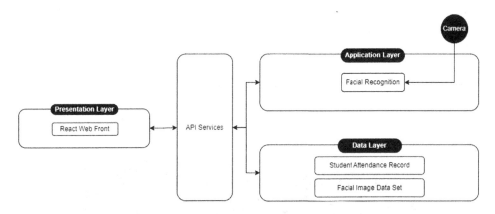

Presentation Layer

The is the front layer of the system where view are populated from the Student Attendance Record using API Services. Moreover, it allows users to view the data in different forms using multiple filter options. In addition, this layer enables users to override attendance statements for students which will directly be reflected into the database using API Services.

Application Layer

The Application layer contains the most predominant module which is the facial recognition system. The facial recognition can be broken to simple steps:

Face Detection: This is where the system accepts images from available video sources and inspects if a face is present and calculates its position on the image. As a result, the output of this step 'Face' and face alignment is done which prepares pre-processed images for the next step.

Feature Extraction: The pre-processed images obtained from the previous step are used to create a set of fiducial points that are made into facial landmarks and are transformed into vectors with specific dimensions.

Face Recognition: This is where the system must recognize the 'Face' from the students present in the database. The database is accessed by reading and/or updating using API services.

Data Layer

The data layer, also known as the database a layer or data access layer is the application's data is kept and maintained. The data mentioned here is the Student Information consisting of IDs, Names, Enrolled Classes, Attendance Record, etc. In addition, the database contains Student's facial data set to train the recognizer in the facial recognition model.

Performing Facial Recognition Using Ensemble Learning

Figure 26.

```
import tensorflow as tf
import numpy as np
import pickle
from keras.models import load_model
import cv2
from facenet_pytorch import MTCNN
```

Import the libraries for image processing and facial recognition.

Image processing function, an image file path is required as input for this function. It reads the picture from BGR to RGB color space using OpenCV's "cv2.imread". By dividing the pixel values by "255.0" to bring them into the range of 0.0 to 1.0, the image is normalized. Using "np.expand_dims", the image is enlarged to add a new dimension, making it suitable for the model input. The "tf.image.adjust_brightness" function is used to generate a new TensorFlow Sequential model that accepts an image as input and applies a brightness adjustment. The model is used to create the adjusted picture by applying it to the input image "model(img)[0].numpy()". "np. clip" is used to clip the altered image to lie inside the range of 0.0 to 1.0. Lastly, using "cv2.cvtColor", the image is then changed back to the BGR color space and the altered image is delivered back.

Figure 27.

```python
def image_processing_1(image):

    # Load the image
    img = cv2.imread(image)

    # Pre-process the image
    img = cv2.cvtColor(img, cv2.COLOR_BGR2RGB)
    img = np.array(img, dtype=np.float32) / 255.0
    img = np.expand_dims(img, axis=0)

    # Create the model
    model = tf.keras.Sequential([
        tf.keras.layers.Input(shape=(None, None, 3)),
        tf.keras.layers.Lambda(lambda x: tf.image.adjust_brightness(x, delta=0.5))
    ])

    # Apply the model to the image
    new_img = model(img)[0].numpy()

    # Post-process the image
    new_img = np.clip(new_img, 0.0, 1.0)
    new_img = np.uint8(new_img * 255.0)
    new_img = cv2.cvtColor(new_img, cv2.COLOR_RGB2BGR)

    return new_img
```

Figure 28.

```python
def check_img_darkness(image):

    # Load the image
    img = cv2.imread(image)

    # Convert the image to grayscale
    gray = cv2.cvtColor(img, cv2.COLOR_BGR2GRAY)

    # Calculate the histogram of the image
    hist = cv2.calcHist([gray], [0], None, [256], [0, 256])

    # Calculate the total number of pixels in the image
    total_pixels = gray.shape[0] * gray.shape[1]

    # Calculate the percentage of pixels that are in the darkest and brightest 5% of the histogram
    darkest_pixels = sum(hist[:13])
    brightest_pixels = sum(hist[242:])
    darkest_percent = darkest_pixels / total_pixels * 100
    brightest_percent = brightest_pixels / total_pixels * 100

    # Check if the image is poorly exposed
    if darkest_percent > 5 or brightest_percent > 5:
        # True if it is poorly exposed
        return True
    else:
        # False if it is well exposed
        return False
```

Image brightness function, an image file path is required as input for this function. With the aid of OpenCV's "cv2.imread", the picture is read. Using "cv2.cvtColor", the image is turned into a grayscale version. Utilizing "cv2.calcHist", the histogram of the grayscale image is calculated. The grayscale image's height and width are multiplied to determine the total number of pixels in the image. The sum of the pixels in the 5% of the histogram bins that are darkest (0–12) and brightest (243–255). By dividing the sum of the values by the total number of pixels and multiplying by "100", the percentages of pixels in the darkest and brightest areas are returned. The function returns "True" if the percentage of pixels in either the darkest or brightest regions is higher than "5", which indicates that the image was not properly exposed. Otherwise, the method returns "False" since the image is thought to be well-exposed if the percentages are both less than or equal to "5".

Figure 29.

```python
def facial_recognition():

    # Read the contents of the pickle file
    with open('class_names.pkl', 'rb') as f:
        # Load the data from the file
        class_names = pickle.load(f)

    # Count for managing print statements for when a face is not detected
    count = 0

    # Confidence threshold
    confidence_threshold = 0.85

    # Load model 1
    model1 = load_model("models/vgg19_model")

    # Load model 2
    model2 = tf.saved_model.load("models/efficientnetb0_model")

    # Initialize MTCNN for face detection
    mtcnn_detector = MTCNN()

    # Initialize webcam
    webcam = cv2.VideoCapture(0)
```

Facial recognition 1, sets up the necessary components for performing facial recognition, including specifying the confidence threshold to remove false positives and set a minimum value to which a bounding box is drawn, loading both pre-trained models, initializing face detection using MTCNN, and setting up the webcam for capturing video input.

Figure 30.

```
# Run loop for live face detection
while True:
    # Capture frame from webcam
    ret, frame = webcam.read()

    # Detect faces using MTCNN
    boxes, _ = mtcnn_detector.detect(frame)

    # Create list to store the detected faces
    faces = []

    # Draw bounding boxes around the detected faces
    if boxes is not None:
        for box in boxes:
            x1, y1, x2, y2 = box.astype('int')
            width = x2 - x1
            height = y2 - y1
            # Increase width and height of bounding box by 12%
            x1 -= int(0.12 * width)
            y1 -= int(0.12 * height)
            x2 += int(0.12 * width)
            y2 += int(0.12 * height)


            face = frame[y1:y2, x1:x2]        # Stores the cropped face within the bounding box into a variable
            cv2.rectangle(frame, (x1, y1), (x2, y2), (0, 255, 0), 2)        # Displays bounding box around face
```

Facial recognition 2, continuously capture frames from a webcam and use the MTCNN algorithm to detect faces in each frame then draw bounding boxes around the detected faces. This code also crops the faces within the bounding boxes and stores them in a list. Finally, display the original frame with the bounding boxes drawn around the faces.

Facial recognition 3, verify that an identified face has a size greater than 0 and that both its width and height are at least 50 pixels. Maintain the face image's aspect ratio and scale it to the desired 224x224 pixel size if the criteria are matched. Use the "check_img_darkness()" function on the cropped face picture that is saved as "bbox_image.jpg". Depending on the outcome, either use "image_processing_1()" to apply image processing to change the brightness of the face image or simply resize the original face image. The variable "img_resized" holds the resulting resized picture.

Figure 31.

```
# Checks whether a face is detected in the frame and if the width and height of the bounding box is greater than 50 pixels
# to filter out false detections
if face.size > 0 and width > 50 and height > 50:

    # Maintain aspect ratio of image
    h, w, _ = face.shape
    scale = max(h, w) / 224
    new_h = int(h / scale)
    new_w = int(w / scale)
    top = (224 - new_h) // 2
    bottom = 224 - new_h - top
    left = (224 - new_w) // 2
    right = 224 - new_w - left

    # Save cropped frame as an image to be passed into the check_img_darkness() function
    cv2.imwrite('bbox_image.jpg', face)
    bbox_img = 'bbox_image.jpg'
    result = check_img_darkness(bbox_img)           # Checks if image is dark enough for processing

    if result:
        processed_img = image_processing_1(bbox_img)         # Image goes into a processing function to alter brightness
        # Resize processed image
        img_resized = cv2.resize(processed_img, (new_w, new_h))
    else:
        # Resize cropped frame
        img_resized = cv2.resize(face, (new_w, new_h))
```

Figure 32.

```
        img_resized = cv2.copyMakeBorder(img_resized, top, bottom, left, right, cv2.BORDER_CONSTANT, value=(0, 0, 0))

        # Normalize image
        img = tf.keras.preprocessing.image.img_to_array(img_resized)
        img = np.expand_dims(img, axis=0)
        img = tf.cast(img, dtype=tf.float32)

        # Append all faces detected in the image
        faces.append(img)

# Checks whether the faces list contains at least one face
if len(faces) > 0:
    count = 0
    # Concatenate the list of preprocessed faces into an array
    faces_array = np.concatenate(faces, axis=0)

    # Use model 1 to make a prediction on the preprocessed faces
    pred1 = model1.predict(faces_array)

    # Use model 2 to make a prediction on the preprocessed faces
    pred2 = model2(faces_array)

    # Compute the average prediction of the two models
    ensemble_preds = np.mean([pred1, pred2], axis=0)

    # Get the predicted classes for each face
    pred_classes = np.argmax(ensemble_preds, axis=1)
```

Facial recognition 4, "cv2.copyMakeBorder()" adds a constant border to the enlarged picture. The image is then expanded, normalized, and converted to an array. The "faces" list is supplemented with the preprocessed face photos. The faces in the list are concatenated into an array if at least one face is found (length of "faces" is higher than 0). To make predictions, the preprocessed faces are then fed into two models ("model1" and "model2"). The predictions from the two models are averaged, then "np.argmax()" is used to determine the predicted classes for every face.

Figure 33.

```
# obtains predicted class and their respective probability
for i, pred_class in enumerate(pred_classes):
    output_class = class_names[pred_class]
    output_prob = ensemble_preds[i][pred_class]

    # Checks whether the predicted probability is above the threshold and below 100% to eliminate processing of anything
    # other than a face
    if ((output_prob >= confidence_threshold) and (output_prob <= 0.99)):
        print(f"Face {i+1}: {output_class}, Probability: {output_prob:.2f}")

elif(count == 0):
    count = 1
    print("Looking for a face...")

# Show frame with bounding boxes
cv2.imshow('Live Face Detection', frame)

# Press 'q' to exit
if cv2.waitKey(1) & 0xFF == ord('q'):
    break

# Release webcam and close window
webcam.release()
cv2.destroyAllWindows()
```

Facial recognition 5, iterate through each detected face's anticipated classes and associated probabilities. Verify whether the anticipated probability is equal to, greater than, or less than the specified confidence level and 0.99. Print the face number, anticipated class, and probability if the conditions are met. Print a message stating that a face is being sought after in the event that no faces are found (count is 0). Display the frame with bounding boxes to finish. The application can be stopped by pressing "q," and when the loop is over, the webcam is released and the window is closed.

Face detection 1, the facial recognition system displaying the bounding boxes around the detected faces.

After facial recognition 1, the GUI displaying the identification of the detected faces from Figure 34.

Face detection 2, the facial recognition system displaying the bounding boxes around the detected faces.

After facial recognition 2, the GUI displaying the identification of the detected faces from Figure 36.

Figure 34.

Figure 35.

API Services

API Services that enable modules to communicate and exchange information securely. In addition, introducing the usage of APIs into the framework of the system makes it much scalable in the future.

Figure 36.

Figure 37.

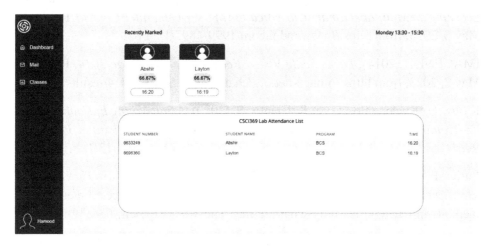

CONCLUSION

In conclusion, AAS is an automated attendance system that uses facial recognition to detect and recognize students in a class and mark their attendance accordingly. The facial recognition and detection system uses a mix of models such as MTCNN and RetinaFace to achieve the highest accuracy possible through the concept of ensemble learning.

REFERENCES

Adjabi, I., Ouahabi, A., Benzaoui, A., & Taleb-Ahmed, A. (2020). Past, Present, and Future of Face Recognition. *RE:view*, *9*(8), 1188. Retrieved June 20, 2023, from https://www.mdpi.com/2079-9292/9/8/1188

Brownlee, J. (2017). *A Gentle Introduction to Transfer Learning for Deep Learning.* Machine Learning Mastery. Retrieved April 2, 2023, from https://machinelearningmastery.com/transfer-learning-for-deep-learning

Chowdhury, M. (2022). *Limitations Of Facial Recognition In Today's World.* Retrieved October 31, 2022, from https://www.analyticsinsight.net/limitations-of-facial-recognition-technology-in-todays-world/

Dulčić, L. (2019). *Face Recognition with FaceNet and MTCNN.* Retrieved November 1, 2022, from https://arsfutura.com/magazine/face-recognition-with-facenet-and-mtcnn/

Haralabopoulos, G., Anagnostopoulos, L., & McAuley, D. (2020). *Ensemble Deep Learning for Multilabel Binary Classification of User-Generated Content.* Retrieved May 6, 2023, from https://www.mdpi.com/1999-4893/13/4/83

IMAGENET. (2014). *Large Scale Visual Recognition Challenge 2014.* Retrieved May 2, 2023, from https://image-net.org/challenges/LSVRC/2014/results

Karlos, S., Kostopoulos, G., & Kotsiantis, S. (2020). *A Soft-Voting Ensemble Based Co-Training Scheme Using Static Selection for Binary Classification Problems.* Retrieved May 6, 2023, from https://www.mdpi.com/1999-4893/13/1/26

Lutins, E. (2017). *Ensemble Methods in Machine Learning: What are They and Why use Them?* Retrieved April 2, 2023, from https://towardsdatascience.com/ensemble-methods-in-machine-learning-what-are-they-and-why-use-them-68ec3f9fef5f

Mohanakrishnan, R. (2021). *Top 11 Facial Recognition Software in 2021.* Retrieved June 20, 2023, from https://www.spiceworks.com/it-security/identity-access-management/articles/facial-recognition-software/

Pintelas, P., & Livieris, L. E. (2020). *Special Issue on Ensemble Learning and Applications.* Retrieved May 6, 2023, from https://www.mdpi.com/1999-4893/13/6/140

RECFACES BLOG. (n.d.). *What Is AI Facial Recognition Tech and How does It Work?* Retrieved October 23, 2022, from https://recfaces.com/articles/ai-facial-recognition

Serengil. (2023). *RetinaFace: Deep Face Detection Library for Python.* Retrieved April 2, 2023, from https://github.com/serengil/retinaface

Simonyan, K., & Zisserman, A. (2015). *Very deep convolutional networks for large-scale image recognition.* Retrieved May 2, 2023, from https://arxiv.org/pdf/1409.1556.pdf

Simplilearn. (2021). *What Is Keras: The Best Introductory Guide To Keras.* Retrieved October 31, 2022, from https://www.simplilearn.com/tutorials/deep-learning-tutorial/what-is-keras

Suneratech. (2021). *What Is AI, ML & How They Are Applied to Facial Recognition Technology.* Retrieved October 23, 2022, from https://www.suneratech.com/blog/ai-ml-and-how-they-are-applied-to-facial-recognition-technology/

Tan, M., & Le, Q. (2019). EfficientNet: Rethinking Model Scaling for Convolutional Neural Networks. *Proceedings of Machine Learning Research.* Retrieved May 2, 2023, from https://proceedings.mlr.press/v97/tan19a.html.

Yegulalp, S. (2022). *What is TensorFlow? The machine learning library explained.* Retrieved November 1, 2022, from https://www.infoworld.com/article/3278008/what-is-tensorflow-the-machine-learning-library-explained.html

YoungWonks. (2021). *What is OpenCV, what does it do and where is it used?* Retrieved November 1, 2022, from https://www.youngwonks.com/blog/What-is-OpenCV

Zvarevashe, K., & Olugbara, O. (2020). *Ensemble Learning of Hybrid Acoustic Features for Speech Emotion Recognition.* Retrieved May 6, 2023, from https://www.mdpi.com/1999-4893/13/3/70

Chapter 5
Advanced Data–Driven Approaches for Intelligent Olfaction

Shiv Nath Chaudhri

https://orcid.org/0000-0002-5436-2977
Santhiram Engineering College, India

Ashutosh Mishra

https://orcid.org/0000-0001-8579-5583
Yonsei University, South Korea

Navin Singh Rajput
Indian Institute of Technology (BHU), India

ABSTRACT

Advanced data-driven approaches have transformed the development of intelligent systems, gaining recognition from researchers and industrialists. Data plays a critical role in shaping intelligent systems, including artificial olfaction systems (AOS). AOS has evolved from manual feature extraction to leveraging artificial neural networks (ANNs) and convolutional neural networks (CNNs) for automated feature extraction. This chapter comprehensively overviews the synergy between data-driven approaches and CNNs in intelligent AOS. CNNs have significantly improved the accuracy and efficiency of scent and odor detection in AOS by automating feature extraction. Exploiting abundant data and leveraging CNN capabilities can enhance AOS performance. However, challenges and opportunities remain, requiring further research and development for optimal utilization of data-driven approaches in intelligent AOS.

DOI: 10.4018/978-1-6684-8696-2.ch005

1 INTRODUCTION

Data science and data analytics play a crucial role in the development of intelligent systems (Drobot, 2020). These disciplines help enhance the performance of conventional systems (Bag et al., 2011) while reducing the overall system design costs (Chaudhri, Rajput, Alsamhi et al, 2022). In today's scenario, the effectiveness of advanced data-driven approaches in developing intelligent systems has been well-proven (Chaudhri, Rajput, Alsamhi et al, 2022; Chaudhri, Rajput, & Mishra, 2022). Additionally, the performance of intelligent systems heavily relies on the presentation of input data. The term "Intelligent Systems" encompasses almost every field of science, engineering, and technology, enabling the creation of smart applications (Ghaffari et al., 2010; Cole, Covington and Gardener, 2011; Gholam Hosseini et al., 2007; Choden et al., 2017). This chapter specifically focuses on artificial olfaction systems (AOS), which rely on electronic gas/odor sensors (Zhang, Wang, Chen et al, 2021). Traditional AOS implementations incorporate conventional pattern recognition techniques with handcrafted feature extraction and selection methods for data processing (Moore et al., 1993). Data processing in such AOS systems relies on statistical and probabilistic methods (Estakhroueiyeh and Rashedi, 2015; Sanaeifar et al., 2014; Sari et al., 2021). However, in artificial neural network (ANN) based AOS systems, advanced data processing utilizes a one-dimensional (1D) feature extraction process (Sari et al., 2021; Mishra, Rajput, and Han, 2018; Ying et al., 2015). In contrast, a 2D feature extraction process provides enhanced and information-rich features that further improve the system's performance (Chaudhri & Rajput, 2022). Hence, advanced data-driven approaches require the transformation of 1D features into 2D features.

The incorporation of several layers of convolutional neural networks (CNN), such as convolutional and pooling layers, involves the use of 2D features, leading to improved performance compared to previous intelligent olfaction systems. CNNs gained popularity due to their remarkable performance on image datasets (LeCun et al., 1998). Images can consist of single-band (e.g., Binary and Grayscale Images) or multi-band (e.g., RGB/False-Color-Composite, Multispectral, Hyperspectral Images) data (LeCun et al., 1998; Chaudhri, Rajput, and Singh, 2020; Ghamisi, Benedicktsson, and Ulfarsson, 2013; Chaudhri et al., 2021). Apart from processing two-dimensional (2D) or three-dimensional (3D) images, one-dimensional (1D) datasets, such as time-series datasets and gas sensor responses, are processed using fully-connected layers-based MLP-ANNs (Mishra & Rajput, 2018). However, ANNs have several disadvantages compared to CNNs, such as allowing only complex fully connected layers and lacking weight-sharing capabilities. This limitation has motivated researchers to harness the power of CNNs for non-imaging datasets. Consequently, the first challenge lies in using CNNs on gas sensor array response datasets. Another challenge involves generalizing the applicability of CNNs independent of the modality of gas sensor array responses, including transient and steady-state responses. If CNNs can be effectively applied to gas sensor responses, they can be utilized to tackle various data-driven problems related to AOS.

This chapter has discussed classification, quantification, drift analysis, real-time processing, resource-constrained scenarios, virtual sensor responses, spatial upscaling, feature extraction, feature selection, and cluster separation. These data-driven strategies aim to overcome the challenges encountered in AOS. The utilization of CNNs provides vast opportunities, especially in the AOS paradigm, to achieve superior performance. Therefore, the subsequent content presents an extensive context that explores the synergy between advanced data-driven approaches and CNNs for intelligent AOS.

1.1 Artificial Olfaction Systems (AOS)

The gas sensors-based Ambient Odor Sensing (AOS) technology is utilized for detecting the presence of various odors and gases in both indoor and outdoor environments. These systems generate output signals that are directly related to the concentration of the detected odor or gas. These signals are commonly referred to as patterns or signatures from gas sensors. Figure 1 illustrates a schematic representation of a traditional AOS system. Typically, the output signals are measured by observing changes in the electrical resistance of the sensing materials within the gas sensors. Consequently, the obtained signals are analyzed to identify the specific gas present (classification) and determine the concentration of the gas (quantification) in the environment. The response of a gas sensor is highly sensitive to several factors, including the type and concentration of the detected gas, the operating temperature and humidity, and the design and materials used in the sensor.

However, gas sensors often encounter slight changes or deviations in their responses, commonly known as drift. These variations can be attributed to factors such as sensitivity to humidity and temperature, as well as the remnants of previously exposed gases. Drift poses a significant challenge in AOS technology, as it can hinder the accuracy and reliability of the system's performance. Traditional AOS systems employ a two-stage procedure to provide final results. In the first stage, drift correction algorithms are applied using statistical and probabilistic methods to compensate for the drift in the sensor responses. Subsequently, in the second stage, the corrected data obtained from the first stage is utilized by the final model for the classification and quantification of the gases. While these modular approaches have been effective, they are not suitable for end-to-end real-time systems. Additionally, the two-stage systems may not be ideal for miniaturized or resource-constrained applications where optimization is crucial. The gas sensors-based AOS technology plays a vital role in detecting and quantifying odors and gases in various environments. However, addressing the issue of drift and optimizing the AOS system for real-time and resource-constrained applications remain ongoing challenges in the field.

Figure 1. A traditional artificial olfaction system (AOS) consists of an array of gas sensor elements for data acquisition. It captures responses from the gas sensor array, which are popularly known as signature patterns. These patterns are then processed in the next stage of data pre-processing to obtain salient features using handcrafted feature extraction techniques. In the last stage of a traditional AOS, the obtained salient features are used to classify and/or quantify the responses using pattern recognition techniques compatible with the 1D architecture of the data.

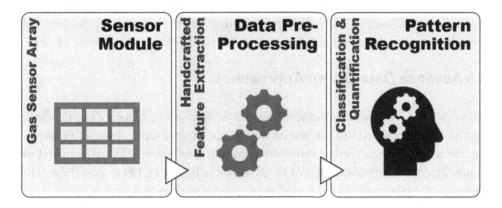

1.2 Challenges in AOS at Data Processing Level

Generally, gas sensors exhibit two types of responses:

1. Steady-State Responses: These responses are crucial when quantifying the area of interest. In other words, to measure the concentration of the gas sample being detected, it is necessary to obtain the stable (steady-state) value of sensor responses. These responses have been used as the primary method since the beginning and are often referred to as the "Gold Standard" responses of gas sensors (Rehman et al., 2020) and (Llobet et al., 1997). If these responses are directly proportional to the gas concentration, they are known as linear responses; otherwise, they are non-linear. Ideally, linear responses are desirable as they allow for accurate measurement of gas concentrations.
2. Transient Responses: These responses are utilized for early qualitative analysis or classification purposes. By applying pattern recognition techniques to transient

responses, the exposed gas can be identified as early as possible. Correct detection is possible through transient responses alone, but accurate estimation without involving steady-state responses is not achievable. It is practically impossible to eliminate all factors that influence sensor responses, leading to drift issues. Consequently, the responses may not be directly proportional to the gas concentration, making them non-linear in nature.

As mentioned earlier, traditional AOS (Analytical Odor Sensing) methods represent data in a 1D architecture. However, in order to achieve enhanced performance, we aim to utilize Convolutional Neural Networks (CNNs). CNNs inherently require data in a 2D architecture to process effectively. Although CNNs can work with 1D data architecture, they are limited to extracting only 1D variations in the data. Therefore, advanced data-driven approaches are necessary to apply 2D CNNs to gas sensor responses in AOS. By implementing these advanced approaches, the focus is on enhancing the qualitative and quantitative analysis capabilities of AOS.

1.3 Advance Data-Driven Approaches

A discussion is presented on advanced data-driven approaches, namely Zero-Padding, Spatial Augmentation, Virtual Sensor Responses, Hybrid Convolutional Features, etc., which have been further utilized to develop intelligent AOS (as depicted in Figure 2), contrasting traditional AOS (as shown in Figure 1). Let us now delve into understanding these advanced data-driven approaches one by one:

Zero-Padding: Zero-Padding is a technique that involves utilizing null or zero values for various purposes. For instance, during data cleaning, corrupted or missing values are replaced with zeroes to render the dataset compatible for further processing. Sometimes, in order to equalize the length of feature vectors, shorter features are padded with additional zero values, ensuring uniform length across all feature vectors. Additionally, when applying convolution operations on images, zero-padding is employed to extend the border of the observed image, covering the edge and corner pixels. A clearer context can be observed from Figure 3. To improve the effectiveness of padding techniques, non-zero values can also be used, in which case the technique is referred to as Non-Zero Padding (Chaudhri, Rajput, Alsamhi et al, 2022; Chaudhri, Rajput, & Mishra, 2022).

Spatial Augmentation: The combination of zero-padding and spatial augmentation has been applied to 1D sensor responses to transform them into a 2D architecture that is compatible with the advanced neural network 2D-CNN to a significant extent. The feature vector length obtained from sensor responses depends on the number of gas sensor elements used in the gas sensor array of AOS. Consequently, we first utilize zero-padding to ensure that the length of the feature vector is equal to the nearest perfect square number. We then convert the 1D feature vector into a 2D architecture with a squared shape. However, the size of the resulting 2D squared architecture may not meet the requirements for utilizing 2D-CNN, which typically necessitates an input size larger than 3×3. Therefore, we employ spatial augmentation to increase the size of the 2D squared feature vector by three times (Chaudhri & Rajput, 2021; Chaudhri, Rajput, Alsamhi et al, 2022). This enhanced version is now compatible with 2D-CNN. The process of spatial augmentation is illustrated in Figure 4.

Figure 2. An intelligent AOS consists of an array of gas sensor elements for data acquisition. The captured responses from gas sensor arrays, popularly known as signature patterns, are processed in the next stage of data pre-processing to obtain salient features using advanced data-driven approaches. Thus, in the final stage of the intelligent AOS, the obtained salient features are used to classify and/or quantify the responses using pattern recognition techniques compatible with both 1D and 2D architectures of data.

Both zero-padding and spatial augmentation techniques are well-established and published, providing a solid foundation for utilizing 2D-CNN (two-dimensional convolutional neural networks) to achieve high performance in gas/odor classification and quantification. Zero-padding and spatial augmentation are widely recognized techniques in the field. Zero-padding involves adding extra zeros around the edges of input data, which helps preserve spatial information during convolutional operations and ensures consistent input dimensions for the CNN. This technique is particularly useful when working with images or other 2D data.

Spatial augmentation, on the other hand, refers to applying various transformations to the input data, such as rotations, translations, and flips. By augmenting the dataset with these transformed versions of the original samples, the model becomes more robust and better generalizes to unseen data. Spatial augmentation helps to address issues like overfitting and improves the network's ability to classify and quantify gases or odors accurately. The utilization of 2D-CNN architectures is a natural fit for gases/odors classification and quantification tasks due to their ability to capture spatial dependencies in the data. CNNs consist of multiple convolutional layers that extract local features from the input, followed by pooling layers that downsampled the representations, and finally, fully connected layers that perform the classification or regression tasks.

Figure 3. A schematic diagram is used to demonstrate the usage of zero-padding in the 1D and 2D data architectures. Zero-padding facilitates uniformity in terms of size and shape.

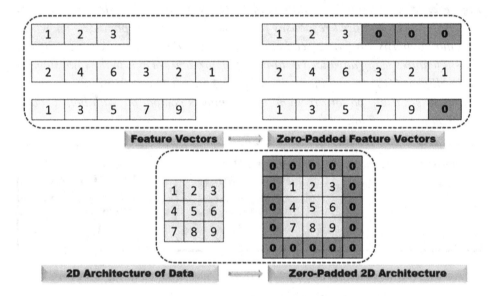

By combining the power of zero-padding and spatial augmentation with 2D-CNNs, researchers, and practitioners have achieved remarkable performance in gases/odors classification and quantification. These techniques enhance the model's ability to learn discriminative features from the input data and improve its overall accuracy and robustness. The well-established and published nature of both zero-padding and spatial augmentation techniques, in conjunction with the utilization of 2D-CNN architectures, forms a strong foundation for achieving high-performance results in gases/odors classification and quantification tasks.

Virtual Sensor Responses: Virtual sensor responses are a form of data augmentation technique that involves generating synthetic gas sensor responses through the use of mathematical formulas and transformation techniques applied to actual physical gas sensor responses. The resulting virtual gas sensor responses are then combined with the original dataset, effectively augmenting the overall data. Numerous techniques for generating virtual sensor responses have been developed in recent studies (Chaudhri, Rajput, & Mishra, 2022; Mishra et al., 2017; Srivastava, Chaudhri, Rajput, & Mishra, 2023). The utilization of virtual sensors not only enhances performance but also offers insights for optimizing gas sensor nodes or AOS.

Figure 4. A schematic diagram is used to demonstrate spatial augmentation, which is the subsequent step after zero-padding. For example, let's consider a 1D feature vector for AOS that consists of eight gas sensors. This feature vector is padded with zeroes by one unit to ensure its length becomes a perfect square number (e.g., 9). Afterward, the padded 1D data architecture is transformed into a 2D data architecture of size 3×3. Subsequently, spatial augmentation is applied to this 2D data, increasing the size of the 2D architecture by three times (e.g., 9×9).

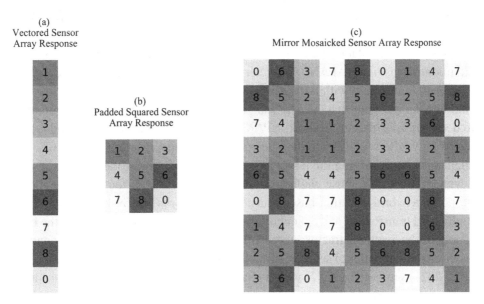

Hybrid Convolutional Features: Convolutional layers are advanced neural network layers designed to overcome the limitations and complexities of fully-connected layers. Convolutions are linear arithmetic operations that can be implemented in 1D, 2D, and 3D feature spaces. Each version of convolutional layers has its own significance depending on the data and desired objective. For example, the 1D convolutional layer performs exceptionally well in learning temporal variations within 1D feature vectors and is frequently utilized for analyzing time-series datasets. On the other hand, the 2D convolutional layer is capable of capturing spectral-spatial variations in the data, making it popular worldwide for analyzing imaging datasets. Lastly,

3D convolutional layers offer insights into both temporal and spectral directions simultaneously, albeit at a higher computational cost.

Researchers have devised various architectures incorporating hybrid neural networks that combine 1D, 2D, and 3D convolutional layers within the same network. Although these networks come with significant computational costs, they have the ability to outperform other methods, making them valuable in certain applications. In the field of AOS (Audio-Visual Speech Recognition), such a hybrid CNN is referred to as a "Drift Tolerant Robust Classifier" (DTRC), which has been shown to outperform several state-of-the-art methods by effectively suppressing the effects of drift. Furthermore, the utilization of these advanced data-driven techniques in different contexts has been demonstrated through established and well-published relevant works (Chaudhri & Rajput, 2022).

Traditional techniques for gas sensing applications are often harmful, inefficient, and relatively complex. As a result, e-nose models with data-driven analysis have come into the picture as non-destructive solutions. In (Kang et al., 2023), based on the e-nose system's data features, the researchers have presented an adaptive pooling attention mechanism (APAM). To determine the tea quality, the planned APAM was finally integrated with a traditional CNN to identify the gas information. The findings demonstrate that APAM can successfully implement adaptive attention to deep gas information. In short, APAM, paired with traditional CNN and e-nose technology, offers an efficient non-destructive gas sensing approach. E-noses face challenges in identifying the target gases to counter the unfavorable effect of drift deviation. To tackle these challenges, in (Pan et al., 2023), the researchers have proposed a hybrid attention-based transformer network (HATN-DA). Inside it, the multi-head transformer and channel-wise attention mechanism serving as the main blocks of the feature extractor successfully capture temporal dependencies and lay focus on the diversities of sensors. In another work, Zhang et al. (Zhang, Cheng, Luo et al, 2021) presented a CNN with a channel attention mechanism to concentrate on the salient properties of the gas and successfully realize gas identification for several baijiu brands. The data gathered by e-nose are often time series and show nonlinearity, dynamics, and redundancy. These qualities make e-nose designing a tedious task using such data. In (Wu et al., 2023), Z et al. have proposed a new regularized spatiotemporal attention (STA)-based long short-term memory (LSTM) to address these issues. The developed algorithm successfully forecasts the nitrogen oxide emissions of a selective catalytic reduction de-nitration system after being compared to other cutting-edge algorithms using artificial data.

2 APPLICATIONS OF DATA-DRIVEN APPROACHES

2.1 Classification and Quantification

In the field of AOS, gas sensors play a crucial role in detecting and quantifying the presence of various gases and odors in the environment. These sensors provide two types of responses: steady-state and transient responses. Initially, researchers relied on steady-state responses to estimate the concentration of observed gases or odors. During this time, they either employed handcrafted feature extraction-based methods or expensive chromatography-spectrometry techniques. However, as technology advanced, transient responses emerged as a valuable tool for early gas/odor class detection. Compared to steady-state responses, transient responses provide a larger amount of data. This abundance of data presented researchers with an opportunity to explore new avenues in gas/odor sensing. Recently, with the rise of Convolutional Neural Networks (CNNs), researchers have begun applying CNNs to transient responses by converting them into image-like structures. The conversion from 1D data to a 2D architecture is relatively straightforward in the case of transient responses, as they naturally possess sufficiently large dimensions.

In a notable study by authors cited as (Kang et al., 2023), a novel approach was proposed to convert steady-state responses into a compatible 2D architecture. This data-driven scheme facilitated the smooth application of CNNs to the converted responses. The researchers achieved high accuracy in the detection (classification) and estimation (quantification) of hazardous gases and odors using this advanced data-driven approach. The approach involved techniques such as spatial upscaling or spatial augmentation, which enhanced the performance of the CNN model. By transforming the steady-state responses into a compatible 2D architecture, the researchers opened up new possibilities for utilizing CNNs in gas/odor sensing applications. The use of CNNs allows for automatic feature extraction, enabling the model to learn discriminative patterns directly from the transformed data. This approach eliminates the need for handcrafted feature engineering, which can be a time-consuming and error-prone process.

The application of CNNs to transient responses and the data-driven conversion of steady-state responses have significantly advanced the field of AOS. These techniques offer a more efficient and accurate means of detecting and quantifying hazardous gases and odors in real-time. Moreover, the use of CNNs provides a scalable framework that can adapt to different sensing environments and gas/odor classes. The difference between qualitative (classification) and quantitative (quantification) data analysis can be understood from Figure 5.

Figure 5. A schematic block diagram showing qualitative (classification) and quantitative (quantification) analysis paradigms

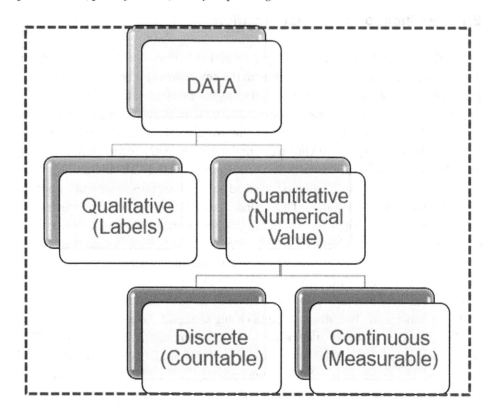

```
# Spatial Upscaling Code Snippet
import numpy as np
# A = response_vector_in_2D_squared_format
def spatial_upscaling(A):
    B = np.fliplr(A)
    C = np.rot90(B,1)
    D = np.flipud(A)
    E = np.rot90(D,1)
    X = np.concatenate((E,D,C),axis=1)
    Y = np.concatenate((B,A,B),axis=1)
    Z = np.concatenate((C,D,E),axis=1)
    upscaled_data = np.concatenate((X,Y,Z),axis=0)
    return upscaled_data
```

```
# Example usage
# A = response_vector_in_2D_squared_format
A = np.asarray(([1,2,3],[2,3,1],[3,1,2]),dtype='float64')
upscaled_data = spatial_upscaling(A)
```

The introduction of transient responses and the application of CNNs to gas/odor sensing has revolutionized the field of AOS. With the ability to convert steady-state responses into a compatible 2D architecture, researchers have achieved high accuracy in detecting and quantifying hazardous gases and odors. These advancements have not only improved the reliability of gas sensors but also opened up new possibilities for real-time monitoring and environmental control. As technology continues to evolve, we can expect further innovations in AOS, driven by the integration of advanced machine learning techniques with sensor data analysis. The spatial upscaling involves transforming the steady-state responses to a higher-resolution format. This process allows for more detailed information to be extracted from the data, enhancing the accuracy of the CNN models. A snippet of Python program code for implementing spatial upscaling is provided below:

In the provided Python code snippet, the **spatial_upscaling** function takes the **response_vector_in_2D_squared_format** as input. The **response_vector** represents the steady-state responses, typically stored in a NumPy array. The function utilizes the NumPy library to perform the spatial upscaling. The resulting upscaled data by three times is then returned. This spatial upscaling technique serves as an example of how researchers have leveraged data-driven approaches to enhance the performance of CNN models for gas sensor applications. By converting the steady-state responses into a compatible 2D architecture and utilizing techniques like spatial upscaling, accurate detection and estimation of hazardous gases or odors can be achieved, opening up new possibilities for AOS technology.

2.2 Gas Sensor Node Optimization

As we are aware, the length of a feature vector does not always align with a perfect square number, necessitating a conversion into a squared 2D shape. To accomplish this, the technique of zero-padding can be employed, enabling the representation of the feature vector to meet the desired length requirements. In previous applications, a sole advanced data-driven approach, such as spatial augmentation, was typically utilized. However, in a notable study (Chaudhri, Rajput, Alsamhi et al, 2022), the authors successfully implemented the optimization of gas sensor nodes by leveraging the synergistic effects of two advanced data-driven approaches, namely zero-padding and spatial augmentation. The study presented in (Chaudhri, Rajput, Alsamhi et al, 2022) sought to enhance the performance of gas sensor nodes through the integration of zero-padding and spatial augmentation techniques. By combining these approaches, the researchers aimed to achieve superior optimization results compared to a baseline approach, both in terms of classification and quantification tasks. The utilization of zero-padding allowed for the transformation of the original feature vector into a squared 2D shape. By adding zero values to the vector, the resulting shape was able to conform to the desired dimensions. This technique proved particularly beneficial when dealing with feature vectors of varying lengths, as it facilitated a consistent input format for subsequent analysis and processing.

Spatial augmentation, on the other hand, involved the manipulation and transformation of the feature vector within the 2D space. By applying geometric operations, such as rotation, scaling, and translation, to the zero-padded feature vector, the researchers aimed to enhance its discriminative properties. This augmentation process effectively expanded the dataset by generating additional variations of the original samples, providing the underlying models with a more diverse and comprehensive set of training data. To assess the effectiveness of the proposed optimization approach, the researchers conducted extensive experiments and evaluations. They compared the performance of the optimized gas sensor nodes against a baseline approach, which likely utilized only a single advanced data-driven technique, such as spatial augmentation. The evaluation encompassed both classification and quantification tasks, representing two fundamental aspects of gas sensor node operation. The results of the study demonstrated the superiority of the optimization approach utilizing the combined effects of zero-padding and spatial augmentation. In comparison to the baseline, the optimized gas sensor nodes exhibited enhanced classification accuracy and improved quantification precision. These findings validated the efficacy of the synergistic integration of advanced data-driven techniques in the context of gas sensor node optimization.

The integration of zero-padding and spatial augmentation techniques showcased promising results in the optimization of gas sensor nodes. The utilization of zero-padding enabled the transformation of feature vectors into a squared 2D shape, while spatial augmentation provided additional variations and improved discriminative properties. By combining these approaches, the researchers achieved superior performance in classification and quantification tasks, surpassing the baseline approach. These findings highlight the potential benefits of employing multiple advanced data-driven techniques in synergy to enhance the performance of sensor systems. Figure 6 shows a general schematic of optimized systems.

Figure 6. A schematic block diagram showing the concept of optimization. It leads to a resource-efficient version of the original systems without a significant compromise in performance.

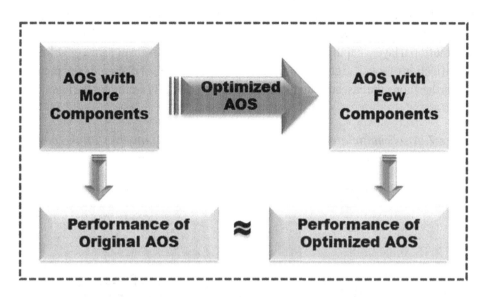

2.3 Designing Drift Tolerant Robust Classifier (DTRC)

In this particular case, the utilization of an advanced data-driven approach known as hybrid convolutional features has been implemented. Originally, the gas sensor array responses of an AOS system are available in a one-dimensional (1D) architecture. However, in order to extract hybrid convolutional features, data must be made available in all three formats: 1D, 2D, and 3D architecture (see Figure 7). In a previous study (Chaudhri & Rajput, 2022), the authors employed a cascaded hybrid Convolutional Neural Network (CNN) that incorporates 1D, 2D, and 3D layers of convolution and pooling. To facilitate the conversion of data, a reshaping layer was applied after each block, ensuring that the data meets the requirements of the subsequent convolutional block. This end-to-end architecture not only effectively mitigates the adverse effects of drift but also enables the utilization of such an architecture in real-time scenarios for the classification and quantification of gases and odors detected by the AOS. The advanced data-driven approach showcased by this model surpasses several existing state-of-the-art methods in terms of performance. By integrating hybrid convolutional features and leveraging the cascaded hybrid CNN architecture, the DTRC demonstrates superior performance compared to other existing methodologies. DTRC tackles the inherent challenges associated with gas sensor arrays, such as drift, noise, and variations in environmental conditions, which often hinder the accurate classification and quantification of gases and odors. The hybrid nature of the convolutional features allows for the extraction of meaningful patterns and discriminative information from the input data. The 1D convolutional layers effectively capture sequential dependencies and temporal dynamics, which are crucial for recognizing changes in gas concentrations over time. The 2D and 3D convolutional layers capture spatial correlations within the sensor array, enabling the identification of specific gas profiles and the discrimination of different odor patterns.

Furthermore, the cascaded architecture of the hybrid CNN facilitates the integration

Figure 7. A schematic architecture of hybrid classifier. It involves all the possible dimensionality-based feature extraction (data analysis) to provide end results.

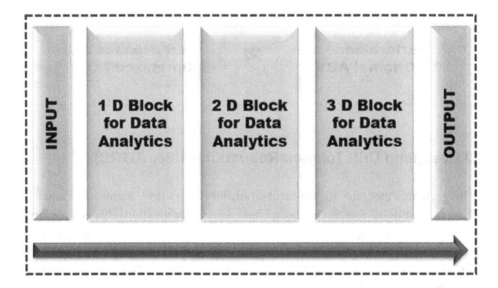

and fusion of features from multiple dimensions, resulting in a comprehensive representation of the sensor array responses. This fusion of information enhances the discriminative power of the model and enables it to accurately differentiate between various gases and odors. The reshaping layers play a pivotal role in this architecture by adapting the data to meet the input requirements of different convolutional layers. By transforming the data from 1D to 2D and 3D formats, the model can effectively leverage the capabilities of each convolutional layer and extract relevant features at multiple scales. The DTRC approach exhibits remarkable potential for real-world applications. Its ability to suppress drift and adapt to changing environmental conditions makes it suitable for deployment in AOS systems used in various domains, such as environmental monitoring, industrial safety, and healthcare. The real-time capabilities of the architecture enable prompt and accurate identification of hazardous gases, allowing for timely preventive measures and intervention. The utilization of hybrid convolutional features and the cascaded hybrid CNN architecture in the DTRC approach present a robust and effective solution for the classification and quantification of gases and odors. By incorporating data from multiple dimensions and leveraging the power of convolutional neural networks, DTRC outperforms existing state-of-the-art methods, paving the way for enhanced gas sensing and odor recognition technologies.

2.4 Virtual Responses

Deriving virtual sensor responses is an advanced data-driven approach that involves calculating synthetic gas sensor responses through the use of formulas or transformations applied to physical (real) gas sensor responses (see Figure 8). The technique of virtual sensor responses offers several advantages, including a reduction in hardware cost and the ability to extract more salient features compared to the raw features obtained from unprocessed gas sensor array responses. In a study conducted by the authors in (Chaudhri, Rajput, & Mishra, 2022), virtual sensor responses were derived using principal component analysis (PCA). The synthetic responses obtained through this method possess an additional feature: they do not require extra effort in feature selection. The selection of virtual sensor responses can be based on the explained variance by principal components, allowing for customization as per specific requirements. This flexibility is not available in the peer technique mentioned in (Mishra et al., 2017). Another recently proposed approach for deriving virtual sensor responses, as described in (Srivastava, Chaudhri, Rajput, & Mishra, 2023), offers the advantage of providing a greater number of virtual sensor responses compared to previously mentioned methods.

Table 1 provides a comprehensive list of both traditional and advanced data-driven approaches. In today's data-driven landscape, Data Engineering has emerged as a prominent subfield of Data Science, gaining increasing popularity with each passing day. Although an extensive body of literature dedicated to the pre- and post-processing of data already exists, the field is continuously evolving, and its full potential has yet to be realized. Recent news, articles, and blogs explicitly emphasize the rapid growth of Data Science as a field, with related job opportunities offering higher wages. Therefore, the study of advanced data-driven approaches holds significant value and promises numerous opportunities for those involved in the field.

With the ever-increasing volume of data being generated, there is a growing demand for innovative techniques that can effectively extract meaningful insights and valuable information from these vast datasets. Advanced data-driven approaches, such as virtual sensor responses, contribute to addressing this demand by providing efficient and cost-effective solutions. By leveraging the power of data analysis and transformation techniques, these approaches enable the extraction of essential features and patterns that may not be readily apparent in raw data. The use of PCA to derive virtual sensor responses offers a robust method for reducing the dimensionality of the data while retaining the most informative features. By capturing the variability of the original gas sensor responses in a lower-dimensional space, PCA facilitates the generation of synthetic responses that encapsulate the essential characteristics of the underlying data. Moreover, the ability to select virtual sensor responses based on the explained variance allows for adaptability and customization to specific application requirements.

Figure 8. A schematic diagram showing virtual sensor responses. Such responses are derived from features from the original ones or in some cases from padded features. These are added to original responses to augment the data as a whole.

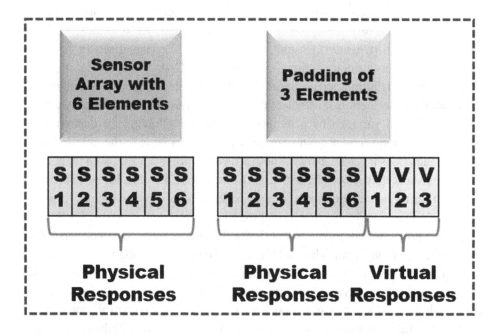

Furthermore, the recently proposed approach for deriving virtual sensor responses, as mentioned in (Srivastava, Chaudhri, Rajput, & Mishra, 2023), expands the range of available virtual sensor responses. This increased diversity can potentially enhance the performance and versatility of data-driven systems that rely on these synthetic responses. By exploring novel methods and techniques, researchers and practitioners in the field of data-driven approaches can continually push the boundaries of what is possible, opening up new avenues for innovation and discovery. The study of advanced data-driven approaches, including virtual sensor responses, holds great promise in the realm of Data Science. These techniques offer valuable insights, reduce hardware costs, and enable the extraction of more salient features from gas sensor array responses. As the field continues to evolve and mature, the importance of advanced data-driven approaches will only grow, presenting exciting opportunities for researchers, practitioners, and businesses alike.

Table 1. Traditional and advanced data-driven approaches

Traditional Approaches	Advanced Approaches
Logarithm (Moore et al., 1993)	NDSRT (Mishra et al., 2017)
Sensor Normalization (Moore et al., 1993)	Mirror Mosaicking (Chaudhri & Rajput, 2021)
Difference (Hoffheins, 1990)	Non-Zero Padding (Chaudhri, Rajput, Alsamhi et al, 2022)
Relative (Gardner, 1991)	TITO (Srivastava, Chaudhri, Rajput, & Mishra, 2023)
Fractional Difference (Gardner, 1991)	Virtual Sensor Responses (Chaudhri, 2022; Chaudhri, Rajput, Alsamhi et al, 2022; Srivastava, Chaudhri, Rajput, & Mishra, 2023)
Array Normalization (Gardner, 1991)	

Thus, advanced data-driven approaches use advanced algorithms and intelligent techniques to extract insights from the data for decision-making. These approaches leverage the power of data analytics, machine learning, data science, data engineering, etc. Data-driven techniques for intelligent olfaction depend on data, as suggested by the name. Due to the distinctive elements that these strategies aim to address, like data dimensionality, data drift, data curation, data engineering, etc. The suggested data-driven approaches are thus restricted to datasets displaying the same problems. For instance, if a data-driven strategy is suggested to address data drift, it will be effective for some other datasets but not for the aspect of data drift.

3 RESULTS AND DISCUSSIONS

Case 1

The authors utilized an integrated array that consists of four gas-sensing elements, which were fabricated using thick-film technology. The purpose of this system was to detect and analyze four different types of hazardous gases. During the experiment, we measured the output signals, also known as sensor responses or signature patterns, by observing the changes in the electrical resistance of the sensing elements. It is worth mentioning that each exposure to hazardous gases involved a different concentration level. To ensure the reliability of our findings, we captured two batches of datasets: one for training and the other for testing. The training dataset, which consisted of 42 samples, was used to train the classification or quantification models. These models were designed to categorize or quantify the presence of specific hazardous gases based on the sensor responses. On the other hand, the testing dataset, comprising 16 samples, was kept separate from the training process. This segregation allowed us to evaluate the performance of the trained models on unseen data, providing a genuine analysis of the qualitative and quantitative models using this dataset.

For further details on the dataset, please refer to Table 2 (Mishra et al., 2018; Rajput et al., 2010). This table provides comprehensive information about the characteristics and parameters of the dataset used in our study. It includes details such as the gas types, their concentrations, and the corresponding sensor responses for each sample. By employing the thick-film technology and capturing the change in electrical resistance of the gas-sensing elements, we were able to create a reliable and accurate system for gas detection and analysis. The integration of multiple sensing elements allowed us to gather a wide range of data points, enhancing the sensitivity and accuracy of our measurements. The availability of both training and testing datasets played a crucial role in our research. The training dataset, with its 42 samples, enabled us to develop and fine-tune our classification and quantification models. This process involved training the models to recognize patterns in the sensor responses and associate them with specific gas types and concentrations.

Once the models were trained, we evaluated their performance using the testing dataset, which consisted of 16 samples that were not included in the training phase. This evaluation provided us with a realistic assessment of the models' capabilities in dealing with unseen data. By examining the models' accuracy, precision, and recall on the testing dataset, we gained valuable insights into their effectiveness and potential for real-world applications. The use of separate training and testing datasets allowed us to train and evaluate classification and quantification models effectively. The dataset details, available in Table 2, provide comprehensive information for a better understanding of our research. Through this work, we aim to contribute to the development of reliable gas detection systems that can enhance safety and protect human health in various industries and environments.

In (Srivastava, Chaudhri, Rajput, Alsamhi et al, 2023), the authors utilized the mentioned dataset and employed an advanced data-driven approach called "spatial upscaling" for high-performance classification and quantification of the hazardous gases/odors under consideration. This dataset consists of samples containing four data points based on the number of sensors in the integrated array. Therefore, each sample can be represented as a 1D data vector as well as a 2D patch of size (2×2).

Table 2. Dataset details (Case 1)

Sensors	Exposed Gas	Training Set	Testing Set	Total Samples
CdS	Acetone	8	2	10
MoO	Carbon Tetrachloride	10	3	13
SnO$_2$	Ethyl Methyl Ketone	12	6	18
ZnO	Xylene	12	5	17

Figure 9. Classification performance in terms of accuracy (%). The spatial upscaling provides competitive performance to its peers.

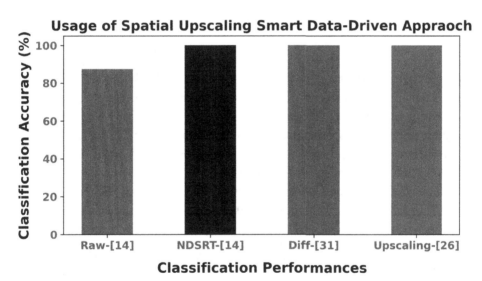

It is evident from the literature that 2D-CNN provides better results compared to its ANN-based counterparts. To classify this dataset using 2D-CNN, each sample needs to have a sufficient spatial dimension size. Hence, spatial upscaling is used to enhance the size of the samples up to three times larger (i.e., 6×6). The authors classified and quantified the dataset using 2D-CNN. Figure 9 clearly shows that the advanced data-driven approach used yields superior results on the processed dataset. Similar to its counterparts, it also provides well-classified results for all samples. This figure presents the classification results in terms of classification accuracy.

Figure 10. The preciseness of classification results in terms of mean squared error (MSE)

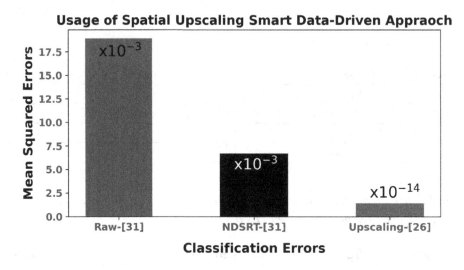

Figure 10 shows how closely the classification results are achieved using different data-driven approaches. Both figures (Figure 9 and Figure 10) display the classification performance. The quantification results are shown in Figure 11. During the quantification of the considered dataset, the squared error for each sample was recorded. Hence, the minimum and maximum squared errors (minSE and maxSE) were noted for the best and worst quantified samples. Moreover, the average of squared errors for all samples was calculated and presented as the mean squared error (MSE). It is evident from Figure 11 that the upscaling approach outperforms the compared technique in terms of quantification.

The same dataset was used in (Chaudhri, Rajput, Alsamhi et al, 2022) for gas sensor array optimization. The dataset was captured from a sensor array consisting of four sensor elements. In this work, it is assessed whether a similar performance can be achieved by using advanced data-driven approaches, using only two significant sensor responses. This allows for the optimization of the sensor array to have only two sensing elements, reducing power consumption by half and chip area by half. The experimental results demonstrate that even with the removal of two responses from less significant sensor elements, classification can still be achieved with all well-classified samples. Although a slight increase in MSE is observed during quantification, the MSE remains within satisfactory levels. In addition to upscaling, another advanced data-driven approach, padding, has been used. Zero-padding has been employed to replace the responses of less significant sensors in order to maintain the sample size. The performance can be observed in Table 3.

Figure 11. Errors for best and worst quantified samples and MSE for the quantification of all samples

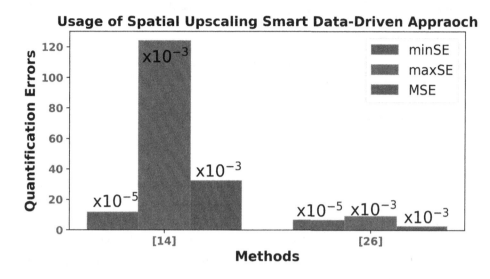

Table 3. Performance on the considered dataset by using upscaling and padding (Chaudhri, Rajput, Alsamhi et al, 2022)

Sensors	Padded Response	Classification Accuracy (%)	Quantification MSE	Overall Performance
4	0	100	$(7.61 \pm 1.66) \times 10^{-3}$	Baseline
3	1	100	$(7.02 \pm 0.86) \times 10^{-3}$	
2	2	100	$(1.64 \pm 0.38) \times 10^{-2}$	−

In (Srivastava, Chaudhri, Rajput, & Mishra, 2023), advanced data-driven approaches have been applied to this dataset to determine virtual sensor responses. Initially, the dataset contains four responses from physical sensors. To augment the dataset and generate new features, transformation algorithms are applied to the original sensor responses. These newly generated responses are referred to as virtual sensor responses. Furthermore, another technique called "NDSRT" (Mishra et al., 2017) has also been applied to the same dataset for virtual sensor responses. A performance comparison of these techniques for generating virtual sensor responses is presented in Table 4.

Table 4. Comparison of virtual sensor responses generation techniques

Technique	Physical Response	Virtual Responses	Tested Classifiers	Performance
NDSRT (Mishra et al., 2017)	4	6	9	1
TITO (Srivastava, Chaudhri, Rajput, & Mishra, 2023)	4	24	9	9

Case 2

In this case, we used another dataset captured using an array of sensors consisting of 16 elements. This dataset is widely recognized as the most popular publicly available dataset (Dua & Graff, 2019) in the research community focusing on artificial olfaction systems, electronic noses, and gas sensor arrays. It contains a total of 13,910 samples divided into ten subsets, created based on the duration of sample capture. The entire duration of sample acquisition spans three years or 36 months. The primary purpose of this dataset is to enable an extensive study of drift in sensor response characteristics (Vergara et al., 2012) and (Rodriguez-Lujan et al., 2014). Originally, each sample was captured as a long 1D time series vector. From this vector, a total of eight features were extracted, including two features for steady-state responses and six features for transient responses. Out of the six extracted features from the transient response, three were obtained for the rising edge (exposure of gas is ON), and three for the decaying edge (exposure of gas is OFF). The exponential moving average was employed for feature extraction. Consequently, each sample consists of a total of 128 (8×16) data points, representing the eight features and 16 sensor elements. Therefore, the samples can still be considered as 1D time-series data vectors with a sufficient length of 128.

Using this dataset, a hybrid convolutional features-based advanced data-driven approach has been implemented. This approach incorporates a hybrid convolutional neural network for classifying the responses in the dataset. The experimental results clearly demonstrate the effectiveness of the proposed methodology, achieving higher classification accuracy by mitigating the negative impact of drift. The proposed approach outperforms not only the baseline but also several state-of-the-art methods, as indicated in (Chaudhri & Rajput, 2022).

Case 3

As per the above discussion, several advanced data-driven approaches require the technique of padding. Conventionally, zero-padding is used, which involves stuffing zero or null values. However, this approach only maintains the shape and size of the data without adding any insight to the information content. To address this limitation, non-zero values can be used for padding. This logical motivation is utilized to propose a non-zero-padding technique based on PCA for generating virtual sensor responses. Two datasets have been used to verify the experimental results. In the first dataset, sensor responses captured for four different gases (carbon monoxide, ethanol, ethylene, and methane) exist. Each observed sample has a different range of concentration. The associated sensor array consists of eight metal oxide (MOX)-based gas sensor elements. This dataset is publicly available at (Dua & Graff, 2019) and contains 640 samples, with 160 samples for each gas. Each sample in this dataset represents a time series vector recorded for a duration of 600 seconds using a sampling rate of 100Hz (Fonollosa et al., 2016). Additionally, this dataset has been divided into two subsets for training and testing purposes, with 80% and 20% of the samples respectively. Each sample in this dataset has eight data points corresponding to the number of sensors in the array. An additional feature is required to make the total number of features in each sample nine. This facilitates the representation of each sample as a 2D squared form (3×3). The additional feature is derived from the first principal component of the original dataset. Subsequently, spatial upscaling is applied to the 2D squared samples to enhance the spatial size to 9×9. Using these modified inputs, the dataset is classified using a 2D-CNN (Chaudhri, Rajput, & Mishra, 2022).

The second dataset, also available at (Dua & Graff, 2019), has been trimmed to implement the study proposed in (Chaudhri, Rajput, & Mishra, 2022). This dataset captures responses for two different gases (ethanol and acetone) and their binary combinations. In addition to these three classes, the ambient air is taken as the fourth class in the dataset. The dataset consists of a total of 58 samples, with 39 used for training and 19 used for testing. Originally, this dataset was captured using an array of 16 MOX-based gas sensors. However, these 16 sensor elements belong to five different categories of the same brand (TGS: Taguchi Gas Sensors) (Ziyatdinov et al., 2015). Therefore, the dataset has been trimmed to include responses from the first five unique sensor elements. Consequently, each sample in the used dataset has five data points. In this scenario, four additional features are required to make the total number of data points in each sample nine. These four additional features are derived from the first four principal components of the trimmed dataset. Similar to the previous dataset, spatial upscaling is applied to make each sample of size 9×9. After modifying this dataset, it is also classified using a 2D-CNN (Chaudhri, Rajput,

& Mishra, 2022). When classifying both datasets, the results show a performance comparison between zero padding and non-zero padding (principal components). It is found that non-zero padding produces performance enhancement.

4 CONCLUSION

The field of advanced data-driven approaches for intelligent olfaction has made significant strides in recent years, revolutionizing the way we understand and utilize the sense of smell. Through the integration of sophisticated technologies, such as machine learning, artificial intelligence, and sensor arrays, researchers have been able to unlock the full potential of olfactory systems for a wide range of applications. One of the key achievements of advanced data-driven approaches is the development of electronic noses or e-noses. These devices mimic the human olfactory system by utilizing arrays of sensors to detect and analyze odor patterns. By leveraging machine learning algorithms, e-noses can not only identify specific odors but also classify and quantify them with high accuracy. This has enormous implications in various industries, including food and beverage, environmental monitoring, healthcare, and even national security. In the food and beverage industry, advanced data-driven approaches have enabled rapid and reliable quality control processes. E-noses can assess the freshness, ripeness, and authenticity of various products, ensuring consumer safety and satisfaction. By providing real-time monitoring and early detection of odor-related issues, these approaches have also facilitated the prevention of spoilage, reduced waste, and improved overall supply chain efficiency.

Environmental monitoring is another area where intelligent olfaction has made a significant impact. By deploying sensor networks and data-driven algorithms, researchers have been able to detect and analyze odor emissions from industrial facilities, waste management sites, and agricultural operations. This proactive approach allows for the identification of potential environmental hazards and the implementation of targeted mitigation strategies. Furthermore, the integration of intelligent olfaction with other sensing technologies, such as gas chromatography and mass spectrometry, has enhanced the accuracy and sensitivity of odor detection, enabling more comprehensive and reliable monitoring systems. In healthcare, advanced data-driven approaches have shown promise in early disease diagnosis and treatment. The ability of e-noses to detect volatile organic compounds (VOCs) associated with specific diseases, such as cancer and respiratory conditions, offers a non-invasive and potentially cost-effective diagnostic tool. By analyzing odor patterns, machine learning algorithms can identify biomarkers and patterns indicative of certain diseases, aiding physicians in making informed decisions and improving patient outcomes.

Moreover, advanced data-driven approaches have contributed to advancements in odor-based human-computer interaction (HCI). By understanding and interpreting human olfactory responses, intelligent systems can personalize user experiences, enhance virtual reality simulations, and create immersive environments. This has implications not only in entertainment and gaming but also in therapeutic applications, such as stress reduction and mood enhancement. While advanced data-driven approaches for intelligent olfaction have demonstrated remarkable achievements, there are still challenges that need to be addressed. The development of more sensitive and selective sensor arrays, the establishment of standardized datasets, and the refinement of machine learning algorithms are ongoing research areas. Additionally, ethical considerations, such as privacy and data security, must be carefully addressed as olfactory data becomes more prevalent and valuable.

At the conclusion of this chapter, the utility of advanced data-driven approaches can be summarized as follows:

Predictive Analytics: By analyzing data and employing statistical models and machine learning algorithms, organizations can predict future outcomes, trends, and behaviors of intelligent systems.

Prescriptive Analytics: This approach surpasses predictive analytics by providing recommendations for the best actions to achieve desired outcomes.

Data Visualization: Visualizing data through charts, graphs, and interactive dashboards aids in quickly comprehending complex information. Data visualization tools empower users to explore and interact with data visually, facilitating improved decision-making.

Real-time Data Analysis: Thanks to the emergence of big data technologies, organizations can process and analyze data in real-time or near real-time.

Automated Decision-making: Advanced data-driven approaches can seamlessly integrate into automated systems to make decisions and take actions without human intervention. This capability proves particularly valuable in scenarios that require rapid, consistent, and large-scale decision-making.

Therefore, these advanced data-driven approaches possess the potential to revolutionize industries and organizations by unearthing valuable insights, enhancing operational efficiency, elevating customer experiences, and driving innovation.

Future research and development in the area of intelligent olfaction using enhanced data-driven methodologies have a number of potential areas. Here are a few of them: future deep learning techniques, federated learning, domain adaptation, transfer learning, automated machine learning (AutoML), multi-modal learning, and interdisciplinary partnerships. These are but a few illustrations of potential future developments in the area of sophisticated data-driven methods for artificial olfaction.

REFERENCES

Bag, A. K., Tudu, B., Roy, J., Bhattacharyya, N., & Bandyopadhyay, R. (2011). Optimization of sensor array in electronic nose: A rough set-based approach. *IEEE Sensors Journal*, *11*(11), 3001–3008. doi:10.1109/JSEN.2011.2151186

Chaudhri, S. N. (2022). *Novel intelligent signal processing approaches for performance enhancement of gas sensor nodes suitable for near real-time resource-constrained scenarios* [Doctoral dissertation]. IIT (BHU).

Chaudhri, S. N., & Rajput, N. S. (2021). Mirror Mosaicking: A Novel Approach to Achieve High-performance Classification of Gases Leveraging Convolutional Neural Network. SENSORNETS, 86-91. doi:10.5220/0010251500860091

Chaudhri, S. N., & Rajput, N. S. (2022). Multidimensional Multiconvolution-Based Feature Extraction Approach for Drift Tolerant Robust Classifier for Gases/Odors. *IEEE Sensors Letters*, *6*(4), 1–4. doi:10.1109/LSENS.2022.3153832

Chaudhri, S. N., Rajput, N. S., Alsamhi, S. H., Shvetsov, A. V., & Almalki, F. A. (2022). Zero-padding and spatial augmentation-based gas sensor node optimization approach in resource-constrained 6G-IoT paradigm. *Sensors (Basel)*, *22*(8), 3039. doi:10.339022083039 PMID:35459024

Chaudhri, S. N., Rajput, N. S., & Mishra, A. (2022). A novel principal component-based virtual sensor approach for efficient classification of gases/odors. *Journal of Electrical Engineering*, *73*(2), 108–115. doi:10.2478/jee-2022-0014

Chaudhri, S. N., Rajput, N. S., & Singh, K. P. (2020). The Novel Camouflaged False Color Composites for the Vegetation Verified by Novel Sample Level Mirror Mosaicking Based Convolutional Neural Network. *IEEE India Geoscience and Remote Sensing Symposium (InGARSS)*, 237-240. 10.1109/InGARSS48198.2020.9358926

Chaudhri, S. N., Rajput, N. S., Singh, K. P., & Singh, D. (2021). Mirror Mosaicking Based Reduced Complexity Approach for the Classification of Hyperspectral Images. *IEEE International Geoscience and Remote Sensing Symposium IGARSS*, 3657-3660. 10.1109/IGARSS47720.2021.9554276

Choden, P., Seesaard, T., Dorji, U., Sriphrapradang, C., & Kerdcharoen, T. (2017). Urine odor detection by electronic nose for smart toilet application. *IEEE 14th International Conference on Electrical Engineering/Electronics, Computer, Telecommunications and Information Technology (ECTI-CON)*, 190-193. 10.1109/ECTICon.2017.8096205

Cole, M., Covington, J. A., & Gardner, J. W. (2011). Combined electronic nose and tongue for a flavour sensing system. *Sensors and Actuators. B, Chemical, 156*(2), 832–839. doi:10.1016/j.snb.2011.02.049

Drobot, A. T. (2020). Industrial Transformation and the Digital Revolution: A Focus on Artificial Intelligence, Data Science and Data Engineering. IEEE, ITU Kaleidoscope: Industry-Driven Digital Transformation (ITU K), 1-11.

Dua, D., & Graff, C. (2019). *UCI machine learning repository*. School of Information and Computer Science, University of California. Available http://archive.ics.uci.edu/ml

Estakhroueiyeh, H. R., & Rashedi, E. (2015). Detecting moldy Bread using an E-nose and the KNN classifier. *IEEE 5th International Conference on Computer and Knowledge Engineering (ICCKE)*, 251-255. 10.1109/ICCKE.2015.7365836

Fonollosa, J., Fernandez, L., Gutiérrez-Gálvez, A., Huerta, R., & Marco, S. (2016). Calibration transfer and drift counteraction in chemical sensor arrays using Direct Standardization. *Sensors and Actuators. B, Chemical, 236*, 1044–1053. doi:10.1016/j.snb.2016.05.089

Gardner, J. W. (1991). Detection of vapours and odours from a multisensor array using pattern recognition Part 1. Principal component and cluster analysis. *Sensors and Actuators. B, Chemical, 4*(1-2), 109–115. doi:10.1016/0925-4005(91)80185-M

Ghaffari, R., Zhang, F., Iliescu, D., Hines, E., Leeson, M., Napier, R., & Clarkson, J. (2010). Early detection of diseases in tomato crops: An electronic nose and intelligent systems approach. *IEEE International Joint Conference on Neural Networks (IJCNN)*, 1-6. 10.1109/IJCNN.2010.5596535

Ghamisi, P., Benediktsson, J. A., & Ulfarsson, M. O. (2013). Spectral–spatial classification of hyperspectral images based on hidden Markov random fields. *IEEE Transactions on Geoscience and Remote Sensing, 52*(5), 2565–2574. doi:10.1109/TGRS.2013.2263282

Gholam Hosseini, H., Luo, D., Liu, H., & Xu, G. (2007). Intelligent processing of E-nose information for fish freshness assessment. *IEEE 3rd International Conference on Intelligent Sensors, Sensor Networks and Information*, 173-177.

Hoffheins, B. S. (1990). *Using sensor arrays and pattern recognition to identify organic compounds (No. ORNL/TM-11310). Oak Ridge National Lab.* ORNL. doi:10.2172/6875143

Kang, S., Zhang, Q., Li, Z., Yin, C., Feng, N., & Shi, Y. (2023). Determination of the quality of tea from different picking periods: An adaptive pooling attention mechanism coupled with an electronic nose. *Postharvest Biology and Technology, 197*, 112214. doi:10.1016/j.postharvbio.2022.112214

LeCun, Y., Bottou, L., Bengio, Y., & Haffner, P. (1998). Gradient-based learning applied to document recognition. *Proceedings of the IEEE, 86*(11), 2278–2324. doi:10.1109/5.726791

Llobet, E., Brezmes, J., Vilanova, X., Sueiras, J. E., & Correig, X. (1997). Qualitative and quantitative analysis of volatile organic compounds using transient and steady-state responses of a thick-film tin oxide gas sensor array. *Sensors and Actuators. B, Chemical, 41*(1-3), 13–21. doi:10.1016/S0925-4005(97)80272-9

Mishra, A., & Rajput, N. S. (2018). A novel modular ANN architecture for efficient monitoring of gases/odours in real-time. *Materials Research Express, 5*(4), 045904. doi:10.1088/2053-1591/aabe09

Mishra, A., Rajput, N. S., & Han, G. (2017). NDSRT: An efficient virtual multi-sensor response transformation for classification of gases/odors. *IEEE Sensors Journal, 17*(11), 3416–3421. doi:10.1109/JSEN.2017.2690536

Mishra, A., Rajput, N. S., & Singh, D. (2018). Performance evaluation of normalized difference-based classifier for efficient discrimination of volatile organic compounds. *Materials Research Express, 5*(9), 095901. doi:10.1088/2053-1591/aad3dd

Moore, S. W., Gardner, J. W., Hines, E. L., Göpel, W., & Weimar, U. (1993). A modified multilayer perceptron model for gas mixture analysis. *Sensors and Actuators. B, Chemical, 16*(1-3), 344–348. doi:10.1016/0925-4005(93)85207-Q

Pan, X., Chen, J., Wen, X., Hao, J., Xu, W., Ye, W., & Zhao, X. (2023). A comprehensive gas recognition algorithm with label-free drift compensation based on domain adversarial network. *Sensors and Actuators. B, Chemical, 387*, 133709. doi:10.1016/j.snb.2023.133709

Rajput, N. S., Das, R. R., Mishra, V. N., Singh, K. P., & Dwivedi, R. (2010). A neural net implementation of SPCA pre-processor for gas/odor classification using the responses of thick film gas sensor array. *Sensors and Actuators. B, Chemical, 148*(2), 550–558. doi:10.1016/j.snb.2010.05.051

Rehman, A. U., Belhaouari, S. B., Ijaz, M., Bermak, A., & Hamdi, M. (2020). Multi-classifier tree with transient features for drift compensation in electronic nose. *IEEE Sensors Journal, 21*(5), 6564–6574. doi:10.1109/JSEN.2020.3041949

Rodriguez-Lujan, I., Fonollosa, J., Vergara, A., Homer, M., & Huerta, R. (2014). On the calibration of sensor arrays for pattern recognition using the minimal number of experiments. *Chemometrics and Intelligent Laboratory Systems, 130*, 123–134. doi:10.1016/j.chemolab.2013.10.012

Sanaeifar, A., Mohtasebi, S., Ghasemi-Varnamkhasti, M., Ahmadi, H., & Lozano Rogado, J. S. (2014). *Development and application of a new low-cost electronic nose for the ripeness monitoring of banana using computational techniques (PCA, LDA, SIMCA, and SVM)*. Available: (http://hdl.handle.net/10662/4367

Sari, I. M., Wijaya, D. R., Hidayat, W., & Kannan, R. (2021). An approach to classify rice quality using electronic nose dataset-based Naïve bayes classifier. *IEEE International Symposium on Electronics and Smart Devices (ISESD)*, 1-5. 10.1109/ISESD53023.2021.9501909

Srivastava, S., Chaudhri, S. N., Rajput, N. S., Alsamhi, S. H., & Shvetsov, A. V. (2023). Spatial Upscaling-Based Algorithm for Detection and Estimation of Hazardous Gases. *IEEE Access : Practical Innovations, Open Solutions, 11*, 17731–17738. doi:10.1109/ACCESS.2023.3245041

Srivastava, S., Chaudhri, S. N., Rajput, N. S., & Mishra, A. (2023). A novel data-driven technique to produce multi-sensor virtual responses for gas sensor array-based electronic noses. *Journal of Electrical Engineering, 74*(2), 102–108. doi:10.2478/jee-2023-0013

Vergara, A., Vembu, S., Ayhan, T., Ryan, M. A., Homer, M. L., & Huerta, R. (2012). Chemical gas sensor drift compensation using classifier ensembles. *Sensors and Actuators. B, Chemical, 166*, 320–329. doi:10.1016/j.snb.2012.01.074

Wu, X., Sun, K., & Cao, M. (2023). A New Regularized Spatiotemporal Attention-Based LSTM with Application to Nitrogen Oxides Emission Prediction. *ACS Omega, 8*(14), 12853–12864. doi:10.1021/acsomega.2c08205 PMID:37065070

Ying, X., Liu, W., Hui, G., & Fu, J. (2015). E-nose based rapid prediction of early mouldy grain using probabilistic neural networks. *Bioengineered, 6*(4), 222–226. doi:10.1080/21655979.2015.1022304 PMID:25714125

Zhang, S., Cheng, Y., Luo, D., He, J., Wong, A. K., & Hung, K. (2021). Channel attention convolutional neural network for Chinese baijiu detection with E-nose. *IEEE Sensors Journal, 21*(14), 16170–16182. doi:10.1109/JSEN.2021.3075703

Zhang, W., Wang, L., Chen, J., Bi, X., Chen, C., Zhang, J., & Hans, V. (2021). A Novel Gas Recognition and Concentration Estimation Model for an Artificial Olfactory System with a Gas Sensor Array. *IEEE Sensors Journal*, *21*(17), 18459–18468. doi:10.1109/JSEN.2021.3091582

Ziyatdinov, A., Fonollosa, J., Fernandez, L., Gutierrez-Galvez, A., Marco, S., & Perera, A. (2015). Bioinspired early detection through gas flow modulation in chemosensory systems. *Sensors and Actuators. B, Chemical*, *206*, 538–547. doi:10.1016/j.snb.2014.09.001

Chapter 6
Just Quit:
A Modern Way to Quit Smoking

Mohammed Furqanuddin Siddiqui
University of Wollongong in Dubai, UAE

Gaurav Gulshan Awatramani
University of Wollongong in Dubai, UAE

Cyril Kunjumon Daniel
University of Wollongong in Dubai, UAE

Rahul Manwani
University of Wollongong in Dubai, UAE

Shwetha Shaji
University of Wollongong in Dubai, UAE

ABSTRACT

One of the leading causes of early death nowadays is smoking. There are many applications available to assist individuals quit smoking, but many are inefficient as they require a lot of user involvement. These programs rely on the user to consistently track their smoking lapses and evaluate their success, which is quite unpleasant and demanding for the user. JustQuit is an application that has been developed for smokers who are motivated to quit. The application's goal is to assist users in effectively quitting smoking by automatically identifying their smoking behavior using a machine learning approach and lowering reliance on the user to monitor their progress. The application offers a novel approach to this issue by gathering data from wearable sensors and utilizing machine learning techniques to predict the user's smoking habit. The software will include elements like a points system, awards, and achievements based on the user's successes acting as a motivation factor.

DOI: 10.4018/978-1-6684-8696-2.ch006

RESEARCH OBJECTIVE

Many adults and young people worldwide struggle with addiction to smoking, and one of the biggest issues is the difficulty in quitting. Despite efforts by medical professionals and health authorities to provide techniques to help people quit, statistics show that only 7.5% of motivated individuals can successfully give up smoking.

The goal of this project is to assist self-motivated smokers in achieving their goal of quitting smoking. Since existing quit smoking applications rely on the user to constantly evaluate their progress and record the number of smoking lapses which is very unpleasant and requires a lot of effort from the user. One of the main objectives of this project was to reduce this dependence on users to track the progress of the user and the way to achieve this objective was using a Machine Learning model.

The application named JustQuit will utilize wearable device sensors, such as accelerometer and gyroscope, to provide users with statistics regarding their smoking habits. This will encourage users to track their smoking behavior and establish daily targets to reduce the number of cigarettes smoked. By using gamification techniques, such as a points system, the application will incentivize users to refrain from smoking and distract them from the urge to smoke. Ultimately, the aim is to support smokers in their efforts to quit smoking.

LITERATURE REVIEW

Smoking is a significant global public health concern responsible for millions of deaths yearly. Smoking is becoming one of the leading causes of early death. According to the World Health Organization, around 8.2 million people die yearly from smoking. (W.H.O., 2022). According to health experts in U.A.E., over 40% of university students began smoking just at the age of 14.

Despite the well-known health risks associated with smoking, many people still find it challenging to quit. The development of digital interventions, such as mobile applications, has provided an opportunity to help people quit smoking. Quit smoking applications are a modern way to allow individuals and assist them in their journey to quit smoking using machine learning technology. Several apps in the market help people reduce or quit their smoking habits. A Digital Intervention to Reduce Smoking in the United Arab Emirates (Abdulrahman et al., 2019) describes a mobile application that helps users quit smoking by providing them with motivational messages and educational materials. Another such application, called Breatheasy, provides users with personalized messages and advice to help them quit smoking. Such applications help users keep track of their smoking habits and provide them with distractions through games and exercise suggestions to help them fight the urge to smoke. Research on quit-smoking applications and the rising trend in the use of digital technology indicate that mobile applications can be a beneficial tool in assisting individuals who wish to quit smoking and require extra help in their journey to reduce their smoking habits.

However, all existing quit-smoking applications require users' input to track their health status and smoking habits. Many, if not all, quit-smoking applications can be ineffective e because they need a high amount of user participation. These applications rely on the user to constantly evaluate their progress and record the number of smoking lapses, which is very unpleasant and requires much effort, making it demotivating for them to use such applications.

The use of smartwatches equipped with accelerometers and gyroscope sensors has gained popularity in various applications such as health monitoring, fitness tracking, and activity recognition. These sensors provide an opportunity to monitor human motions, and machine learning algorithms can be used to detect various activities.

Carrino et al. (2019) explored the collection and processing of data from wearable devices in heterogeneous and multiple-user scenarios. The authors demonstrated using machine learning algorithms such as Long Short Term Memory (LSTM) and CNN to detect various activities such as walking, running, and cycling using the accelerometer and gyroscope sensors of smartwatches. The results showed that the models achieved an accuracy of 95% and 97%, respectively. Zeng et al. (2020) developed a deep learning-based human activity recognition system using smartwatch sensor data. In their research, LSTM and Gated Recurrent Unit (G.R.U.) models were used to classify various activities and provide the user's health status. The study showed that the models achieved an accuracy of 91.3% and 91.8%, respectively. Many health and fitness applications use the built-in sensors of smartwatches and wearable devices to detect human activities. The same approach can be used to detect the smoking behaviors and patterns of the users.

Combining the applications of existing machine learning models such as LSTM and CNN with the benefits of using mobile applications to assist people who wish to quit smoking, this research explores the development of a quit-smoking application that automatically detects the user's smoking behaviors and patterns in real-time with the help of accelerometer and gyroscope sensors of smartwatches. In addition, the application could also provide the user with real-time distractions to users through games, comics, and exercise suggestions. The automatic detection of users' smoking behaviors eliminates the need for constant manual input from the users and provides much reliable data.

MATERIALS AND METHODS

The project deals with time series data, so LSTM was found to be the best model. The wearable used could be a Fitbit or any watch with Wear OS. To get the raw data from a smartwatch's accelerometer and gyroscope hardware sensors, the Android sensor framework from the android.hardware package was utilized. The mobile application was developed using Android Studio or React Native on a Windows machine. Python scripts were used to collect sensor data, and Firebase was used as the database on Google Cloud.

Python was the primary language for implementing SVM due to its precision, conciseness, and extensive range of libraries and frameworks, making it convenient, adaptable, and straightforward to use.

DATASET

A custom dataset was created which included human activity data. To track the smoking action performed using the hand gestures of the user, accelerometer and gyroscope data was collected from the Android smartwatch.

Twenty three participants were chosen for the data collection process which included male and female users across different age groups to prevent biases on the dataset. The dataset included the X,Y, and Z axis sensor values of accelerometer and gyroscope streaming at the rate of 100 tupes per second from the smartwatch.

The target class of the classification "Smoking" included two values "Smoking" and "Not Smoking" indicating the action of the user at the particular instant. Data was collected in a supervised environment where the participants were instructed to perform smoking action as well as non-smoking actions such as eating, drinking, walking, running, standing and sitting.

LOADING THE DATA

Two folders were created pertaining to the smoking and non-smoking data of 23 participants. The data was then merged into a single table as shown below maintaining the order of the tuples relating to each user. The total number of tuples in the table was 292068.

The data was imported to a dataframe using the pandas library within which the read_csv() function was used to read the .csv files generated from the IOT sensor.

Figure 1. snippet of the data extracted from the IOT sensors in the smartwatch

Unnamed: 0	Milliseconds	Time	AX	AY	AZ	GX	GY	GZ	Smoking
0	74506	2:50:02.073 PM	-0.088585	-9.129091	3.756502	-0.521679	0.009774	-0.007330	Smoking
1	74516	2:50:02.083 PM	-0.253785	-9.200917	3.727772	-0.548557	0.028100	-0.018326	Smoking
2	74527	2:50:02.094 PM	-0.375890	-9.021352	3.622427	-0.575435	0.056200	-0.021991	Smoking
3	74537	2:50:02.104 PM	-0.474052	-8.815451	3.732560	-0.637743	0.074526	-0.015882	Smoking
4	74547	2:50:02.114 PM	-0.490811	-8.841787	3.586514	-0.723264	0.076969	-0.013439	Smoking

EXPLORATORY DATA ANALYSIS

EDA is an initial step for performing data analysis to get insights about the data in the form of visual representation and statistical summaries. EDA is an essential part when performing ML models as it helps to remove erroneous data and understand the patterns and trends in data.

The columns of data which were not relevant in the training phase of the machine learning model were omitted from the dataframe using the pandas drop() function. These included the columns "Milliseconds" and "Time".

Figure 2. Information regarding attributes in dataframe

```
In [4]: df.info()

        <class 'pandas.core.frame.DataFrame'>
        RangeIndex: 292068 entries, 0 to 292067
        Data columns (total 7 columns):
         #   Column   Non-Null Count   Dtype
        ---  ------   --------------   -----
         0   AX       292068 non-null  float64
         1   AY       292068 non-null  float64
         2   AZ       292068 non-null  float64
         3   GX       292068 non-null  float64
         4   GY       292068 non-null  float64
         5   GZ       292068 non-null  float64
         6   Smoking  292068 non-null  object
        dtypes: float64(6), object(1)
        memory usage: 15.6+ MB
```

All the features in the dataset were float64 datatype except the target class which was of object datatype. Categorical features are not supported to be fed into the machine learning models, therefore the Smoking class was label encoded to 0 and 1. It was also confirmed that there are no missing values in the dataset which otherwise would need to be omitted before performing the training.

Figure 3. Number of samples for each target class, smoking and non-smoking

```
In [3]: df['Smoking'].value_counts().plot(kind='bar', title='Training examples by activity type');
```

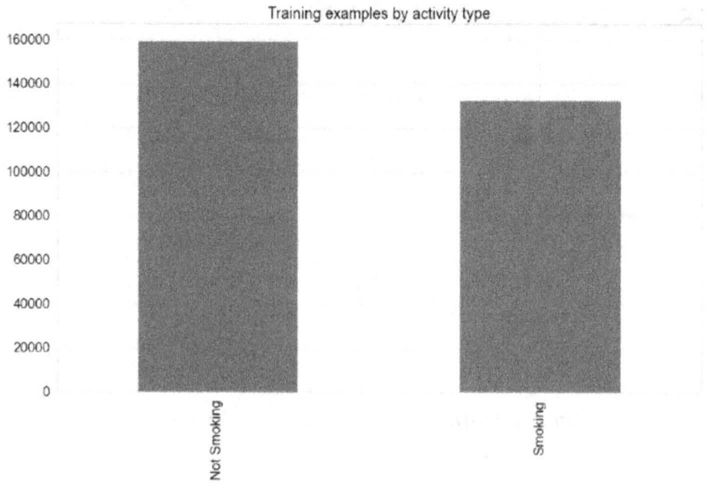

The count of smoking and no-smoking samples in the dataset were kept close to each other to avoid bias or overfitting to a certain target class.

Figure 4. Statistical information regarding attributes

```
In [10]: df.describe()
Out[10]:
```

	AX	AY	AZ	GX	GY	GZ
count	292068.000000	292068.000000	292068.000000	292068.000000	292068.000000	292068.000000
mean	-0.531061	-5.167527	2.824547	-0.008911	0.011113	0.006510
std	7.094421	3.425186	3.408683	1.034778	0.676951	1.141799
min	-30.767885	-43.030987	-23.130383	-12.767083	-5.004208	-7.325496
25%	-7.728483	-6.852205	1.106121	-0.321315	-0.172264	-0.249233
50%	0.107739	-4.618415	2.540248	0.000000	0.007330	-0.001222
75%	5.839458	-3.248932	4.673482	0.309098	0.212581	0.246790
max	23.997084	15.298949	46.334984	15.234980	5.535661	7.743328

The describe() method describes the data in the dataframe by providing statistical insights which helps to determine the potential outliers in the dataset and the average values of each feature.

Figure 5. Correlation of smoking class with attributes in the table

```
In [36]:  df.corr()['Smoking']

Out[36]:  AX           0.400437
          AY           0.048069
          AZ          -0.287589
          GX           0.003786
          GY           0.022703
          GZ          -0.001259
          Smoking      1.000000
          Name: Smoking, dtype: float64
```

The correlation() method helps to find the relation between the features of the dataframe and how closely they are interdependent on each other. In the above table, it is clearly seen that the X axis of the accelerometer has the highest correlation with the target class followed by the Z axis. Among the features relating to the gyroscope sensor, the Y axis has the highest correlation followed by X axis.

The difference is clearly seen when the smoking and non-smoking activity data is compared in the graphical form. There is a pattern which can be observed in the sensor values recorded during the smoking duration.

The displots above show that the data is fairly normalized across all the axes of the sensor data, therefore techniques such as binning, normalization is not required. It can also be observed that as this data pertains to a streaming data from the sensor, it does contain an abundance of outliers.

Outliers is an observation or a set of observations wherein the data point is far away from the rest of the observations (Engineering Statistics Handbook, 2019). Usually outliers are considered as erroneous data which are handled by techniques such as binning, or removing the values. But in this case of streaming data from a sensor, it is expected that when testing in the real world, the data streamed will also contain many outliers. Applying any methods to handle the outliers, would degrade the performance of the Machine Learning model as it would not relate to the data streamed when testing the model in the real world.

Figure 6. Graphical representation of smoking samples

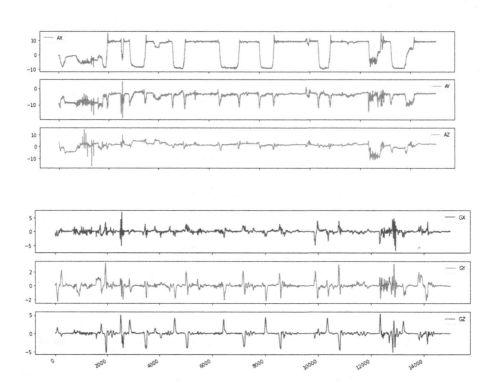

"Smoking" column which is categorical is converted to numeric data 0 and 1 where 0 represents "not smoking" and 1 represents "smoking".

APPROACH USING CNN

```
#Frames Building
import scipy.stats as stats
```

The scipy.stats library contains a number of frequency statistics, probability distributions which used in the functions below.

Figure 7. Graphical representation of non-smoking samples

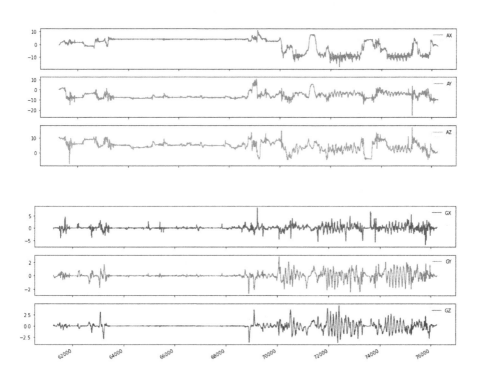

The average time observed during the data collection process for a smoking puff was 4 seconds. Therefore, the frame size of the window was taken to be the same. The data streaming program in the IOT device was programmed to stream sensor data at the rate of 100 tuples/second. Once the 400 tuples are processed, the window slides by 200 tuples creating a sliding window approach on the dataframe.

Based on the correlation metrics between the features and target class, only the accelerometer X, Y, Z axis and the Y axis of the gyroscope was considered to train the model. The mode of the target class value was calculated based on the 400 tuples used and assigned as a result corresponding to the particular window.

```
X,y = get_frames(df,frame_size,hop_size)

X.shape,y.shape

((1459, 400, 4), (1459,))
```

```
df.shape

(292068, 7)
```

Figure 8. Displots of different attributes to check if the data is normalized

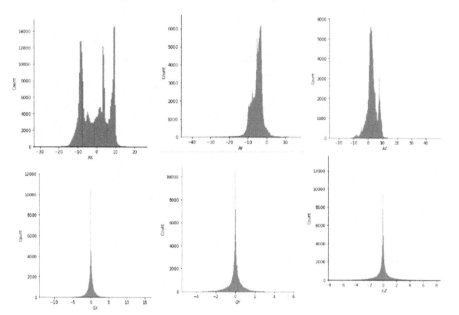

Figure 9. Change of categorical target column to numeric value

```
df.head()
```

	AX	AY	AZ	GX	GY	GZ	Smoking
0	-0.088585	-9.129091	3.756502	-0.521679	0.009774	-0.007330	Smoking
1	-0.253785	-9.200917	3.727772	-0.548557	0.028100	-0.018326	Smoking
2	-0.375890	-9.021352	3.622427	-0.575435	0.056200	-0.021991	Smoking
3	-0.474052	-8.815451	3.732560	-0.637743	0.074526	-0.015882	Smoking
4	-0.490811	-8.841787	3.586514	-0.723264	0.076969	-0.013439	Smoking

→

```
df.head()
```

	AX	AY	AZ	GX	GY	GZ	Smoking
0	0.560199	0.581209	0.387055	0.437304	0.475716	0.485649	1
1	0.557183	0.579978	0.386641	0.436344	0.477455	0.484920	1
2	0.554953	0.583056	0.385124	0.435384	0.480121	0.484677	1
3	0.553161	0.586586	0.386710	0.433159	0.481859	0.485082	1
4	0.552855	0.586135	0.384607	0.430105	0.482091	0.485244	1

The size of the dataframe after dividing into windows is 1459 samples of either smoking or non-smoking data.

Building and Training the CNN Model

Convolution Layer

This layer is responsible for extracting the feature maps from the input data provided using the kernel provided. The feature maps are generated by sliding the kernel over the input data and performing matrix multiplication and summing up the result. The convolution is performed on 3D input shapes (freeCodeCamp.org, 2018).

Figure 10. Function to implement sliding window approach on the dataframe

```
Fs=100
frame_size = Fs*4
hop_size = Fs*2
```

```
def get_frames (df, frame_size, hop_size):
    N_FEATURES = 4
    frames = []
    labels = []
    for i in range(0, len(df)-frame_size, hop_size):
        x=df['AX'].values[i: i+frame_size]
        y=df['AY'].values[i: i+frame_size]
        z = df['AZ'].values[i: i+ frame_size]
        w = df['GY'].values[i: i+ frame_size]

# Retrieve the most often used Label in this segment
        label = stats.mode(df['Smoking'][i: i + frame_size])[0][0]
        frames.append([x, y, z,w])
        labels.append(label)

#Bring the segments into a better shape

    frames= np.asarray(frames).reshape(-1, frame_size, N_FEATURES)
    labels = np.asarray(labels)
    return frames, labels
```

For the below case, 2 convolution layers were taken into consideration with a kernel size of 2 and activation function 'relu'. The activation function helps to make the output non-linear.

Flattening Layer

The flattening layer is used to convert the feature maps into 1D shape to be fed into the fully connected dense layers (freeCodeCamp.org, 2018).

The Fully Connected Layer

The dense layer or the connected layers is the final step in the CNN network in which each neuron is connected to every other neuron on the subsequent layer. These layers help in the prediction of the output class based on the preceding convolution and flattening layers (freeCodeCamp.org, 2018).

Figure 11. Training the CNN Model and producing the confusion matrix

Diving the dataset into Train and Test
Converting the dimension of the input from 2D to 3D to be fed into the convolution network.

```
from sklearn.model_selection import train_test_split
```

```
X_train, X_test, y_train, y_test = train_test_split(X,y,test_size=0.3, random_state=101, stratify=y)
```

```
X_train.shape, X_test.shape
```

```
((1021, 400, 4), (438, 400, 4))
```

```
X_train= X_train.reshape(1021, 400, 4,1)
X_test=X_test.reshape(438, 400, 4,1)
```

```
X_train[0].shape
```

```
(400, 4, 1)
```

Importing required libraries to perform convolution, Flattening, and creating the Dense Network

```
import tensorflow as tf
from keras.models import Sequential
from keras.layers import Dense
from tensorflow.keras.optimizers import Adam
from tensorflow.keras.layers import Conv2D, MaxPool2D
from tensorflow.keras.layers import Flatten, Dense, Dropout, BatchNormalization
```

Creating the convolve layers for feature extraction, then flattening to be able to feed into the Dense Network

```
model =Sequential()
model.add(Conv2D(8,(2,2),activation='relu', input_shape=X_train[0].shape))
model.add(Conv2D(16,(2,2),activation='relu'))
model.add(Flatten())

model.add(Dense(64, activation='relu'))
model.add(Dense(16, activation='relu'))
model.add(Dense(2, activation='softmax'))
```

Using the Adam Optimizer to update the weights relating to the neurons and fitting the model

```
model.compile(optimizer='adam', loss= 'sparse_categorical_crossentropy',metrics=['accuracy'])
```

```
history= model.fit(X_train,y_train,epochs=20,verbose=1)
```

Evaluating the model based on test data

```
model.evaluate(X_test,y_test)
```

```
14/14 [==============================] - 0s 8ms/step - loss: 0.2817 - accuracy: 0.8881
```

```
[0.28174087405204773, 0.888127863407135]
```

Plotting the confusion metrics to judge the performace of the model

```
from mlxtend.plotting import plot_confusion_matrix
from sklearn.metrics import confusion_matrix
```

```
y_pred = np.argmax(model.predict(X_test), axis=1)
```

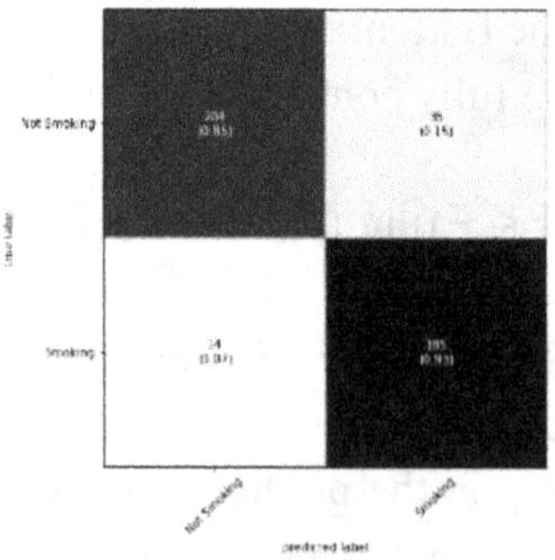

Performance Metrics

The performance of the model can be calculated using a confusion matrix. This gives an overview regarding the actual values and the predictions performed by the trained model by means of True Positive, True Negative, False Positive, False Negative.

Figure 12. Confusion matrix relating to CNN classification model

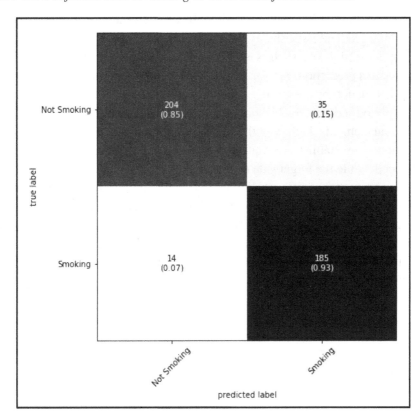

The accuracy of the train dataset was 91% and for the test dataset, the accuracy was 88%.

Accuracy can be calculated using the confusion matrix above using the formula

(TP+TN)/(TP+TN+FP+FN) (Beheshti, 2022).

Other performance metrics, such as precision, recall, F1 score can be calculated using the formulas as below.

Precision: TP/(TP+FP)
Recall: TP/(TP+FN)
F1 score: 2X(Precision X Recall) / (Precision+Recall)
(Beheshti, 2022)

APPROACH USING LONG SHORT-TERM MEMORY (LSTM)

LSTM, or Long Short-Term Memory, is a kind of RNN structure that aims to address the vanishing gradient issue that typical RNNs face.LSTMs are highly effective in managing sequential data, such as natural language processing, speech recognition, and time-series prediction.

LSTMs function by preserving a memory cell that can store information for an extended period and selectively modify or forget that data. The LSTM cell comprises three critical elements, including the input gate, forget gate, and output gate.

The input gate establishes the quantity of fresh data that should be included in the memory cell, while the forget gate decides which data to remove from the memory cell. The output gate specifies the amount of data to output from the memory cell.

Each of these gates is established using a sigmoid function that uses the current input, previous hidden state, and current memory cell state. The gates produce intermediate values utilized to modify the memory cell and hidden state.

To sum up, LSTMs use a memory cell with input, forget, and output gates to selectively store, forget, and output data, allowing them to more effectively handle sequential data and long-term dependencies than typical RNNs.

Figure 13. Sliding window approach on the dataframe

```
N_TIME_STEPS = 400
N_FEATURES = 4
step = 200
segments = []
labels = []
for i in range(0, len(df) - N_TIME_STEPS, step):
    ax = df['AX'].values[i: i + N_TIME_STEPS]
    ay= df['AY'].values[i: i + N_TIME_STEPS]
    az= df['AZ'].values[i: i + N_TIME_STEPS]
    gy= df['GY'].values[i: i + N_TIME_STEPS]
    label = stats.mode(df['Smoking'][i: i + N_TIME_STEPS])[0][0]
    segments.append([ax, ay, az,gy])
    labels.append(label)
```

N_TIME_STEPS = 400 and N_FEATURES = 4: These are constants that define the number of time steps and the number of features (sensor measurements) that will be used for each segment of data.

step = 200: This defines the number of time steps to move forward in each iteration of the loop. This means that each iteration will process a segment of data that is 200 time steps away from the previous one.

segments = [] and labels = []: These are empty lists that will be filled with the processed segments of data and their corresponding labels.

for i in range(0, len(df) - N_TIME_STEPS, step):: This is a loop that iterates over the entire dataset, processing segments of data with a fixed number of time steps and features, and skipping over a fixed number of time steps between segments.

ax = df['AX'].values[i: i + N_TIME_STEPS], ay= df['AY'].values[i: i + N_TIME_STEPS], az= df['AZ'].values[i: i + N_TIME_STEPS], and gy= df['GY'].values[i: i + N_TIME_STEPS]: These lines extract the sensor measurements for each segment of data from the original dataset (df). Each variable (ax, ay, az, and gy) contains an array of sensor measurements for one of the four features.

label = stats.mode(df['Smoking'][i: i + N_TIME_STEPS])[0][0]: This line calculates the label for the segment of data by finding the most common value in the Smoking column of the original dataset (df) for the corresponding time steps.

segments.append([ax, ay, az,gy]) and labels.append(label): These lines add the processed segment of data and its label to the corresponding lists (segments and labels).

Overall, these steps are processing the raw sensor data into segments of fixed length with a fixed number of features, and assigning each segment a label based on the most common smoking activity during that segment. The resulting segments and label lists can be used to train our Long Short Term Memory (LSTM) model to classify smoking activity based on sensor data.

Building Long Short-Term Memory (LSTM) Model

These steps are defining a function create_LSTM_model in TensorFlow for creating a LSTM model for classifying the smoking activity based on the pre-processed data generated by the previous code snippet. Overall, these steps define a TensorFlow function that creates an LSTM model for classifying smoking activity based on the preprocessed input data. The function takes the preprocessed input data as an argument, applies two LSTM layers to the hidden layer outputs, and computes the final output using an output layer with N_CLASSES=2 output units. The resulting model can be trained using TensorFlow's optimization algorithms and evaluated on a test set to assess its performance.

Figure 14. Creating the LSTM model

```
N_CLASSES = 2
N_HIDDEN_UNITS = 64
def create_LSTM_model(inputs):
    W = {
        'hidden': tf.Variable(tf.random_normal([N_FEATURES, N_HIDDEN_UNITS])),
        'output': tf.Variable(tf.random_normal([N_HIDDEN_UNITS, N_CLASSES]))
    }
    biases = {
        'hidden': tf.Variable(tf.random_normal([N_HIDDEN_UNITS], mean=1.0)),
        'output': tf.Variable(tf.random_normal([N_CLASSES]))
    }

    X = tf.transpose(inputs, [1, 0, 2])
    X = tf.reshape(X, [-1, N_FEATURES])
    hidden = tf.nn.relu(tf.matmul(X, W['hidden']) + biases['hidden'])
    hidden = tf.split(hidden, N_TIME_STEPS, 0)

    # Stack 2 LSTM layers
    lstm_layers = [tf.contrib.rnn.BasicLSTMCell(N_HIDDEN_UNITS, forget_bias=1.0) for _ in range(2)]
    lstm_layers = tf.contrib.rnn.MultiRNNCell(lstm_layers)

    outputs, _ = tf.contrib.rnn.static_rnn(lstm_layers, hidden, dtype=tf.float32)

    # Get output for the last time step
    lstm_last_output = outputs[-1]

    return tf.matmul(lstm_last_output, W['output']) + biases['output']
```

Training the CNN Model

These steps are for training and evaluating the Long Short-Term Memory (LSTM) model using TensorFlow:

N_EPOCHS = 50 and BATCH_SIZE = 1024 are hyperparameters that specify the number of epochs to train for and the batch size for each training iteration.

saver = tf.train.Saver() creates an instance of the Saver class, which can be used to save and restore the trained model.

history is a dictionary used to store the training history, including the train and test loss and accuracy for each epoch.

sess=tf.InteractiveSession() creates an interactive session, which allows us to execute TensorFlow operations.

sess.run(tf.global_variables_initializer()) initializes all the variables in the TensorFlow graph.

train_count = len(X_train) calculates the number of training examples in the training set.

The for loop runs for N_EPOCHS and trains the model on batches of size BATCH_SIZE. It uses the optimizer to minimize the loss function, which is defined earlier in the code.

After each epoch, the accuracy and loss are calculated for both the training and test sets and stored in the history dictionary.

Figure 15. Training the CNN model

```
N_EPOCHS = 50
BATCH_SIZE = 1024
saver = tf.train.Saver()

history = dict(train_loss=[],
                    train_acc=[],
                    test_loss=[],
                    test_acc=[])

sess=tf.InteractiveSession()
sess.run(tf.global_variables_initializer())

train_count = len(X_train)

for i in range(1, N_EPOCHS + 1):
    for start, end in zip(range(0, train_count, BATCH_SIZE),
                          range(BATCH_SIZE, train_count + 1,BATCH_SIZE)):
        sess.run(optimizer, feed_dict={X: X_train[start:end],
                                       Y: y_train[start:end]})

    _, acc_train, loss_train = sess.run([pred_softmax, accuracy, loss], feed_dict={
                                        X: X_train, Y: y_train})

    _, acc_test, loss_test = sess.run([pred_softmax, accuracy, loss], feed_dict={
                                        X: X_test, Y: y_test})

    history['train_loss'].append(loss_train)
    history['train_acc'].append(acc_train)
    history['test_loss'].append(loss_test)
    history['test_acc'].append(acc_test)

    if i != 1 and i % 10 != 0:
        continue

    print(f'epoch: {i} test accuracy: {acc_test} loss: {loss_test}')

predictions, acc_final, loss_final = sess.run([pred_softmax, accuracy, loss], feed_dict={X: X_test, Y: y_test})

print()
print(f'final results: accuracy: {acc_final} loss: {loss_final}')
```

The final predictions, accuracy, and loss are calculated using the trained model and the test data.

Figure 16. Accuracy of the test data after 50 epochs

```
epoch: 1 test accuracy: 0.4006849229335785 loss: 3.7987856864929292
epoch: 10 test accuracy: 0.5445205569267273 loss: 1.398408055305481
epoch: 20 test accuracy: 0.6335616707801819 loss: 1.3380966186523438
epoch: 30 test accuracy: 0.6917808055877686 loss: 1.2167613506317139
epoch: 40 test accuracy: 0.7808219194412231 loss: 1.1065274477005005
epoch: 50 test accuracy: 0.8082191944122314 loss: 1.054443597793579

final results: accuracy: 0.8082191944122314 loss: 1.054443597793579
```

As we can see after each epoch the accuracy increases and the final accuracy comes around 80%.

Confusion Matrix

```
LABELS = ['Snoking','Non-Smoking']
max_test = np.argmax(y_test, axis=1)
max_predictions = np.argmax(predictions, axis=1)
confusion_matrix = metrics.confusion_matrix(max_test, max_predictions)
plt.figure(figsize=(16, 14))
sns.heatmap(confusion_matrix, xticklabels=LABELS, yticklabels=LABELS, annot=True, fmt="d");
plt.title("Confusion matrix")
plt.ylabel('True label')
plt.xlabel('Predicted label')
plt.show();
```

Finally, we create a confusion matrix to evaluate the performance of our model as shown below:

Figure 17. Confusion matrix for LSTM model

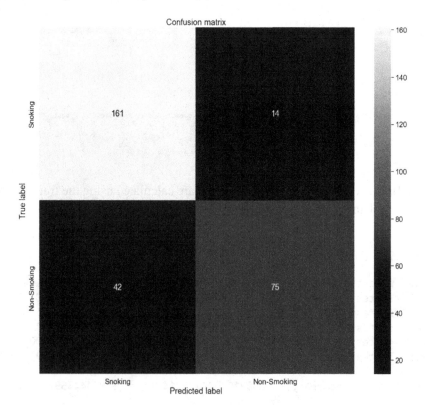

EVALUATION AND DISCUSSION

Although it can be observed that CNN has provided better accuracy results when compared to LSTM, there were several reasons why LSTM was considered more relevant to this particular prediction and why it performed better than CNN in real life scenarios.

The reason for using Convolution Neural Network as it uses a sliding window approach in image classification. As the model for this project also required a sliding window approach on the dataframe, it was felt suitable to test using CNN. However, it is crucial to note that CNN classification models are best suited for image classification and do not account for sequential dependencies as seen in the smoking data patterns (Grogan, 2021) .

On the other hand, although LSTM provided slightly lower accuracy than CNN, it was observed that it performed significantly well in real life testing. The reason being, LSTM accounts for sequences in a time series. Smoking behavior of the user can be a time series data as it relates to the patterns of smoking the user has, which is taken into consideration in LSTM classification (Grogan, 2021).

CONCLUSION AND FUTURE IMPROVEMENTS

The goal of the JustQuit application is to assist addicted chain smokers in breaking their smoking habit and adopting a healthier lifestyle. To put this concept into practice, sensor data is gathered from the smartwatch, which records the user's hand motions and uses Deep Learning Long Short Term Memory (LSTM) model to recognise smoking action. When smoking is detected, the user receives notifications on his smartphone that serve as distractions. Memory games, humorous stories, and suggested workouts are just a few of the misdirection activities. The user would be able to set daily or monthly goals in order to maintain his level of motivation during his quest to stop smoking. The user will be rewarded with exciting vouchers if the goals were attained, which can be redeemed at either stores or restaurants.

Listed below are certain features we anticipate to include in the future:

- Support for multiple OS

Currently we have decided to implement our application in the android OS, but we would be planning to implement our application in iOS and other wearable OS which would make the application accessible to a wider range of users.

- Consider additional features such as heart rate, O2 from the wearable device for training the testing the ML model

As per the current situation, our application would be relying on the data we retrieve from the accelerometer and gyroscope sensors, however if we do detect at the later stage of the project that the accuracy of the model may be improvised by making use of more additional features, we may add them to train our ML model. Time factor would be a major constraint to implement this feature.

- Video Consultation with health experts

Currently, our application will provide the user with the contact details of the medical experts and help him to set appointments using the intelligent chatbot, however in future we would be adding a provision so that the users may speak to the experts virtually from within the application. Several security and legal aspects would be taken into consideration to implement this feature.

- Providing the users with certified medical plans to quit the addiction of smoking

JustQuit provides the feature to the users to set their own targets/goals from their profile section and then based on their goal, would provide statistics whether the user is achieving them or not. In future, under the supervision of the authorized medical authorities, we would be setting up recommended plans within the application which the user may select and give up the craving of smoking effectively.

- Providing Community Chats and Leader board charts

One of the main sources of reliability of applications that users depend on are user reviews and feedback. In future, when our application would have been used by several users to achieve their goals, we would be providing a community chats section and also leader board charts which would motivate the user to use the application and quit smoking.

REFERENCES

Azizur Rahman, S. (2020). Mobile for health: A digital intervention to reduce smoking in the United Arab Emirates. *2020 IEEE 44th Annual Computers, Software, and Applications Conference (COMPSAC)*. 10.1109/COMPSAC48688.2020.0-171

Beheshti, N. (2022). *Guide to Confusion Matrices & Classification Performance Metrics*. Medium. Available at: https://towardsdatascience.com/guide-to-confusion-matrices-classification-performancemetrics-a0ebfc08408e#:~:text=Confusion%20 matrices%20can%20be%20used

Benouis, M. (2019). Behavioural smoking identification via hand-movement dynamics. *2019 IEEE SmartWorld, Ubiquitous Intelligence & Computing, Advanced & Trusted Computing, Scalable Computing & Communications, Cloud & Big Data Computing, Internet of People and Smart City Innovation (SmartWorld/SCALCOM/ UIC/ATC/CBDCom/IOP/SCI)*. doi:10.1109/SmartWorld-UIC-ATC-SCALCOM-IOP-SCI.2019.00309

de Arriba-Pérez, F., Caeiro-Rodríguez, M., & Santos-Gago, J. (2016). Collection and processing of data from wrist wearable devices in heterogeneous and multiple-user scenarios. *Sensors (Basel)*, *16*(9), 1538. doi:10.339016091538 PMID:27657081

Engineering Statistics Handbook. (2019). *7.1.6. What are outliers in the data?* Nist. gov. Available at: https://www.itl.nist.gov/div898/handbook/prc/section1/prc16.htm

Finkelstein, J., & Wood, J. (2013). Interactive Mobile System for Smoking Cessation. *2013 35th Annual International Conference of the IEEE Engineering in Medicine and Biology Society (EMBC)*. Available at: 10.1109/EMBC.2013.6609714

freeCodeCamp.org. (2018). *An intuitive guide to Convolutional Neural Networks*. Available at: https://www.freecodecamp.org/news/an-intuitive-guide-to-convolutional-neural-networks260c2de0a050/#:~:text=The%20term%20 convolution%20refers%20to

Grogan, M. (2021). *CNN-LSTM: Predicting Daily Hotel Cancellations*. Medium. Available at: https://towardsdatascience.com/cnn-lstm-predicting-daily-hotel-cancellations-e1c75697f124#:~:text=Forecasting%20without%20LSTM%20layer

Mohan, B. A. (2021). Breatheasy - An Android application to quit the smoking. *2021 IEEE International Conference on Distributed Computing, VLSI, Electrical Circuits and Robotics (DISCOVER)*. Available at: 10.1109/DISCOVER52564.2021.9663588

Ortis, A., Caponnetto, P., Polosa, R., Urso, S., & Battiato, S. (2020). A report on smoking detection and quitting technologies. *International Journal of Environmental Research and Public Health*, *17*(7), 2614. doi:10.3390/ijerph17072614 PMID:32290288

Senyurek, V., Imtiaz, M., Belsare, P., Tiffany, S., & Sazonov, E. (2019). Cigarette smoking detection with an inertial sensor and a smart lighter. *Sensors (Basel)*, *19*(3), 570. doi:10.339019030570 PMID:30700056

Who.int. (2022). *Tobacco*. Available at: https://www.who.int/news-room/fact-sheets/detail/tobacco

Chapter 7

Naive Bayes Classification for Email Spam Detection

Zain Syed
University of Wollongong in Dubai, UAE

Omar Taher
University of Wollongong in Dubai, UAE

ABSTRACT

Email is one of the cheapest forms of communication that every internet user utilizes, from individuals to businesses. Because of its simplicity and wide availability, it is vulnerable to threats by perpetrators through spam with malicious intents, known to have resulted in huge financial losses and threatened the privacy of millions of individuals. Not all spam emails are malicious; however, they are a nuisance to users regardless. Because of these reasons, there is a dire need for good spam detection systems that are automatically able to identify emails as spam. This chapter aims to do exactly that by proposing a Naïve Bayes approach to create a spam detection system by using a combination of the Enron Email dataset and the 419 fraud dataset. The datasets are lemmatized in order to boost performance in terms of execution time and accuracy. Grid search is one technique adopted to maximize accuracy. Finally, the model is evaluated through various metrics and a comparative analysis is performed.

DOI: 10.4018/978-1-6684-8696-2.ch007

INTRODUCTION

In 2021, it was revealed that 3,026,626 emails were sent every second, 67% of them being spam (Andre, 2021). Email spams have been known to cost businesses up to $20.5 billion each year (What's on the Other Side of Your Inbox - 20 SPAM Statistics for 2022, 2022). With humongous amounts of spam being generated day by day, it is crucial for powerful anti-spam filtration systems to be developed in order to prevent such drastic losses.

Text classification is the fundamental concept behind spam detection. Machine learning, natural language processing (NLP) and artificial intelligence come hand in hand to classify all kinds of text with an unsurpassed accuracy. Unlike rule-based classification approaches which classify text into groups manually based on a set of handcrafted linguistic rules, machine learning text classification actually learns to make classifications based on past observations or pre-labeled examples given to the classifier as training data (Text Classification: What It Is and Why It Matters, 2014). Such classifiers are able to learn different associations between texts and establish that a particular output is expected for a particular input. The first step in this process is feature extraction or vectorization, which will be further elaborated in detail below, after which the feature sets along with their predefined labels, or "tags" are used to train the model. This in turn will produce a classifier model that can successfully sort text into different categories, be the classification binary or multiclass. Once the model is thoroughly trained with enough training samples, test data will be provided which will be transformed into feature sets after which accurate predictions are made. Text classification through machine learning and NLP techniques is much faster and efficient as compared to human-crafted rule systems, which consist of more than a few flaws.

In this paper, a Naïve Bayes model was created upon a grid search technique using the tf-idf matrix as the feature extraction method. The model is trained to differentiate spam from ham emails with a high accuracy rate. Section 2.1 to 2.3 gives an overview on the basic pre-requisites needed to understand the working of various aspects and concepts that will be used further in the paper. Section 3 lists out a number of research papers that proposed different ideas and approaches using various classification methods and even a few deep learning approaches to tackle the issue of email spam detection. The accuracies of each are listed out which will be later compared to this study's results in Section 5, which dissertates the results of the proposed model and involves a comparative analysis, linking other research papers' outcomes with the currently discussed model. Section 4 consists of a list of subsections that together aim to describe the methodology behind the suggested approach to the problem. Finally, Section 6 concludes the paper by restating the problem and providing a final overview of how it had been approached and solved.

2.1 Naïve Bayes Classification

The Bayesian Classification is a mathematical classifier based on Bayes Theorem in probability that determines the credible target for a given feature. Naïve Bayes is a significantly less complicated extension of classifiers that make a "naïve" assumption of the features involved, which are independent to each other. Although it may seem like an irrational assumption, it has proven to yield eminent outcomes on par with far more intricate algorithms. Efficacious applications of NB have been implemented including but not limited to, text classification, weather forecasting, biometrics identification and news article categorization. Let's have a deeper comprehension on how the algorithm works by understanding Bayes' Theorem (Rish, 2001).

Bayes' Theorem is a probabilistic theory that enables calculations of certain probabilities that evince the impact of an event in contrast to another (also known as Conditional Probability).

It can be written as (Garg, 2013):

$$P\left(A|B\right) = \frac{P\left(B|A\right) \times P\left(A\right)}{P\left(B\right)} \tag{1}$$

Where,

P(A): Probability of the event A occurring
P(B): Probability of the event B occurring
P(A | B): Probability of the event A occurring given the event B
P(B | A): Probability of the event B occurring given the event A

In Eq. 1, P(B) is the probability of A having no information on the event of A. Thus, there can be a hypothesis of A being true or false, thus, Bayes' Theorem can also be written as:

$$P\left(A|B\right) = \frac{P\left(B|A\right) \times P\left(A\right)}{P\left(B|A\right) \times P\left(A\right) + P\left(B|-A\right) \times P\left(-A\right)} \tag{2}$$

Where,

P(A): Probability of the event A occurring while being false
P(B | A): Probability of the event B occurring given the event A is false

Based on this theorem (Eq. 2), a feature variable can be classified to its target class assuming all other features are independent to each other. Although Naïve Bayes gives staggering results while classifying corpora with limited number of data and document fragments (Muhammad, Bukhori & Pandunata, 2019), one of its weaknesses is that it is prone to yield low accuracies considering the selection of independent variables and probability evaluation that may not run optimally (Nur Hayatin, Gita Indah Marthasari & Nuarini, 2020).

2.2 Text-Vectorization

The significance of data has proliferated to every aspect of our lives. Amongst the different representations of data, the textual form is ceaselessly the most widespread, especially considering its usage in communication across diverse platforms. It is imperative to utilize the ability of machines to generate imperceptible insights by transmuting the data in a form that is conveniently transparent to the computers. One of the preliminary methods involved in converting text documents in a way that is machine-readable, is by vectorization (Singh & Shashi, 2019).

Text-Vectorization is almost a prerequisite to any Natural Language Processing (NLP) task that involves solving text based problems mathematically. These vectorizers can range from very lucid to really complex models (Singh & Shashi, 2019). An unsophisticated and basic approach to build such vectors would be to generate a numerical representation of all words in the lexicon using binary encoding. This method is called One-hot Encoding and should be avoided as it would lead to dimensional disaster and data sparsity. Some of the more common methods to represent a vector make use of word frequency for each term in a document. Although most of these approaches still fail to solve problems such as dimensionality reduction and feature extraction of text semantics, they are commonly used to solve most classification problems. (Yang et al. 2022). A brief explanation of such methods are as follows:

2.2.1 Bag of Words

In general classification of documents, a Bag of Words (or commonly known as BoW) is a vector representation of term frequencies. It retrieves word occurrences for each sentence or document while considering word duplicates but disregards grammar and its sequence. This form of numerical representation is usually enforced in classification methods where the features used are based on the frequency of each term (Wisam Abdulazeez Qader, et al., 2019). Consider an example of a paragraph containing two sentences that are as follows:

"The moon is bright. It seems to be really bright."

The Bag of Words representation for this corpus is shown in Table 1.

Table 1. Bag of words representation

Documents	be	bright	is	it	moon	really	seems	the	to
The moon is bright	0	1	1	0	1	0	0	1	0
It seems to be really bright	1	1	0	1	0	1	1	0	1

2.2.2 Word2Vec

The Word2Vec model is a word vector generation method that makes use of word embeddings and consists of skip-gram and Continuous Bag of Words (CBOW). It is designed to contain a disseminated emotion of words that map them to vectors with describable dimensions. Since the context is contemplated while training, a less dense dimensional vector with text semantics is produced. Each term in a document is intrinsically established as a word sequence (Yang et al. 2022).

$$d = [d^{(1)}, d^{(1)}, \ldots, d^{(j)}, \ldots, d^{(i)}]$$

Where,

d(j) indicates word at jth position
d(i) indicates word at last position

To acquire the word vector, a mapping association should be established between the observed word and its context. This is trained using a neural network where the hidden layer weight procured during training is the word vector itself (Yang et al. 2022).

Apart from these models, the Term Frequency - Inverse Document Frequency (TF-IDF), Doc2Vec (an extension of Word2Vec), pre-trained models like Bidirectional Encoder Representations from Transformers (BERT), Embedding from Language Model (ELMo) and many other models are also used to solve various NLP tasks and in most cases help in the classification of textual data (Singh & Shashi 2019).

2.3 Hyper-Parameter Tuning

Hyperparameters are a deliberate group of choices that precisely influence the training and outcome of machine learning models resulting in a substantial increase in the model's performance. Since the choices are dataset specific and there are no conventional set of parameters that would yield maximum performance, it is essential for an ML model to have the right hyperparameter setting. Most parameters have an extensive scale of values that can be specified. These can be selected based on default values proposed by the developer of the concerned ML algorithm or by finding values suggested by research authors working on a project within a similar domain. For either case, the model may not perform well considering the differences in each set of data. Another approach can be carried out by performing manual search. This requires prior knowledge and experience with the algorithm. Generally, these preconditions are strenuous to accomplish. Therefore, a systematic gradual tuning scheme that requires no expertise or profound knowledge would be a far more favorable alternative (Pannakkong et al. 2022). Some of the widely used hyper-parameter optimization techniques include Grid Search, Random Search, Bayesian Hyper-parameter Optimization with HyperOpt (Shekhar, Bansode & Salim).

3. LITERATURE REVIEW

Malicious and non-malicious spamming through email platforms has become a widespread nuisance for internet users worldwide, the former of which is known to have resulted in severe consequences such as great financial or budgetary misfortunes for businesses, organizations and even individuals. Despite the fact that not all spam messages are malicious, the separation of spam from hamemails are a huge convenience to individuals and organizations alike, as such emails are usually undesired and not given much attention to. As the development of spam emails continues to grow at an alarming rate, the need for viable phishing and spam recognition systems also increases. Several machine learning algorithms have already been developed for the purposes of anti-spam email filtering. Some examples of which are perceptron-based neural model techniques such as single-layered perceptron (SLP) and multi- layered perceptron (MLP), logical algorithms such as decision trees and random forest classification, and statistical learning techniques such as instance-based techniques and Bayesian networks. Despite the employment of several of the aforementioned classifiers, Naïve Bayes classifiers were found to be particularly popular in commercial and open-source spam filters (Metsis & Paliouras, n.d.). This would be due to the machine learning classifier's simplicity and ease of implementation, accuracy and its linear computational complexity.

Hassan, Mirza and Hussain (2017) used Weka (Waikato Environment for Knowledge Analysis), a software that contains tools for data pre-processing, classification, etc. in combination with the Naïve Bayes classifier model to identify spam emails using a custom dataset that included only the header field attributes from emails such as "Subject", "To", "From", "Date", etc. The authors of the research paper supported the decision to extract the header and disregard the body by claiming that concentrating on the body section of emails when conducting spam filtration is "time consuming and inefficient". Although the main goal of the study was to determine whether a machine learning approach would yield better accuracies as compared to a non-machine learning approach, one conclusion that can be drawn after comparison with other similar studies is that, the elimination of the bodies of emails would not produce as accurate results as previously thought.

One such paper that was discovered to be against the idea of identifying spam emails only through the header sections while ignoring the body completely, was authored by Abiramasundari, Ramaswamy and Sangeetha (2021). In this study, the author claims that not all header features can be useful in identifying spam and may instead result in memory wastage and higher processing time, leading to inefficiency. The reasoning behind this claim is that various businesses such as tourism packages, loan providers, educational institutes, etc. try to approach multiple users for the purpose of aiding business development, and such emails are sent through genuine sources (Abiramasundari, 2021). Therefore, a system that concentrates only on headers would not be able to accurately serve its purpose.

Moving on from the header versus body argument, Abiramasundari's research paper focuses on designing a classification system that proposes Rule Based Subject Analysis (RBSA) and Semantic Based Feature Selection (SBFS) to analyze spam terms and reduce the number of features required for the classification process. The dataset used was the Enron Email Dataset (the same as the one used in this proposed model) from which 5132 emails were used in the study. Four classification algorithms were implemented, namely, Support Vector Machine (SVM), Multinomial NB, Gaussian NB, and Bernoulli NB. The accuracies that were produced were 97%, 95%, 88%, and 87% respectively.

Another paper proposed a framework for spam email detection using machine learning based Naïve Bayes algorithm in combination with computational intelligence-based Particle Swarm Optimization (PSO), which is a stochastic optimization technique and is used for heuristic global optimization of parameters of the Naïve Bayes algorithm (Parmar et al., 2020). The Ling-Spam dataset was chosen to perform the classification of emails into classes of either ham or spam. The accuracy was found to be quite impressive, standing at 95.50%.

Hassan (2017) proposed a unique concept of investigating the effect of combining text clustering using K-means algorithm with various supervised classification mechanisms (such as K-Nearest Neighbor, Support Vector Machine, Naïve Bayes, Logistic Regression, etc.) and find out if this increases the classification accuracies. The dataset in question was the Enron Spam Dataset. The author's findings show that the conjunction of K-means clustering with supervised classifiers does not necessarily improve the classification of ham and spam for all mails. In addition, when the performance was found to be improved by clustering for the few cases that it did, the accuracy scores were found to be increased very slightly and did not seem worth it as compared to the amount of time it took to build the model that combined the two mechanisms together in the first place. The highest accuracy was found to be produced by the SVM classifier model combined with K-means clustering, with a score of 97.97%.

Soni (2020) made use of an improved intermittent Region-based Convolutional Neural Network model (RCNN) to propose an email spam recognition model named "THEMIS". The structure of emails is initially examined. After which, this model is capable of extracting emails at the header, body, word and character level and then utilizes these powerful functionalities to assess whether an email contains malicious or phishing intents or not. The exploratory outcome reveals that the precision of THEMIS is at an extraordinary rate of 99.84%, which is by far the most successful model as compared to the models of all the other research papers and studies mentioned in this literature review.

More recently, Sahmoud and Mikki (2022) conducted a research where a spam detector model was built using the pre-trained transformer model BERT (Bidirectional Encoder Representations from Transformers), a deep learning model, to classify emails by using the ability of the system to take the context of the email content into its perspective. The model was also trained using several different corpuses such as Enron Emails, SpamAssassin, Ling-Spam, and SMS spam collection corpus. This particular model was discovered to yield staggering accuracies ranging from 97.83% up to 99.28% for each of the different datasets (Sahmoud et al., 2022).

To summarize, the fight against spam emails has spurred the development of diverse machine learning techniques and algorithms. While Naïve Bayes classifiers remain popular due to their simplicity and effectiveness, there is an ongoing debate regarding the efficacy of solely relying on email headers for spam identification. As mentioned in this literature review, multiple research studies have explored alternative approaches, such as rule-based subject analysis, semantic feature selection, and deep learning models like RCNN and BERT, to improve accuracy rates for models aimed towards solving the issue of the classification of spam and ham emails. While significant progress has been made, the challenge of combating spam emails continues as spammers constantly evolve their tactics. Future research should focus on combining the strengths of different approaches to create robust and efficient spam detection systems that can adapt to the ever-changing landscape of email spamming.

4. METHODOLOGY

This section of the paper meticulously demonstrates the implementation of an approach to classify emails into spam or ham utilizing python and its relevant libraries for NLP, Machine Learning and Hyperparameter Tuning. In Figure 1, a flowchart demonstrating the same is illustrated.

Figure 1. Flowchart for the approach

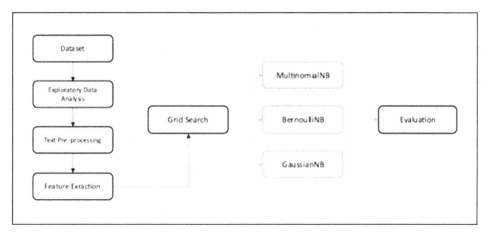

4.1 Study Dataset

The proposed research makes use of two datasets, one containing legit or ham emails and the other containing spam emails. Details of both corpuses are described below.

The Enron email dataset (Cukierski, 2015), a corpus containing approximately 500,000 emails generated by around 150 employees of the Enron Corporation, was used for the purpose of this study. The data had been collected by the Federal Energy Regulatory Commission during its investigation of Enron's collapse in 2001. The dataset initially was found to have a number of integrity issues and privacy concerns, which were later resolved as part of a redaction effort as per requests of the affected employees. This dataset is one of the only substantial collections of "real" email that is publicly available online. Most studies in this field of research are conducted on synthetic data due to an inadequate and real enough benchmark. The Enron email dataset is a touchstone for research in the field of spam detection among others.

The second dataset used in this study is the Fraudulent Email Corpus (Tatman, 2017) which consists of fraudulent emails containing criminally deceptive information with respect to the "Nigerian Letter" or "419" fraud, which cost its victims over $1 million in financial losses in 2016. The dataset is a collection of more than 2500 fraudulent "Nigerian Letters" with phishing intentions from 1998 to 2007.

Both corpuses have a similar structure so they are both preprocessed the same way and the bodies of these emails are extracted, after which they are combined into one single corpus. However, before the conjunction of the two datasets, sampling is performed on both datasets to randomly extract 2000 samples from each, resulting in a final corpus of 4000 emails.

4.2 Text Pre-Processing

Text pre-processing is a mandatory step in any Natural Language Processing task to retain the pivotal words and label them accordingly. To achieve this, various NLP libraries such as Natural Language Toolkit (NLTK), spaCy, email and re (for regular expressions) were used. Figure 2 shows the different stages involved in the pre-processing of text in this approach.

Figure 2. Pre-processing steps

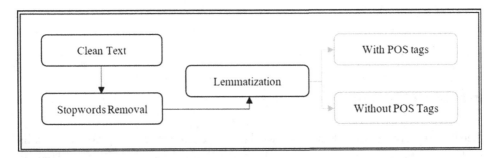

4.2.1 Cleaning the Text

Prior to cleaning the text, as mentioned above, the format of each email in the dataset was examined and it was observed that the messages were followed by some metadata such as the sender's and receiver's address, date, subject, type of encoding, along with other data that was irrelevant to this particular study. To extract the content of the messages (also referred to as payload), the "email" library of python was employed. The cleaning process consists of basic text preparation techniques as mentioned below:

- *Lowering of cases:* If the same word exists with different cases such as either upper or sentence case, two different instances for the same word would be created by the system. To avoid this, all the words in the corpus were transformed into lowercase to begin with.
- *Regex cleaning:* Removal of symbols, punctuations and digits is performed using a basic regular expression statement (from the re library), as this specific domain does not require the presence of such characters.
- *Tokenization (using basic python split):* This is done to break up paragraphs and extract meaningful elements (also referred to as tokens) that can be utilized to perform various -other tasks.
- *Stop words removal:* Stop words are the less significant words that exist in a sentence. The removal of these words depends entirely on the dataset and the task performed. In this approach, these words have no significance in the classification process, therefore, they are removed. NLTK has incorporated an easy-to-use subclass called "stopwords" that contains a list of pre-set stop words to be deleted. This list is referred to during the process of tokenization and the matching words are eliminated.
- *Basic lemmatization:* Basic lemmatization (using WordNetLemmatizer from NLTK) is performed on the tokenized version of the corpus. Although this does not change much, it is a common practice to change the plural form of certain words to singular form, such as by removing the letter 's' towards the end.

To combine this multi-step process, a single function was created that expects the corpus as its input and a regular expression that can be applied to clean the text.

4.2.2 Lemmatization With POS Tags

Lemmatization is a technique used to combine the analogous words in a way that can be identified as a single element (commonly referred to as the word's "lemma") (Divya Khyani & S, 2021). Table 2 shows an example of a few words and their lemmas. Using spaCy's tokenizer, each word was tokenized along with its POS tag. After which, they are compared to a user-defined list of tags, consisting of nouns, adjectives and verbs, to be lemmatized to. Due to computational constraints, the number of tags in this study were restricted to only three.

Table 2. Example of words and their vocabulary form (lemma)

Words	Lemma
Corpora	corpus
Playing	play
Played	play
Plays	play
Different	differ

4.3 TF-IDF Vectorizer

Term Frequency – Inverse Document Frequency or TF-IDF is a vectorizer utilized extensively for feature extraction and text mining to analyze key correlations between words in a selection of documents (Das & Chakraborty, n.d.). A step-by-step explanation on how the vectorizer works is delineated below. As the name suggests, TF refers to the word count where higher values imply more significance to a document (Kim & Gil, 2019). Consider an example where two documents, A and B, contain the word "Hadoop". If document A and B consist of 1000 and 10000 words respectively, there is a high probability that "Hadoop" is more occurring in B. However, this does not imply that B is more significant than A. Therefore, there is a need to normalize the term frequency for each document which is resolved by dividing it by the total number of words in that document (shown in Eq. 3) (Kim & Gil, 2019).

$$TF\left(word \middle| doc\right) = \frac{Frequency\ of\ word\ in\ doc}{No.\ of\ words\ in\ doc} \tag{3}$$

The problem of finding the importance of words across documents persists. To achieve this, document frequency (DF) is used. This measures the significance of documents in a corpus by counting the occurrences of a term in it (shown in Eq. 4) (Kim & Gil, 2019).

$$DF\left(word \middle| doc\right) = \frac{Frequency\ of\ word\ in\ doc}{No.\ of\ words\ in\ doc} \tag{4}$$

Since the objective is to know the relevance of a word, the inverse of DF is taken into account. For almost all commonly occurring words, the IDF gives a low score with a relative weightage. However, when analyzing a large dataset, the IDF value spikes which may cause problems. Another complication that may occur is if a fixed vocabulary is chosen, some documents may not contain these terms, resulting in the DF to return zero. To deal with these issues, the log of IDF is taken to dampen the effect of high values and the denominator (containing DF) is increased by 1 to avoid dividing by zeroes (shown in Eq. 5) (Das & Chakraborty, n.d.).

$$IDF\left(word\,\middle|\,docs\right) = \log \frac{No.\,of\,docs}{Frequency\,of\,word\,in\,docs + 1} \tag{5}$$

Using Eq. 6 in the spam detection dataset, a vectorizer that identifies the significance of terms in each document is obtained. Using python's sci-kit learn (sklearn) library, the TF-IDF matrix and vector is acquired with ease. This would assist in classifying emails into ham or spam by utilizing the vocabulary derived.

$$TFIDF = TF \times IDF$$

4.5 Exploratory Data Analysis (EDA)

EDA is a vital step in data analysis to uncover underlying patterns and identify abnormalities in a dataset. It is considered good practice to first comprehend the data and then perform the data mining tasks. Initially, the extraction of overlapping words between the two categories and removing them (if there exist any) was taken into consideration. This was done to reduce the number of common terms between ham and spam as it would lead to misclassification if two emails of opposing categories have the same terms. This was achieved by taking the top twenty frequent words from both classes (using basic python and pandas) and visualizing them (using subplots in matplotlib). As can be seen in Figure 3, the common words are 'please', 'company' and 'know'. These are identified and removed using python list functions. One thing to note is that the word 'enron' was found to be very specific to this dataset and had the highest weightage among ham emails. Due to this specificity, this word was removed.

Another feature considered was the correlation between the length of the message and its respective category. This association was tested because it was noticed that a number of similar researches in the field discovered a relationship between the length of the message and its class. Analyzing the correlation matrix plotted using python libraries such as Seaborn and Matplotlib, the resultant scores appeared to be weak being as low as 0.1 or 10% (refer Figure 4).

Figure 3. Visualization for overlapping words between ham(left) and spam(right)

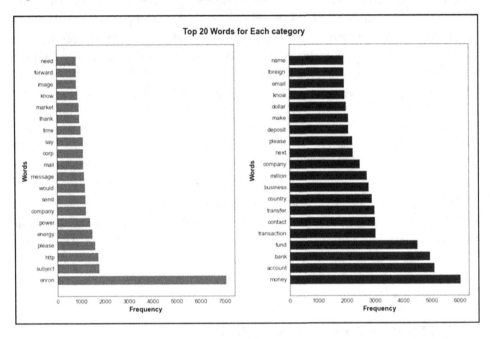

Figure 4. Correlation matrix for length of message and its category

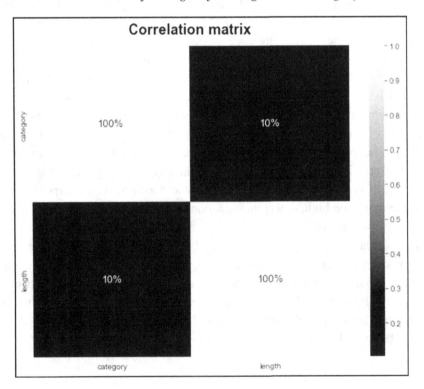

4.6 Grid Search for Variants of Naïve Bayes

4.6.1 Types of Naïve Bayes

To perform the classification, three variants of Naïve Bayes are used as explained below:

- B*ernoulli Naïve Bayes:* Based on binary data, the Bernoulli model excels in feature sets where each token has the value 0 or 1 (Raschka, 2014). For example: the features indicate whether a word exists in a document.
- *Multinomial Naïve Bayes:* Identical to Bernoulli but performs well in scenarios where the features may have values more than 1 (Raschka, 2014). For example: the features indicate the frequency of each term in a document.
- *Gaussian Naïve Bayes:* The above two algorithms deal with categorical features, Gaussian Naïve Bayes stands out when the presumed independent variables are continuous in nature (Raschka, 2014). For example: the commonly used Iris dataset contains continuous features with class variables containing categories of the Iris flower.

Given these points, Multinomial ought to be better performing than Bernoulli and Gaussian. To further analyze these models a grid search is performed using various appropriate parameters.

4.6.2 Grid Search

The Grid Search is a Hyper Parameter Tuning method that iterates through every permutation of parameter combinations where the parameter space is examined and divided into a grid-like structure. Each space in the grid is assessed as hyperparameters to compute its optimum value (Shekhar et al., 2022). Although it is an exhaustive optimization tool, it is preferred over Random Search for this use case since it explores every possible combination rather than randomly selecting hyperparameters. Both the selection of models and the grid search is implemented with ease using the sci-kit learn library.

4.7 Evaluation

In this section, the evaluation metrics used for analyzing the best Naïve Bayes model are demonstrated. The predictions are evaluated in terms of accuracy, precision, recall, f1 score and Receiver Operator Characteristic (ROC) supported by its Area Under Curve (AUC). Before understanding how each of these metrics work, some fundamental concepts regarding outcomes need to be elaborated. Taking into consideration an example from the current study regarding email spam classification, the "true" value refers to the binary classification of 1 (in this case, spam), whereas "false" refers to 0 (ham). Bearing in mind that positives indicate a correct prediction and negatives indicate the opposite, a true positive signifies a correct spam classification, and vice versa in terms of true negatives. The same logic is applied to the classification of ham emails as regards to false positives and false negatives. Using these notions, a brief explanation of each metric is given below:

- *Accuracy*

This is the most common metric and perhaps the easiest to understand. It calculates the proportion of results that are correct (refer Eq. 7) (Chowdhury & Schoen, 2020).

Accuracy = True Positives + True Negatives / Total Predictions   (7)

- *Precision*

Precision indicates the ratio of correctly classified outcomes to the total predicted values -(refer Eq. 8) (Chowdhury & Schoen, 2020).

Precision = True Positives / True Positives + False Positives   (8)

- *Recall*

Recall stipulates the ratio of correctly classified outcomes to just the actual values (refer Eq. 9) (Chowdhury & Schoen, 2020).

Recall = True Positives / True Positives + False Negatives   (9)

- *F1 score*

Ideally, a model with both high precision and recall would be the desired result. However, there would be a trade-off between the two metrics, meaning the model can either be tweaked to increase precision, but at the expense of weaker recall or vice versa. F1 score is the combination of the two metrics into one by calculating their harmonic -mean. (Refer Eq. 10) (Chowdhury & Schoen, 2020)

F1 = 2 X precision X recall / precision + recall   (10)

ROC – AUC Curve and Score

The ROC curve is a performance metric for classification models that can be calculated for different threshold settings. It plots the True Positive Rate (TPR) against the False Positive Rate (FPR). TPR, also known as sensitivity or recall, calculates the True Positives for all truth values (refer Eq. 11, whereas the calculation of FPR is done by taking the difference of Specificity from 1 (refer Eq. 12).

$$TPR = Sensitivity = TP / TP + FN \tag{11}$$

$$FPR = 1 - Specificity = FP / TN + FP$$

Area Under Curve (AUC) is a measure of separability. The higher the curve, the better the predictions of the model. Figure 5 shows an example of ROC-AUC for models A, B and C. As the graph illustrates, it is quite evident that model A has performed the best since it has the largest AUC.

Figure 5. Example of ROC-Curve with AUC
Source: Zach (2021)

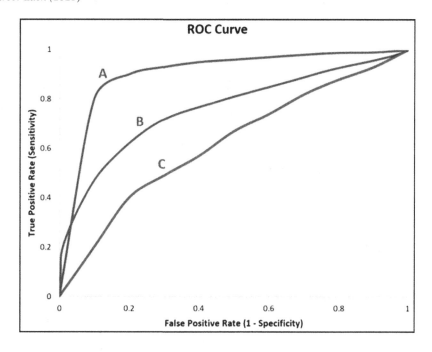

5. RESULTS AND DISCUSSION

In this section, the results of the aforementioned models are interpreted followed by a comparative analysis of this paper with similar researches. The results for the GridSearchCV indicating the best hyperparameter choices for each model along with its pre-eminent scores are shown in Table 3.

Table 3. Results from GridSearchCV

Model	Best Parameters	Best Score
Bernoulli NB	'alpha': 0.00001, 'binarize': 0.0, 'fit_prior': True	0.988750
Multinomial NB	'alpha': 0.1, 'class_prior': [0.7, 0.3], 'fit _prior': True	0.992500
Gaussian NB	'var_smotthning': 0.0081113083078968712	0.984062

Analyzing these outcomes, the Multinomial Naïve Bayes model ostensibly yielded the best scores. Using the predictions obtained from the Grid Search, all these models are further evaluated using the various methods mentioned in Section 4.7. For each model, the classification report summarizing the accuracy, precision, recall and f1-score is illustrated below:

Table 4. Classification report for Bernoulli Naïve Bayes

	Precision	Recall	F1-Score	Support
Not Spam	0.985112	1.000000	0.992500	397
Spam	1.000000	0.985112	0.992500	403
Accuracy			0.992500	800
macro avg	0.992556	0.992556	0.992500	800
weighted avg	0.992612	0.992500	0.992500	800

Table 5. Classification report for multinomial Naïve Bayes

	Precision	Recall	F1-Score	Support
Not Spam	0.992500	1.000000	0.996236	397
Spam	1.000000	0.992556	0.996264	403
accuracy			0.996250	800
macro avg		0.996278	0.996250	800
weighted avg	0.996278	0.996250	0.996250	800

Table 6. Classification report for Gaussian Naïve Bayes

	Precision	Recall	F1-Score	Support
Not Spam	0.989691	0.967254	0.978344	397
Spam	0.968447	0.990074	0.979141	403
accuracy			0.978750	800
macro avg	0.979069	0.978664	0.978743	800
weighted avg	0.978989	0.978750	0.978746	800

To visualize a more comprehensible representation of the metric scores for each model, a bar graph (shown in Figure 6) has been plotted where the models and the scores are denoted by the x and y axes respectively.

Figure 6. Comparison of all metrics for each model

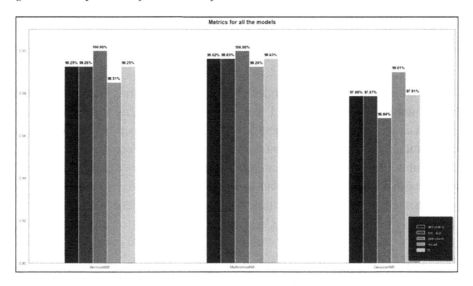

On examining the above figure and tables, it can be deduced that Multinomial outperforms both Bernoulli and Gaussian Naïve Bayes algorithms. This is due to the fact that the overall scores for its accuracy, ROC-AUC, precision, recall, and f1-score are higher in comparison to that of the other two models. In addition to this, the ROC curve plotted using True Positive Rate and False Positive Rate is given in Figure 7. The curve which is the closest to TPR of 1 has the highest AUC score belonging to the Multinomial NB model, further supporting the previously mentioned claim.

Figure 7. ROC curve along with the AUC scores for each model

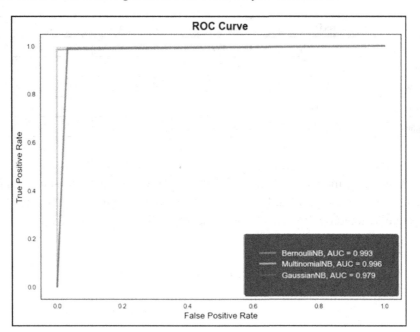

A semantic and rule-based model via supervised learning was suggested by Abiramasundari, Ramaswamy and Sangeetha (2021). In this paper, Rule Based Subject Analysis (RBSA) and Semantic Based Feature Selection (SBFS) methods are integrated with classification models such as Support Vector Machine (SVM), Multinomial, Bernoulli and Gaussian Naïve Bayes. These models were tested on the Enron dataset where the highest accuracy of 97% was observed for the SVM model.

Another approach based on semantic methods using efficient email classification is proposed by Bahgat, Rady and Gad (2017). In this study, several classification models were used to predict the outcome of spam and ham emails for the Enron dataset in an efficient manner. These include Naïve Bayes, Logistic Regression, SVM, J48, Random Forest and Radial Basis Function network. Out of the mentioned algorithms, SVM was identified as the best performing algorithm with an accuracy of 94%.

Comparing the above results to the outcomes produced in this paper, the Multinomial Naïve Bayes model outperforms both the SVM models with an accuracy of 99.62% and a ROC-AUC score of 99.60%.

6. CONCLUSION AND FUTURE RECOMMENDATIONS

The current problem statement, email spam detection, has risen to become one of the most demanding research topics due to an increase in cybercrime with recent advancements in technology. Various classification methods have been developed and trained upon different datasets for this purpose using both machine learning and deep learning techniques combined with a wide variety of feature selection methods, preprocessing approaches, optimization algorithms, etc., as discussed in Section 3, which are all factors that together contribute to the performance of the model. However, it is very difficult to achieve a model that is 100% accurate and perfectly filters out spam emails due to the numerous complexities of the English language such as sarcasm, evolving terminologies in slang among others. Nevertheless, several models have already been developed with considerably high-performance scores. To conclude the findings of this paper, out of the three Naïve Bayes models that were used to perform the classification on a total of 4000 emails in the dataset, the Multinomial NB model proved to be the best classifier with an accuracy of 99.62%, with Bernoulli NB and Gaussian NB following not too far behind with scores of 99.25% and 97.88% respectively. Other evaluation parameters used to assess the performance of the models included precision, recall, and f1-score. It is believed that the reason for such high accuracies across all NB models was due to the use of the most optimal parameters obtained from the output of the hyper-parameter tuning algorithm and the initial lemmatization using POS tags of the corpus. Additionally, the identification and removal of overlapping words between the two classes, namely spam and ham, is also believed to be a contributing factor as to the high accuracy of the Bayesian models.

Needless to say, there is plenty of room for improvement for any proposed model. Spammers are getting more and more intelligent in the way they phrase their messages, making them seem as legitimate as possible in order to scam individuals and organizations. The datasets that were used to train the proposed model included spam emails that used a formal tone. Other types of spam messages may include informal sentiments, sarcasm, or other non-professional slang, which is unlike the spam messages the model in this study has been trained on. In such scenarios, the model in question would perform poorly and would not yield the same accuracies as compared to professional-toned emails. To resolve this issue, the model would be needed to be trained on different spam datasets, containing both formal and informal sentiments. This would ensure the model is able to accurately classify any kinds of spam email it comes across in the future regardless of the level of formality. Other popular spam datasets that are commonly used in anti-spam filtering systems include Spambase, Ling-Spam dataset, and SpamAssassin, to name a few. All these datasets could be combined into one corpus, as other research papers have done previously to further improve the performance of the model. The feature extraction and selection methods play a fundamental role in the performance of the classification. As explained previously in Section 4.3, TF-IDF only takes into consideration the frequency of the words. Using word2vec instead would consider the context of each of the words in the corpus, which would allow the model to perform more generically even on different datasets. To further improve on this, transformer-based models such as BERT or ELMo can be used as they are capable of considering multiple contexts for a particular word, a functionality that is not available in word2vec. Moreover, machine learning models tend to have a directly proportionate relationship between their performance and the size of the dataset. The model in this study was trained upon a dataset of 4000 emails. In the future, another factor that could be considered for the improvement of the system could be increasing the number of emails it is trained upon. It may not be possible to achieve a complete 100% accurate model for any scenario, but every advancement towards the improvement of crucial systems like spam detection systems is worth working on as it is a sensitive field which could easily lead to disastrous consequences.

REFERENCES

Abiramasundari, S., Ramaswamy, V., & Sangeetha, J. (2021). *Spam filtering using Semantic and Rule Based model via supervised learning.* Retrieved from https://www.annalsofrscb.ro/index.php/journal/article/view/1405/1174

Andre, L. (2021, June 15). *You are on the internet almost daily. You check your email, send replies, maybe browse websites and even click.* https://financesonline.com/how-much-data-is-created-every-day/

Bahgat, E. M., Rady, S., Gad, W., & Moawad, I. F. (2018). Efficient email classification approach based on semantic methods. *Ain Shams Engineering Journal, 9*(4), 3259–3269. doi:10.1016/j.asej.2018.06.001

Chowdhury, S., & Schoen, M. P. (2020, October 2). *Research Paper Classification using Supervised Machine Learning Techniques.* ResearchGate. https://www.researchgate.net/publication/346853360_Research_Paper_Classification_using_Supe rvised_Machine_Learning_Techniques?enrichId=rgreq-1c98526e9543b39049d181d973 ede8c2- XXX&enrichSource=Y292ZXJQYWdlOzM0Njg1MzM2MDtBUzoxM DUxMTgzNTY1MjY2OTQ1Q DE2Mjc2MzMxMDA0ODI%3D&el=1_x_3&_ esc=publicationCoverPdf

Cukierski, W. (2015). *The Enron Email Dataset.* Kaggle.com. https://www.kaggle.com/datasets/wcukierski/enron-email-dataset

Das, B., & Chakraborty, S. (n.d.). *An Improved Text Sentiment Classification Model Using TF IDF and Next Word Negation. https://arxiv.org/pdf/1806.06407.pdf*

Divya Khyani, & S, S. B. (2021, January 7). *An Interpretation of Lemmatization and Stemming in Natural Language Processing.* ResearchGate. https://www. researchgate.net/publication/348306833_An_Interpretation_of_Lemmatization_ and_ Stemming_in_Natural_Language_Processing#:~:text=What%20is%20 Lemmatization%3F,adds% 20meaning%20to%20particular%20words

Garg, B. (2022). *Design and Development of Naive Bayes Classifier.* Ndsu.edu. https://doi.org/http://hdl.handle.net/10365/23048

Hassan, D. (2017). Investigating the Effect of Combining Text Clustering with Classification on Improving Spam Email Detection. In Intelligent Systems Design and Applications (Vol. 557, pp. 120–128). essay, Springer International Publishing AG 2017. doi:10.1007/978-3-319-53480-0_10

Hassan, M., Mirza, W., & Hussain. (2017). Header Based Spam Filtering Using Machine Learning Approach. *International Journal of Emerging Technologies in Engineering Research, 5.* https://www.ijeter.everscience.org/Manuscripts/Volume-5/ Issue-10/Vol-5-issue-10-M-21.pdf

Kim, S.-W., & Gil, J.-M. (2019). Research paper classification systems based on TF-IDF and LDA schemes. *Human-Centric Computing and Information Sciences, 9*(1). doi:10.1186/s13673-019-0192-7

Kumari, A., & Shashi, M. (2019, August). *Vectorization of Text Documents for Identifying Unifiable News Articles.* SAI Organization. https://www.researchgate. net/publication/334884108_Vectorization_of_Text_Documents_for_Iden tifying_ Unifiable_News_Articles

Metsis, V., & Paliouras, G. (2006). *Spam Filtering with Naive Bayes -Which Naive Bayes?* https://userweb.cs.txstate.edu/~v_m137/docs/papers/ceas2006_paper_ corrected.pdf

Muhammad, A. N., Bukhori, S., & Pandunata, P. (2019). Sentiment Analysis of Positive and Negative of YouTube Comments Using Naïve Bayes – Support Vector Machine (NBSVM) Classifier. *2019 International Conference on Computer Science, Information Technology, and Electrical Engineering (ICOMITEE).* 10.1109/ ICOMITEE.2019.8920923

Nur, Marthasari, & Nuarini. (2020). Optimization of Sentiment Analysis for Indonesian Presidential Election using Naïve Bayes and Particle Swarm Optimization. *Jurnal Online Informatika, 5*(1), 81–88. https://join.if.uinsgd.ac.id/index.php/join/article/view/558/148

Pannakkong, W., Thiwa-Anont, K., Singthong, K., Parthanadee, P., & Buddhakulsomsiri, J. (2022, January). Hyperparameter Tuning of Machine Learning Algorithms Using Response Surface Methodology: A Case Study of ANN, SVM, and DBN. *Mathematical Problems in Engineering, 2022*, 1–17. doi:10.1155/2022/8513719

Parmar, N., Sharma, A., Jain, H., & Kadam. (2020). Email Spam Detection using Naïve Bayes and Particle Swarm Optimization. *International Journal of Innovative Research in Technology*, 1–7.

Raschka, S. (2014). *Naive Bayes and Text Classification I Introduction and Theory.* https://arxiv.org/pdf/1410.5329.pdf

Rish, I. (2001). *An Empirical Study of the Naïve Bayes Classifier.* ResearchGate. https://www.researchgate.net/publication/228845263_An_Empirical_Study_of_the_Naive_Bayes_Classifier

Sahmoud, T., & Mikki, M. (2022). *Spam Detection Using BERT.* Retrieved November 30, 2022, from https://arxiv.org/ftp/arxiv/papers/2206/2206.02443.pdf

Shekhar, S., Bansode, A., & Salim, A. (2022, January). *A Comparative study of Hyper-Parameter Optimization Tools.* https://arxiv.org/pdf/2201.06433.pdf

Soni, A. N. (2019). Spam e-mail detection using advanced deep convolution neural network algorithms. Journal for Innovative Development in Pharmaceutical and Technical Science.

Tatman, R. (2017). *Fraudulent E-mail Corpus.* Kaggle.com. https://www.kaggle.com/datasets/rtatman/fraudulent-email-corpus

Text Classification. (2014). What it is And Why it Matters. *MonkeyLearn.* https://monkeylearn.com/text- classification/

Wisam, Ameen, & Ahmed. (2019, June). *An Overview of Bag of Words: Importance, Implementation, Applications, and Challenges.* ResearchGate. https://www.researchgate.net/publication/338511771_An_Overview_of_Bag_of_WordsImportance_Implementation_Applications_and_Challenges

Yang, X., Yang, K., Cui, T., & He, L. (2022, February 11). *A Study of Text Vectorization Method Combining Topic Model and Transfer Learning*. ResearchGate. https://www.researchgate.net/publication/358585623_A_Study_of_Text_Vectorization_Method_C ombining_Topic_Model_and_Transfer_Learning

Zach. (2021, August 9). *How to Interpret a ROC Curve (With Examples)*. Statology. https://www.statology.org/interpret-roc-curve/

Chapter 8
Using SVM and CNN as Image Classifiers for Brain Tumor Dataset

Maryam Zia
University of Wollongong in Dubai, UAE

Hiba Gohar
University of Wollongong in Dubai, UAE

ABSTRACT

Brain tumors make up 85% to 90% of all primary central nervous system (CNS) malignancies. Over a thousand people are diagnosed with cancer each year, and brain tumors are one of those fatal illnesses. It is challenging to diagnose this because of the intricate anatomy of the brain. Medical image processing is expanding rapidly today as it aids in the diagnosis and treatment of illnesses. Initially, a limited dataset was utilized to develop a support vector machine (SVM) model for the classification of brain tumors. The tumors were classified as either present or absent. As the dataset was small, the SVM model achieved great accuracy. To increase the dataset's size, data augmentation, an image pre-processing technique was used. Due to the SVM's limitations in producing high accuracy over a large dataset, convolutional neural network (CNN) was used to produce a more accurate model. Using both SVM and CNN aided in drawing comparisons between deep learning techniques and conventional machine learning techniques. MRI scans were used for tumor classification using the mentioned models.

DOI: 10.4018/978-1-6684-8696-2.ch008

BRAIN TUMOR CLASSIFICATION USING SUPPORT VECTOR MACHINE

Research Background

Among health problems, brain tumors are by far the most frequent. Primary brain tumors are detected in about 4,170 people under the age of 15 per year. A brain tumor consists of a collection of aberrant brain cells. There are several subtypes of brain tumors, and both benign and malignant variants exist. When a brain tumor becomes large enough, it presses on neighboring brain tissue or spreads to other areas of the brain, putting the patient at risk for severe complications, including high intracranial pressure.

Magnetic Resonance Imaging

Magnetic resonance imaging (MRI) is a medical imaging technology that creates extremely clear pictures of the body's anatomical structures, such as the brain. These detailed pictures are produced using a large, powerful magnet, radio waves, and a computer. As opposed to computed tomography (CT) scans, which employ X-ray radiation that can be harmful to human tissue, MRI scans pose no such risk to the brain. Radiologists routinely use MRI to identify brain tumors because it provides a cross-sectional view of the brain and distinguishes between healthy and malignant tissue more precisely. MRI is also favored by patients as it is a painless, non-invasive, and non-harmful diagnostic procedure.

Support Vector Machines

Based on the principles of statistical learning, Support Vector Machine (SVM) is a supervised machine learning algorithm that can be applied for both classification and regression applications. However, its primary application is in classification tasks. SVM's central idea is to utilize hyperplanes to build decision boundaries for classifying data points. The hyperplane separates into two classes, each of which may be assigned to data points that lie on either side of it. The hyperplane's location and orientation can be affected by the data points called support vectors, which are those points that are nearest to the hyperplane. The margins of the classifiers are optimized using these support vectors. Also, the hyperplane's location will shift if the support vectors are removed. Some advantages of SVM are increased speed and compatibility with unstructured and semi-structured data types, including text, images, and trees. SVM also works effectively with small datasets (in the thousands), which is a constraint, as we will see later in this research.

Convolutional Neural Networks

Convolutional Neural Networks (CNNs) is a form of neural network that are commonly used to solve image processing problems. One key feature that sets CNN apart from other neural networks is its ability to recognize patterns using its hidden layers. Convolutional layers, pooling layers, and fully connected layers are the three primary CNN layer types. The foundation of a CNN is the convolutional layer, which is made up of multiple feature maps and may be customized through the application of different kernels. Its objective is to learn a set of features that characterize the inputs. Adding a pooling layer can have the same impact as a supplementary feature extractor, reducing the size of feature maps while simultaneously boosting their resilience. Layers of convolution and pooling are stacked on top of one another to extract high-level features from inputs, often positioned between two convolutional layers. CNN typically has one or more fully connected layers serving as the classifier. All the neurons in the preceding layer are copied into the current layer, and each neuron in the latter is linked to all the neurons in the former. An output layer comes after the final fully connected layer. SVM is common and may be used in conjunction with CNNs to accomplish a variety of classification jobs.

Research Objective

In the process of image classification, it is necessary to first extract relevant features from them and use those features to search for patterns in the training data. The most prevalent method for detecting brain tumors from MRI images is to employ machine learning algorithms, as they are both more practical and have higher predictive accuracy. As technology progresses, deep learning algorithms are also being employed more frequently in image classification procedures since they reduce the need for constant human interaction. The objective of this research is to compare and contrast the performance of a SVM model and a CNN model on a dataset consisting of MRI brain scans in terms of accuracy. The report's findings would highlight which classification method performs better when determining whether a brain is healthy or displays signs of cancer.

LITERATURE REVIEW

Jia and Chen (n.d.) created a Fully Automatic Heterogeneous Segmentation using a Support Vector Machine to detect and isolate brain cancers (FAHS-SVM). A classification method called a probabilistic neural network classification system has been utilized for training and testing the performance of tumor identification in

MRI images. This model employs a multi-spectral brain dataset with an emphasis on automated segmentation of meningiomas. Their findings, which indicate that the system is both efficient and effective, amount to an accuracy rate of roughly 98.51% when distinguishing between aberrant and normal tissue.

Kumar et al. (2017) delve into the practice of classifying and segmenting the brain tumor area. The retrieved features were then utilized to train the artificial neural network to identify the tumor type. Classification learner software was employed to evaluate the efficacy and contrast different classifiers like K-NN, SVM, and Trees. According to the study's findings, the SVM classifier performs better than competing methods.

Sungheetha and Sharma (2020) employed the Gabor transform alongside soft and hard clustering to locate boundaries in CT and MRI scans, since this approach is prevalent for photos with dynamic variations. The K-means clustering approach was used to classify a dataset consisting of 75,000 medical scans based on their shared features. In addition, fuzzy C clustering was used to characterize the images as histogram features, allowing for even more precise image segmentation. The researchers discovered that fuzzy C means were susceptible to noise and were much slower than the K means.

Vani et al. (2017) used the SVM algorithm to extract tumors from medical scans. Additionally, a SVM-based object detection prototype was designed in Simulink for the purpose of classifying the medical images as malignant or benign. After evaluating a test set of 54 images, they found an accuracy rate of 82%, with only 10 inaccuracies.

Santos and Santos (2022) proposed an approach based on a network of artificial neural networks (ANN) for identifying tumors in MRI brain scans. When they were training the model, they used the activation function that was applied to the input features and the hidden layers. The test size consisted of 753 MRI scans. According to the authors of the study, the accuracy of the model, which scored 89% overall on the test, may be enhanced by including additional image data.

Khan et al. (2021) wanted to detect brain malignancies in their early stages; thus, this study proposes to input the deep features extracted from MRI scans into a SVM classifier. After the images had been segmented, they were sent to a convolutional neural network, also known as a CNN, for the purpose of deep feature extraction. In addition, the SVM classifier was given the most effective deep features selected by the approach known as mRNR (minimum Redundancy Maximum Relevance). Initial results showed 98.76% accuracy when the sample set was applied to the CNN, followed by the FLC. In the subsequent stage, they employed mRMR for feature selection and then ran it through the SVM model, which resulted in an accuracy of 99.79%.

Ucuzal et al. (2019) created a free, publicly accessible, web-based application that employs deep learning to detect and diagnose brain tumors using MRI data. They implemented the deep learning method using the Python Keras Library as their platform of choice. Their experimental findings on the training dataset revealed an accuracy of 98%. With the exception of sensitivity, all performance indicators were greater than 91% on the testing dataset.

Hasan et al. (2019) put into practice a methodological model for the purpose of spectral classification of hyperspectral pictures. An SVM-Linear, an SVM-RBF, and a deep learning architecture consisting of principal component analysis (PCA) and convolutional neural networks (CNN) were employed to first extract nearby spatial regions. Images in the dataset having noise and superfluous information were removed using PCA. They employed PCA optimization for spatial regions to generate features because the CNN and SVM models may not be able to extract features at different scales. For the Hyperspec-VNIR Chikusei datasets, the SVM-RBF model had the highest accuracy of 98.84% out of the three models.

Baranwal et al. (2020) wanted to better understand the differences between meningioma, glioma, and pituitary tumors, so they sought to implement CNN, Linear SVM, and Polynomial SVM to categorize the malignancies. They built on Google Colab and used the Python library TensorFlow for their analysis. Following pre-processing, the images in the dataset are randomly split into three groups: training (60%), validation (20%), and testing (20%). When compared to Polynomial SVM (82% accuracy) and Linear SVM (80% accuracy), CNN attained the highest overall accuracy of 95%.

Guo et al. (2017) constructed a basic convolutional neural network (CNN) for use in image classification using the MINIST and cifar-10 datasets as benchmarks. Also examined were several optimization algorithms for finding the most effective parameters for use in image classification, as well as a variety of learning rate sets. A 0.66% error rate was achieved by their CNN. Despite having a lower recognition rate than competing approaches, their network architecture is straightforward and their memory requirements for tuning parameters are low. They also indicate that the shallow network has a decent recognition impact.

METHODOLOGY

Classification of Brain Tumors requires the detection of multiple images to identify the presence of an area with abnormal cell growth. The purpose of this study is to automate the detection of Brain Tumors from MRI scans. Doctors and patients must wait longer for results because intraoperative pathology analysis is time-consuming. (NCI Staff, 2012) Thus, Brain Tumors can be accurately identified using Artificial

Intelligence. (NCI Staff, 2012) Considering the reasoning behind AI in diagnostics, this study proposes a multi-step structure. Due to their accuracy and convenience, machine learning algorithms are the most common method for detecting brain tumors in MRI images. (Dhole & V. Dixit, 2022) In this study, a brain MRI scan was the primary input for the machine learning model's training. The dataset was intricately visualized so that familiarity with the data would aid in understanding the model for an accurate model. Utilizing various image pre-processing techniques, the image scan dataset was analyzed and enhanced. The subsequent steps provide a comprehensive overview of the various training techniques used for the SVM model.

Materials and Methods

Support Vector Machine (SVM) was one of the optimal models that could be employed given the size of the dataset used in this study. Since SVM only accepts 2D data, the 3D dataset was converted to 2D. It is a supervised learning algorithm that is primarily employed for data classification. In this study, the two categories were Brain Tumor Presence and Brain Tumor Absence.

Python was the primary programming language utilized for the SVM implementation. This language was chosen because of its precision and conciseness. In addition, it offered a vast array of libraries and frameworks. Overall, it was very convenient, adaptable, and simple to use and implement.

Table 1. Libraries

Name	Usage
Pandas	Pandas are used for data manipulation and data analysis, data cleaning, data manipulation, and data transformation.
NumPy	NumPy is an open-source library that contains arrays of multiple dimensions. It offers many built-in functions like mathematical functions, linear algebra, and random sampling.
MatplotLib	The primary function of Matplotlib is to facilitate data exploration and visualization. It enables the identification of data patterns, trends, and correlations.
Seaborn	Seaborn is constructed atop Matplotlib. It is utilized to create appealing and informative statistical graphics
OpenCV	OpenCV is a Python library that concentrates on computer vision.
Tensorflow	Python's TensorFlow is a free, open-source machine learning library. It emphasizes the training and inference of deep neural networks. It employs multidimensional arrays, also known as tensors, to perform multiple operations on a given input.
Keras	Keras is a Python-based API for deep learning that operates on top of the TensorFlow machine learning platform. Keras is primarily used for developing deep-learning models.
Sckit-learn	Scikit-learn is a library for data analysis that provides a number of effective machine learning and statistical analysis tools.

Dataset

The dataset used to develop the framework in this study is titled "Br35H: Brain Tumor Detection 2020." It was obtained from Kaggle, a website with over 50,000 publicly accessible datasets. Ahmed Hamada, a data scientist, made the MRI images of brain tumors available in this dataset. There are three folders, with the "yes" folder representing brain scan images with tumors, the "no" folder representing brain scan images without tumors, and the "pred" folder representing brain scan images that may have tumor.

This research report utilized only the "yes" and "no" folders with a total of 3000 pictures evenly divided between both classes. Figure 1 depicts a sample brain scan of a brain without tumors, whereas Figure 2 depicts a brain with tumors.

Figure 1. No tumor detected brain scan

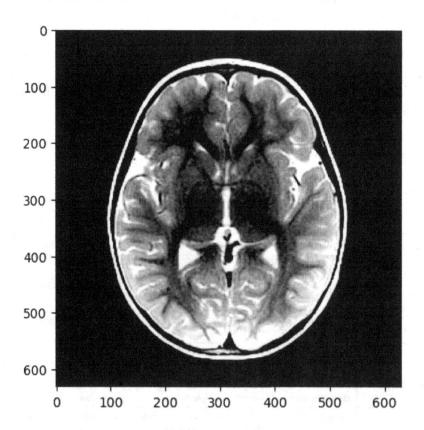

Figure 2. Tumor detected brain scan

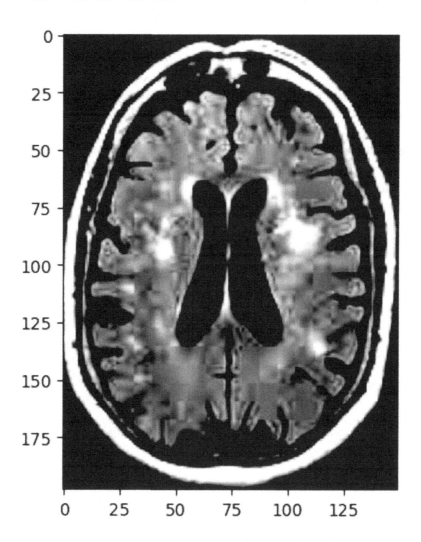

Loading the Data

The data was loaded into two lists (X and Y) using Python's OS module, which allows users to use operating system-specific functionality and the open-cv library. OS assisted in iterating through and identifying current directories, paths, and retrieving their contents, while open-cv assisted in reading and displaying the images. List X included the images and list Y corresponded to the labels of those images.

Exploratory Data Analysis (EDA)

Exploratory Data Analysis (EDA) is a method that employs visual techniques to analyze data. With the aid of statistical summaries and graphical representations, it is used to discover trends, patterns, or to verify hypotheses. Use of EDA is essential during the implementation of any machine learning model because it improves data comprehension and helps to identify errors. Several data visualization techniques were employed in this study to aid in the understanding of the dataset.

Class balance identification was accomplished by assigning a specific number of images to each class (Brain Tumor & No Brain Tumor). The information was then plotted on a bar chart.

Figure 3. Class balance identification

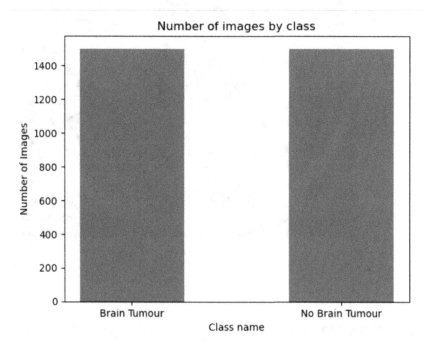

Image size visualization was performed on the raw dataset. It was observed that image size differed between the two classes. Using scatter plots, the data was portrayed graphically (See Figure 4a, 4b, and 4c).

Figure 4.

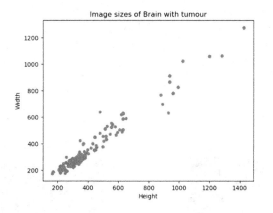

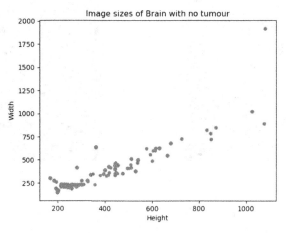

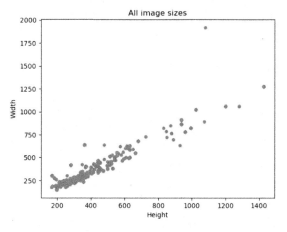

Images observation was accomplished by selecting an image from each class. This method of visual representation demonstrated that background, brightness, and orientation are variable characteristics in different images (See Figure 1 and Figure 2).

Edge detection is a method for locating the boundaries of images' objects. It works by detecting brightness discontinuities (Sikarwar, 2015).

Figure 5. Edge detection

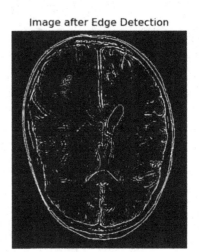

Histogram of oriented gradients is a statistical technique for counting the occurrences of a certain type of gradient orientation throughout a specified area of an image. It is employed in the fields of computer vision and image processing for the goal of object detection.

Data Pre-Processing

Pre-processing refers to operations performed on images at the most fundamental level of abstraction. (N. Vani et al, 2017) Techniques for image pre-processing can be used to enhance the performance of machine learning models. (A. Akinyelu, 2022) Raw data images can be in various formats; therefore, image pre-processing helps to standardize input data to improve the accuracy of any model. This is done to improve the quality of images and convert them into a format that is suitable for machine processing. This step also contributes to the elimination of unwanted noise and the improvement of the input images' overall appearance. Overall, this strategy improves classification precision and accelerates the training process. (Miglani, 2021) Several of the following image preprocessing techniques were utilized for this study.

Figure 6. Histogram of gradients

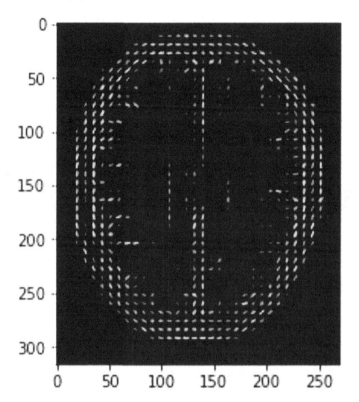

Resizing of images was performed as while examining data, it was discovered that images are of various sizes, so resizing was performed. Consequently, this step ensured that all image sizes are uniform.

Conversion of images was done from 3D to 2D because the library (SKlearn) used for this project only accepts 2D images.

Feature scaling was applied to normalize the range of independent variables or data features. Prior to scaling, the maximum value in this study was 255 and the minimum value was 0; after scaling, the maximum value became 1 and the minimum value remained 0, defining a range from 0 to 1.

Data augmentation was performed to increase the size of the dataset from 3000 images to 14993 images. It is a method in data analysis that involves creating new, synthetic data by combining existing data with slightly altered copies of the original data. When training a machine learning model, it helps prevent the model from overfitting. By augmenting the dataset, it can be seen that SVM is not scalable for large data sets, highlighting the necessity to switch to deep learning models like CNN. Figure 8 shows the results of Data Augmentation.

Figure 7. Data augmentation results

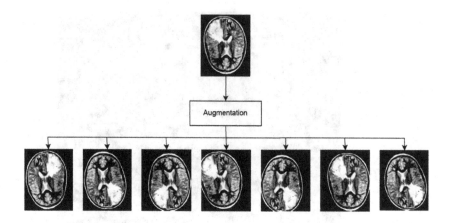

Performance Metrics

Performance metrics quantify the machine learning model's effectiveness. Metric selection influences the comparison and measurement of machine learning algorithm performance. (Sunasra, 2018) Since the problem addressed in this study was related to classification that produces discrete output, it consists of metrics that compare discrete classes. (Bajaj, 2022) Classification Metrics evaluate the performance of a model and indicate how good or bad the classification is, but each metric evaluates it differently. (Bajaj, 2022) Several metrics were used to assess the performance of the machine learning model in this study. The ones utilized are listed below.

Confusion Matrix

This is one of the metrics used to determine the model's correctness and precision. It demonstrates four items that are called True Positive, True Negative, False Positive, and False Negative.

True Positive (TP).
It predicts the number of correctly predicted positive class samples by the machine learning model.

True Negative (TN).
It predicts the number of predicted negative class samples.

False Positive (FP).

It predicts the number of incorrectly predicted negative class samples by the model.

False Negative (FN).

It predicts the number of incorrectly predicted positive class samples.

Classification report.

This is another metric used to evaluate the performance of machine learning models. It illustrates precision, recall, f1-score, support, and precision.

Precision.

It is the ratio of the predicted true positives to total positives.

Recall.

It is the proportion of the predicted positives that match the actual number of positives.

f1-score.

It combines precision and recall into a single measure by using TP/(TP+FN)

Support.

It represents the number of actual occurrences of the class within the dataset.

Accuracy.

It can be defined as the ratio of correct predictions to total predictions multiplied by 100.

Grid Search

Grid search is a technique used to determine the optimal hyperparameters of a model, resulting in the most precise predictions (Joseph, 2018). A model hyperparameter is an attribute of a model whose value cannot be derived from data (Joseph, 2018). SVM, the machine learning model used in this study, has hyperparameters as well. The hyperparameters values identified were "C" and "gamma" values. Grid Search trained the model using a dictionary of these identified parameters.

Support Vector Machine (SVM) Implementation

Figure 9 outlines the steps that were taken to implement the SVM Model for the classification of brain tumors in this study.

Figure 8. SVM implementation

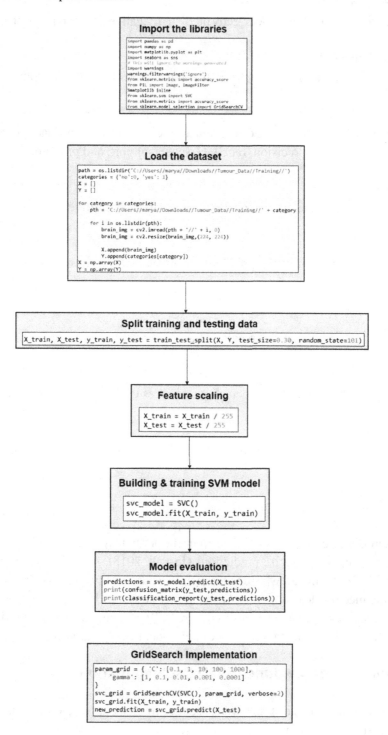

Convolutional Neural Network (CNN)

Architecture

The convolutional neural network requires a two-dimensional image and the image's class, such as an image with a brain tumor and an image without a brain tumor. input. Data patterns or rules are extracted from the images to assist with the output prediction after training the model. CNN architecture consists of a multitude of convolution layers, pooling layers, and dense layers. This can be visualized in Figure 9.

Figure 9. CNN architecture

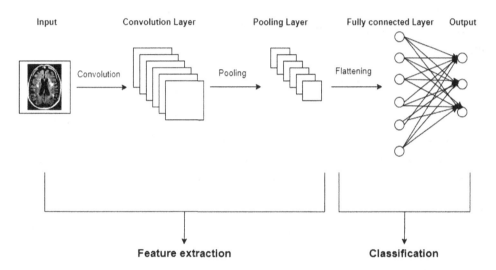

Convolution Layer

This is the first layer of the architecture, which transforms the input image in order to identify its features and then separates them. This method is also known as Feature Extraction. This is accomplished by applying filters or feature detectors to generate feature maps using the 'Relu' function. Feature detectors or filters assist in identifying various image features such as edges, vertical lines, horizontal lines, bends, and corners. Between the input image and a filter of a particular size MxM, the mathematical operation of convolution is performed. By dragging the filter over the input image, the dot product is calculated between the filter and the portions of the input image proportional to the filter's size (MxM). The generated feature map is passed to the subsequent layer, which assists the model in learning additional image features.

Pooling Layer

This is the layer that follows the convolution layer. This reduces the size of the feature maps and summarizes the features produced by the convolution layer. There are two types of pooling layers: maximum pooling and average pooling. Max Pooling is accomplished by selecting the highest value from each pool. The returned image is sharper than the original image, as Max pooling preserves the most prominent features of the feature map. The average pooling layer calculates the pool's mean value. Average pooling preserves the mean values of the map's features. It smooths the image while maintaining the essence of the image's features. The Pooling layer functions as a connection between the Convolutional Layer and the fully connected layer.

Fully Connected Layer

A Fully Connected Layer (also known as a dense layer) is a layer in which each neuron is connected to each neuron in the layer beneath it. Typically, fully connected layers are used at the end of a CNN to predict the image class based on the extracted features from the preceding convolutional and pooling layers.

Dropout

This layer addresses the issue of overfitting, which occurs when the performance of a model on the training data negatively impacts its performance on the validation data. This layer addresses the issue by eliminating neurons during the training process, thereby reducing the size of the model. It leads to an improvement in performance.

Activation Functions

Activation Functions are a crucial parameter of a CNN model because they determine which information of the model should advance and which information should not be inputted until the end of the network. They are responsible for learning the relationships between network variables. The activation functions ReLU, Softmax, TanH, and Sigmoidal are common. Each is responsible for a particular function. Sigmoid and softmax functions are preferred for binary classification, while softmax is used for multiclass classification.

Implementation

Figure 11 depicts the various Python programming steps required to construct, train, and test a CNN model for Brain Tumor classification.

Figure 10. CNN implementation results

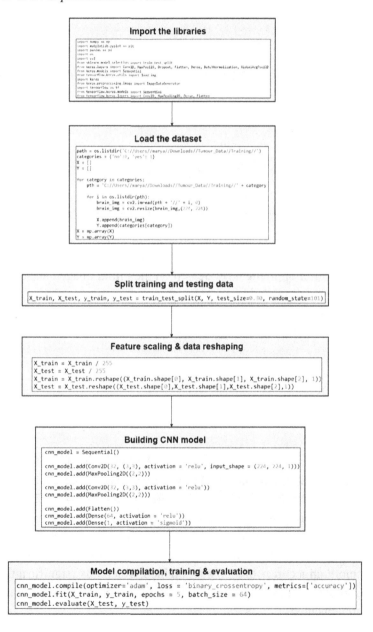

SVM Result before applying Grid Search on the initial dataset.

Figure 11.

```
1  print(confusion_matrix(y_test,predictions))
2
3  # 442 True positives
4  # 36 False positives
5  # 15 False negatives
6  # 407 True negatives
7  # Total of 51 inaccuracies and 849 accuracies out of a sample size of 900
```

```
[[442  36]
 [ 15 407]]
```

```
1  # PRECISION measures how many positives are predicted correctly from the total amount of positive predictions. TP/(TP+FP)
2  # RECALL measures how many positives are predicted correct from the real amount of positives. TP/(TP+FN)
3  # F1-SCORE combines precision and recall into a single measure.
4  # SUPPORT is the number of actual occurences of the class in the dataset.
5
6  print(classification_report(y_test,predictions))
```

```
               precision    recall  f1-score   support

           0       0.97      0.92      0.95       478
           1       0.92      0.96      0.94       422

    accuracy                           0.94       900
   macro avg       0.94      0.94      0.94       900
weighted avg       0.94      0.94      0.94       900
```

SVM results after applying Grid Search on the initial image dataset.
SVM result on augmented image dataset.
CNN result on the initial image dataset.
CNN result on augmented image dataset.

EVALUATION AND DISCUSSION

Accuracy of SVM

The SVM was trained using the training data following a 70:30 split of the training data and testing data. The trained SVM model was then applied to the test data to evaluate the model. With 442 TP, 407 TN, 36 FP, and 15 FN, 94% accuracy was achieved. In an effort to improve accuracy, Grid Search was implemented, which increased accuracy to 97% with 446 TP, 407 TN, 12 FP, and 15 FN values. After implementing Data Augmentation, the size of the dataset tripled. On performing SVM once more, an accuracy of 83% was obtained, which was a significant reduction. After being dissatisfied with the results, CNN implemented a deep-learning strategy was then implemented.

Figure 12.

```
1  print(confusion_matrix(y_test, pred))
2  # 466 True positives
3  # 407 True negatives
4  # 12 False positives
5  # 15 False negatives
6  # Total of 27 inaccuracies and 873 accuracies out of a sample size of 900
```

```
[[466  12]
 [ 15 407]]
```

```
1  # Grid search increased accuracy by 3%
2  print(classification_report(y_test, pred))
```

	precision	recall	f1-score	support
0	0.97	0.97	0.97	478
1	0.97	0.96	0.97	422
accuracy			0.97	900
macro avg	0.97	0.97	0.97	900
weighted avg	0.97	0.97	0.97	900

Figure 13.

```
1  print(classification_report(y_test,predictions))
```

	precision	recall	f1-score	support
0	0.84	0.88	0.86	4220
1	0.82	0.77	0.80	3102
accuracy			0.83	7322
macro avg	0.83	0.82	0.83	7322
weighted avg	0.83	0.83	0.83	7322

```
1  print(confusion_matrix(y_test,predictions))
```

```
[[3713  507]
 [ 715 2387]]
```

Figure 14. Model evaluation

```
1  cnn_model.evaluate(X_test, y_test)

29/29 [==============================] - 3s 102ms/step - loss: 0.0805 - accuracy: 0.9856

[0.08051609992980957, 0.9855555295944214]
```

Figure 15. Model evaluation

```
1  cnn_model.evaluate(X_test, y_test)

229/229 [==============================] - 25s 109ms/step - loss: 0.5157 - accuracy: 0.9127

[0.5156838297843933, 0.9127287864685059]
```

Accuracy of CNN

CNN's model was constructed using multiple layers. EarlyStopping and ModelCheckpoint were used to enable early stopping to conserve computational resources while ensuring the model's performance was maintained. The model was trained with a 99.5% accuracy and 0.03 loss. The loss is the sum of the errors made for each training or validation sample. The objective of the training procedure is to minimize loss value. After evaluating the model, it was determined that it has a 98.5% accuracy when utilizing normal image data. The model was then retested using augmented image data, and its accuracy was determined to be 91%.

Comparison of SVM and CNN

After testing SVM and CNN, it was determined that the traditional machine learning model for image recognition, such as SVM, has a several advantages, but also a number of shortcomings. CNN's approach to deep learning gives high accuracy as a result. The SVM performed exceptionally well with the initial image dataset and yielded a 97% accuracy. However, when data augmentation was applied to the dataset, which significantly increased the number of images, SVM accuracy dropped to 83%. In contrast, CNN achieved an accuracy of 98.5% with the initial image dataset and 91.0% with the augmented dataset. Both CNN values are greater than those of SVM, indicating that CNN is significantly more powerful than SVM.

CONCLUSION AND FUTURE IMPROVEMENTS

The presence of a brain tumor has a profound impact on every individual. As a result, MRI image identification remains a field of rapid technological development and complexity in medical research. The goal of this study was to create a model that improves tumor classification efficiency. This research demonstrates the utility of machine learning algorithms in the medical field. It also emphasizes the superiority of deep-learning techniques like CNN over conventional machine-learning techniques like SVM. The training data for both models was prepared using techniques such as image preprocessing and EDA. First, the trained SVM model was applied to the test data, resulting in a 94% accuracy rate. Because of the sensitive nature of the data, the grid search method was used to improve the test set, resulting in a 97% increase in accuracy. The dataset was augmented using data augmentation to improve the model's accuracy even further. The use of SVM on augmented data yielded an accuracy of 83%. CNN, a deep-learning technique, was used in this study and achieved 98.5% accuracy on the initial dataset and 91% accuracy on the augmented images dataset.

Several enhancements can be made to this model to increase its efficiency. This model's performance can also be improved by testing it with a DICOM dataset. Digital Imaging and Communications in Medicine (DICOM) is a method for storing and transmitting medical imagery. It also contains relevant metadata. Lastly, segmentation techniques that emphasize the extraction of features can be utilized. This can help in identifying the type of brain tumor present.

REFERENCES

Akinyelu, A., Zaccagna, F., Grist, J., Castelli, M., & Rundo, L. (n.d.). *Brain Tumor Diagnosis Using Machine Learning, Convolutional Neural Networks, Capsule Neural Networks and Vision Transformers, Applied to MRI: A Survey*. Retrieved December 1, 2022, from https://www.mdpi.com/2313-433X/8/8/205

Bajaj, A. (2022, November 14). *Performance Metrics in Machine Learning* [Complete Guide]. Neptune.ai. Retrieved December 5, 2022, from https://neptune.ai/blog/performance-metrics-in-machine-learning-complete-guide#:~:text=Performance%20metrics%20are%20a%20part,a%20metric%20to%20judge%20performance

Baranwal, S., Jaiswal, K., Vaibhav, K., Srikantaswamy, R., & Kumar, A. (2020, September 1). *Performance analysis of Brain Tumour Image Classification using CNN and SVM*. IEEE Xplore. doi:10.1109/ICIRCA48905.2020.9183023

Borole, V., Nimbhore, S., & Kawthekar, S. (2015, September). Image Processing Techniques for Brain Tumor Detection: A Review. *International Journal of Emerging Trends & Technology in Computer Science*. Retrieved December 4, 2022, from https://www.ijettcs.org/Volume4Issue5(2)/IJETTCS-2015-10-01-7.pdf

Dhole, N., & Dixit, V. (2022). *Review of brain tumor detection from MRI images with hybrid approaches*. Springer Link. Retrieved December 2, 2022, from https://linkspringer-com.ezproxy.uow.edu.au/article/10.1007/s11042-022-12162-1

Guo, T., Dong, J., Li, H., & Gao, Y. (2020, March 10). *Simple Convolutional Neural Network on Image Classification*. IEEE Xplore. Retrieved December 28, 2022, from doi:10.1109/ICBDA.2017.8078730

Hassan, H., Shafri, H., & Habshi, M. (2019). A Comparison Between Support Vector Machine (SVM) and Convolutional Neural Network (CNN) Models For Hyperspectral Image Classification. *IOP Conference Series: Earth and Environmental Science*. Retrieved December 20, 2022, from 10.1088/1755-1315/357/1/012035

Jia, Z., & Chen, D. (n.d.). *Brain Tumor Identification and Classification of MRI images using deep learning techniques*. IEEE Xplore. Retrieved December 5, 2022, from https://ieeexplore.ieee.org/stamp/stamp.jsp?arnumber=9166580

Joseph, R. (2018, December 30). *Grid Search for model tuning*. Towards Data Science. Retrieved December 1, 2022, from https://towardsdatascience.com/grid-search-for-model-tuning-3319b259367e

Khan, A., Nazarian, H., Golilarz, N., Addeh, A., Li, J., & Khan, G. (2021, January 15). *Brain Tumor Classification Using Efficient Deep Features of MRI Scans and Support Vector Machine*. IEEE Xplore. Retrieved December 5, 2022, from https://ieeexplore.ieee.org/abstract/document/9317509

Kumar, T., Rashmi, K., Ramadoss, S., Sandhya, L., & Sangeetha, T. (2017, October 19). *Brain tumor detection using SVM classifier*. IEEE Xplore. Retrieved December 3, 2022, from https://ieeexplore-ieee-org.ezproxy.uow.edu.au/stamp/stamp.jsp?tp=&arnumber=8071613

Matthew, A., Tan, K., Suharyo, P., & Gunawan, A. (2022, July 25). *A Systematic Literature Review: Image Segmentation on Brain MRI Image to Detect Brain Tumor*. IEEE Xplore. Retrieved December 1, 2022, from https://ieeexplore-ieee-org.ezproxy.uow.edu.au/stamp/stamp.jsp?tp=&arnumber=9829177

Miglani, A., Madan, H., Kumar, S., & Kumar, S. (2021). *A Literature Review on Brain Tumor Detection and Segmentation.* IEEE Xplore. Retrieved December 3, 2022, from https://ieeexplore-ieee-org.ezproxy.uow.edu.au/stamp/stamp.jsp?tp=&arnumber=9432342

Preetha, R., & Suresh, G. (2014). *Performance Analysis of Fuzzy C Means Algorithm in Automated Detection of Brain Tumor.* IEEE Xplore. Retrieved December 1, 2022, from https://ieeexplore-ieee-org.ezproxy.uow.edu.au/stamp/stamp.jsp?tp=&arnumber=6755100

Santos, D., & Santos, E. (2022, January 25). *Brain Tumor Detection Using Deep Learning.* Medrxiv. Retrieved December 5, 2022, from https://www.medrxiv.org/content/medrxiv/early/2022/01/25/2022.01.19.22269457.full.pdf

Staff, N. C. I. (2020, February 12). *Artificial Intelligence Expedites Brain Tumor Diagnosis during Surgery.* National Cancer Institution. Retrieved December 5, 2022, from https://www.cancer.gov/news-events/cancer-currents-blog/2020/artificial-intelligence-brain-tumor-diagnosis-surgery

Sunasra, M. (2017, November 11). *Performance Metrics for Classification problems in Machine Learning.* Medium. Retrieved December 4, 2022, from https://medium.com/@MohammedS/performance-metrics-for-classification-problems-in-machine-learning-part-i-b085d432082b

Sungheetha, A., & Sharma, R. R. (2020). GTIKF- Gabor-Transform Incorporated K-Means and Fuzzy C Means Clustering for Edge Detection in CT and MRI. *Journal of Soft Computing Paradigm.* doi:10.36548/jscp.2020.2.004

Ucuzal, H., Yasar, S., & Colak, C. (2019, December 16). *Classification of brain tumor types by deep learning with convolutional neural network on magnetic resonance images using a developed web-based interface.* IEEE Xplore. Retrieved December 5, 2022, from https://ieeexplore-ieee-org.ezproxy.uow.edu.au/stamp/stamp.jsp?tp=&arnumber=8932761

Vani, N., Sowmya, A., & Jayamma, N. (2017, July 7). Brain Tumor Classification using Support Vector Machine. *International Research Journal of Engineering and Technology.* Retrieved December 5, 2022, from https://www.irjet.net/archives/V4/i7/IRJET-V4I7367.pdf

Zuccarelli, E. (2020, December 29). *Performance Metrics in Machine Learning — Part 1: Classification.* Towards Data Science. Retrieved December 5, 2022, from https://towardsdatascience.com/performance-metrics-in-machine-learning-part-1-classification-6c6b8d8a8c92

Chapter 9
Amazon Product Dataset Community Detection Metrics and Algorithms

Chaitali Choudhary
University of Petroleum and Energy Studies, India

Inder Singh
University of Petroleum and Energy Studies, India

Soly Mathew Biju
University of Wollongong in Dubai, UAE

Manoj Kumar
ⓘ https://orcid.org/0000-0001-5113-0639
University of Wollongong in Dubai, UAE

ABSTRACT

Community detection in social network analysis is crucial for understanding network structure and organization. It helps identify cohesive groups of nodes, allowing for targeted analysis and interventions. Girvan-Newman, Walktrap, and Louvain are popular algorithms used for community detection. Girvan-Newman focuses on betweenness centrality, Walktrap uses random walks, and Louvain optimizes modularity. Experimental results show that the label propagation algorithm (LPA) is efficient in extracting community structures. LPA has linear time complexity and does not require prior specification of the number of communities. However, it focuses on characterizing the number of communities rather than labeling them. K-clique performs well when the number of communities is known in advance. Louvain excels in modularity and community identification. Overall, community detection algorithms are essential for understanding network structures and functional units.

DOI: 10.4018/978-1-6684-8696-2.ch009

1 INTRODUCTION

Subsystems that integrate other subsystems in a hierarchical framework constitute complex systems. Herbert A. Simon made the observation that hierarchical organisation is essential to the growth and development of complex systems as early as 1962. Many complex systems may be described as graphs or networks, where the basic building blocks and relationships between them are represented by nodes and links, respectively. Subsystems in a network appear as subgraphs with dense internal links but weak external linkages (Lancichinetti & Fortunato, 2009). Communities are what are referred to as these subparagraphs, and they are present in many networked systems. Communities explain the internal organisation of a network and imply the presence of certain connections between nodes that may not be immediately apparent via direct empirical testing. Communities may include collections of related websites, linked groups of people in social networks, biochemical routes in metabolic networks, etc. These factors have led to the detection of communities in networks becoming a fundamental subject in network research. People use the internet constantly in their daily lives. A complex network is made up of several individual users who interact in a complex way.

Complex networks' community structure is one of its most essential properties (Zhang et al., 2019; Chen et al., 2019; Li et al., 2020; Khan et al., 2016; Zhao et al., 2019; Zhao et al., 2021; Zhu et al., 2020; Zhao et al., 2017). In several disciplines of study, community identification in complex networks has gained attention. However, connections between nodes from the same community are often many while those from different communities are frequently few. The edge in an unweighted network does not take into consideration the strength of the connection between the nodes; it just indicates the fact that there is a link between them. However, many edges in actual networks often have strong or weak links, such as the number of transactions between buyers and sellers in the commodities trading network and the number of citations between authors in the citation network. As a result, research on weighted networks has practical applications.

The conventional community-finding method ignores the links between nodes and their second-order neighbours and only considers the relationships between nodes and their near neighbours. This lowers the community detection's accuracy. A person's friends' friends are more likely to be his friends than other individuals in a real social network. Similar to this, a node's second-order neighbours may influence whether it belongs to a community. High-dimensional similarity matrices cannot represent the main features of the network typology when grouping similarity matrices. As a result, this study offers a very accurate weighted network approach for community identification that is based on deep learning. This method gets the high-dimensional network similarity matrix first, which contains the information on the nodes' second-order neighbours' similarity, and then performs a dimension reduction on it. To get a precise network community structure, the software ends by doing a cluster analysis on the resultant low-dimensional feature matrix. The main contributions of this article are as follows:

1. By comparing the similarities between the nodes and the things they jointly purchased, preprocess the data. The similarity between the nodes is accounted for by the processed matrix.
2. On a simple Amazon co-purchase data set, a number of community detection techniques are used, and fundamental evaluation parameters are computed.
3. Varied Amazon data sets of various sizes have been the subject of many experiments. The amortised approach proposed in this study may provide a more exact community structure than traditional methodologies, according to experimental results.

Girvan-Newman, Walktrap, and Louvain are three popular community detection algorithms used in social network analysis.

1. Girvan-Newman Algorithm: The Girvan-Newman algorithm is based on the concept of edge betweenness centrality. It iteratively removes edges with the highest betweenness centrality, gradually breaking down the network into smaller communities. The algorithm calculates the betweenness centrality for all edges and removes the edge with the highest value at each iteration until the network is fragmented into distinct communities. Girvan-Newman is effective at detecting communities with well-defined boundaries but can be computationally expensive for large networks.
2. Walktrap Algorithm: The Walktrap algorithm is a hierarchical community detection method that employs random walks on the network. It starts by treating each node as an individual community and then simulates random walks to explore the network's connectivity patterns. The algorithm calculates the similarity between nodes based on their random walk trajectories and progressively merges similar communities. This process continues until a desired level of community structure is obtained. Walktrap is known for its ability to detect communities of various sizes and handle networks with overlapping or hierarchical community structures.
3. Louvain Algorithm: The Louvain algorithm is a fast and scalable method for community detection. It is based on modularity optimization, which measures the quality of community structure in a network. The algorithm iteratively optimizes the modularity by moving nodes between communities to maximize the overall modularity score. Louvain uses a two-step approach: first, it identifies

small communities by optimizing modularity locally within each community; then, it constructs a new network where each community is represented as a single node, and the process is repeated at a higher level. This hierarchical approach allows Louvain to efficiently detect communities in large networks while maintaining good modularity scores.

In summary, Girvan-Newman focuses on edge betweenness centrality, Walktrap utilizes random walks to detect communities of various sizes, and Louvain optimizes modularity through a hierarchical approach. Each algorithm has its strengths and limitations, and the choice of algorithm depends on the specific characteristics of the network and the goals of the analysis.

2 RELATED WORK

Graph segmentation-based techniques, spectral clustering-based algorithms, modularity-based algorithms, and label propagation-based algorithms are the four primary categories of popular community discovery methods. The fundamental idea behind the first three methods is to recursively split or merge a complex network. Thus, a community structure is created from the complex network.

Recent work in the field of community detection has focused on evaluating and improving the performance of existing algorithms as well as developing new metrics for assessing community detection results. Researchers have explored various aspects of community detection, including algorithm scalability, accuracy, robustness to noise, and the ability to handle complex network structures.

One area of focus has been on evaluating the quality of community detection results. Traditional metrics such as modularity, conductance, and normalized mutual information (NMI) have been widely used. However, researchers have recognized the limitations of these metrics and have proposed new evaluation measures. For example, the Surprise metric measures the extent to which the detected communities deviate from a random null model, providing a more comprehensive assessment of community structure (Huang et al., 2021).

Another significant area of research is the development of scalable algorithms capable of handling large-scale networks. As networks continue to grow in size and complexity, there is a need for efficient community detection algorithms. Researchers have explored techniques such as parallelization, distributed computing, and graph summarization to tackle the scalability challenge (Liu et al., 2023).

Furthermore, there has been an increased emphasis on community detection in dynamic and evolving networks. Traditional community detection algorithms are often designed for static networks and may not capture temporal dynamics effectively.

As a result, researchers have proposed dynamic community detection algorithms that consider the evolving nature of networks and track community changes over time (Alotaibi & Rhouma, 2022).

In addition to algorithmic advancements, researchers have also focused on addressing real-world challenges and applications of community detection. This includes studying community detection in specific domains such as social networks, biological networks, and recommendation systems. Understanding the unique characteristics and requirements of these domains has led to the development of specialized algorithms and evaluation metrics tailored to their specific needs.

Overall, the latest work in community detection revolves around improving algorithm performance, developing new evaluation metrics, addressing scalability challenges, considering dynamic networks, and applying community detection to various real-world applications. This research aims to enhance our understanding of complex network structures and their functional units, enabling better analysis, prediction, and decision-making in diverse domains.

A novel approach to community finding based on graphical models was developed by (Zare et al., 2021) Zare et al. The proposed approach, PFCD, considered both nodal properties and network architecture. The varied effects of nodal properties on community designs are looked at in our proposed framework. The proposed model is derived through an efficient probabilistic method. To effectively handle the latent variables, the model's parameters were found using the block-coordinate descent method. Our model exposes the relative significance of each feature on the organisation of communities in line with the discrimination of feature influence on community development. The experimental results on synthetic networks supported the PFCD technique's superiority to traditional methods for community discovery. Additionally, a variety of small to large real-world network datasets and customary evaluation measures were used to analyse the proposed model. The results on real networks showed the suggested model's excellent performance and offered very encouraging outcomes for the identification of community structures based on a network aligned with nodal features. Future research should focus on extending the suggested approach to temporal networks and developing a representation learning mechanism to automatically identify network structural properties.

Li et al. (Li et al., 2021) proposed a WCD network approach in an attempt to use deep learning for network WCD. By taking into consideration the similarity between nodes and second-order neighbours, their method first generates a second-order neighbour similarity matrix. The deep sparse autoencoder and deep learning technique are utilised to get the low-dimensional feature matrix of the weighted network. The community detection results are then shown using the K-means method. In comparison to conventional community discovery strategies, the experiment findings demonstrate that the WCD method is more modular and can be implemented in a fair period of time.

3 CLUSTERING EVALUATION METRICS

Since clustering is often performed independently, it's critical to have an objective function or quality metric to assess the results. Different distance-based functions across the data points are often used to assess the quality of clustering in clustering in various fields. We need to have different metrics for clustering in a graph, however, since graphs are non-Euclidean data and the connections in the graph are significantly more significant than the distance between the data points. To put it another way, the quality metric must be specified across the connectedness of the network.

3.1 Clustering Coefficient

The degree to which nodes in a graph prefer to cluster together is indicated by the clustering coefficient of the network. Evidence reveals that nodes often form closely knit communities with a very high density of linkages in most real-world networks, and particularly social networks. This chance is often higher than the typical probability of a connection randomly forming between two nodes. In order to estimate each network's relative interconnectivity, the clustering coefficient has been used to each network evaluated in this article.

3.2 Cut and Normalized-Cut

In general, if nodes and edges are closely linked to one another, they are seen as belonging to the same community (or cluster); if not, they are seen as coming from distinct communities. Therefore, it makes sense to arrange the graph's nodes into groups where they have the greatest number of connections to one another and the fewest connections with other groups. The "cut" of the graph is defined as the total weights of edges across various groups. In other terms, a "cut" is the total weight of edges that are removed from a graph in order to entirely divide it into distinct sub-graphs. The "cut" of a graph G into two disjoint sets A and B may be calculated mathematically as:

$$cut(A, B) = \sum_{e \in E} w_e \tag{1}$$

3.3 Modularity

When doing community discovery, modularity assesses the network or graph's structural integrity. It gauges how well a network is divided into modules (communities). High modularity networks feature sparse connections between nodes in different modules but dense connections between nodes within modules. The idea that random graph topologies shouldn't follow a community structure leads to the usage of the notion of modularity to assess the division of a network into communities. The introduction of graph modularity as a quality function allowed for the evaluation of community compactness. This is how the modularity Q is defined:

$$Q = \frac{1}{2m}\sum_{i,j}(A_{i,j} - \frac{k_i k_j}{2m}\delta(s_i s_j)) \tag{2}$$

Because the graph adjacency matrix defines the connectivity of the graph, A_j is the actual number of edges connecting any two nodes. And the expression $(k_i * k_j)/2m$ calculates the expected number of edges (assuming edges are randomly placed) between any two nodes, or the probability of an edge existing between node i and node j if edges are randomly placed.

Therefore, modularity may be conceptualised as the discrepancy between the number of edges that really exist and those that would be anticipated if edges were distributed randomly between every pair of nodes in a community (or cluster). When the community is completely separated from the rest of the network and has no fully linked nodes, modularity has a value between [-0.5, 1] and is at its maximum.

3.4 Partition Quality

A quality function is a function that identifies each graph division with a numerical value. By using the quality function's score, one may rank partitions in this manner. High-scoring partitions are deemed "excellent," therefore the partition with the highest score is unquestionably the finest. However, it is important to remember that it is impossible to say whether one partition is superior to another since the answer relies on the notion of community and/or quality function that is used. If there is an elementary function q that, for every graph partition P, then a quality function Q is additive.

$$Q(p) = \sum_{c \in p} q(c) \tag{3}$$

where P's partition C is a generalised cluster. Performance P is an illustration of a quality function. It counts the number of pairs of vertices that are correctly" interpreted," that is, two vertices that belong to the same community and are connected by an edge, or two vertices that belong to different communities but are not connected by an edge.

4 GRAPH PARTITIONING ALGORITHMS

It is well known that finding the optimal graph partitioning solution is NP complete. In other words, a brute-force approach is the only known efficient method that can solve this issue. In layman's words, attempting every combination is the only way to ensure the optimal answer. Due to the size of graphs, practically any combination of graph clustering methods may be tested exhaustively (e.g., using brute force). As a result, several effective methods have been presented throughout the years to discover approximations of solutions for graph clustering.

4.1 Traditional Methods

4.1.1 Graph Partitioning

In parallel computing, circuit partitioning and architecture, and the design of various serial algorithms, such as methods for solving partial differential equations and sparse linear systems of equations, graph partitioning is a crucial problem. The graph partitioning problem has several NP-hard variations. Furthermore, the requirement that the clusters be of similar size is often imposed. This NP-hard issue is known as minimal bisection. One of the early methods developed, the Kernighan-Lin algorithm is still widely used, usually in conjunction with other approaches. Because the number of groups and, in certain situations, even their sizes must be provided as input and are, in theory, unknown, graph partitioning algorithms are not suitable for community discovery. Instead, one would want an algorithm that can generate this data as part of its output.

4.1.2 Spectral Clustering

The normalized-cut eigenvalue/eigenvector decomposition over the normalised graph Laplacian may be approximated via spectral clustering. The connectedness of a graph is shown by the eigenvalues. We can understand the variation as we go along a graph using its eigenvalues. There is never a smaller eigenvalue than zero.

The number of zeroes eigenvalues reveals how many linked components there are in the graph.

4.1.3 Partitional Clustering

Another common family of techniques for locating clusters among a collection of data points is partitional clustering. Here, a fixed number of clusters, let's say k, is allocated. Each vertex of the points is a point because they are contained in a metric space, and every pair of points in the space has a determined distance between them. The separation between vertices is gauged by the distance. In order to optimise or minimise a cost function based on distances between points and/or from points to centroids, i.e., appropriately specified places in space, it is necessary to divide the points in k clusters into smaller groups. K-means clustering is the most often used partitional approach in the literature.

4.2 Divisive Algorithms

The two main types of community identification techniques are agglomerative and divisive methods. Aggregative methods often start with a network that only contains nodes from the original graph. As edges are added to the graph one at a time, stronger edges take priority over weaker ones. The weight or strength of an edge is decided differently depending on how an algorithm is implemented. The idea behind dividing methods is to keep taking edges away from the original graph. The stronger edges are first filed away. The edge weight computation is done at each step because the weight of the remaining edges changes when one edge is removed. Communities, also known as clusters of closely connected nodes, are the result of a given number of steps.

4.2.1 Girvan Newman

Although people are adept at spotting unique or recurring patterns among a small number of components, the structure of large, interconnected networks makes it almost difficult to do such fundamental tasks manually. Visually identifying clusters of closely connected nodes is straightforward, but scripting these jobs requires more complex techniques. These clusters of closely connected parts may be observed in a number of networks that make use of community identification techniques. One of the most popular community detection techniques was introduced by M. Girvan and M. E. J. Newman. They assert that node groups in a network are closely tied to one another both within communities and across communities. The Girvan-Newman approach for the identification and investigation of community structure is based on repeatedly removing edges that have the highest number of shortest paths between nodes passing through them. The graph's edges are removed one at a time, and as a result, the network breaks apart into communities.

4.3 Modularity Based

4.3.1 Louvain's Method

The Louvain method is a quick approach for improving graph modularity. In a two-phase iterative procedure, it maximises a graph's modularity. It begins phase 1 by giving each node in the network a unique community. Following that, the algorithm assesses the change in the graph's modularity when:

- node i is removed from its original community
- node i is inserted into the community of its neighbouring node j
- Phase 1 repeats until there is no increase in modularity and the local maximum is hit.

4.3.2 Greedy Modularity Maximization

Clauset-Newman-Moore will be used for this task. Using greedy modularity maximisation, identify the community split that has the greatest degree of modularity (Clauset et al., 2004). Greedy modularity maximisation begins with each node in its own community and continuously combines the two communities that provide the highest modularity until no further growth in modularity is possible (a maximum). Two keyword arguments may vary the halting condition. Cutoff is a lower bar that stops the procedure from moving on after a specified number of communities have been reached (used to save computation time). Even if subsequent communities reach their maximum modularity, the number of communities is limited at best n, enabling you to continue until only n communities are left.

4.4 For Overlapping Communities

4.4.1 Clique Percolation

Palla et al. (Palla et al., 2005) developed the technique known as Clique Percolation Method (CPM) to locate overlapping communities inside networks (2005, see references). This R code first finds k-person communities, after which it generates a clique network. Each linked element in the clique graph will serve as a representation for one community. The algorithm performs the following operations:

- Find all cliques in the graph that are k in size first.
- build a network with nodes that are cliques of size k.
- If two nodes (cliques) have k-1 common nodes, add edges.
- Every linked part is a community

4.4.2 Label Propagation

A quick approach for locating communities in a network is the Label Propagation Algorithm (LPA). It does not need an objective function that has been predefined or knowledge of the communities in order to discover these communities; instead, it uses network structure alone as its guide (Zhang et al., 2017) .LPA creates communities based on the principle of label propagation by spreading labels over the network.

The approach is based on the idea that although a single label may easily take over an area of sparsely linked nodes, it will take longer to do so in a region of highly connected nodes. Labels will get trapped inside of a tightly linked cluster of nodes, and those nodes that have the same label at the conclusion of the algorithms may be seen as belonging to the same community. This is how the algorithm operates:

- Each node is created with a distinct community label (an identifier).
- They spread across the network.
- Each node changes its label to the one to which the greatest number of its neighbours belong at the end of each propagation cycle. Ties are severed in a predictable yet random manner.
- When each node has the majority label of its neighbours, LPA converges.
- If either convergence or the user-specified maximum number of iterations is reached, LPA comes to an end.

5 PROPOSED METHODOLOGY

The Amazon dataset was obtained by Julian McAuley, UCSD. The data was categorised and included meta data (product information) and reviews.

Table 1. Time comparison of various community detection algorithms

Community Detection Algorithms	Size of Graph	Time
Louvain	351 nodes and 4900 edges	0.046948
	1097 nodes and 34754 edges	0.365119
	4099 nodes and 135190 edges	1.526322
KLB	351 nodes and 4900 edges	0.031185
	1097 nodes and 34754 edges	0.217588
	4099 nodes and 135190 edges	1.848037
GNM	351 nodes and 4900 edges	21.5433
	1097 nodes and 34754 edges	473.2074
	4099 nodes and 135190 edges	23223.42
K Clique	351 nodes and 4900 edges	0.018439
	1097 nodes and 34754 edges	0.069855
	4099 nodes and 135190 edges	0.705794
LPA	351 nodes and 4900 edges	0.003555
	1097 nodes and 34754 edges	0.029723
	4099 nodes and 135190 edges	0.607998
Walktrap	351 nodes and 4900 edges	0.015641
	1097 nodes and 34754 edges	0.567884
	4099 nodes and 135190 edges	16.08991

5.1 Pre-Processing

Python was used to create adjacency lists from the pre-processed data. An initial weighted bigraph is created based on client input. Then, two more graphs were created, one for products and the other for reviews. Each node represents a product in the product graph, and each link represents a pair of products that have each been judged by a single reviewer. Each node represents a reviewer in the reviewer graph, and each link represents a pair of reviewers who bought the same product.

Figure 1. Cleaned data

	asin	title	CC_score	description	also_bought
0	2168100	Wilton Reception Gift Card Holder, White	4.734585	Attractively keeps the wedding gift cards toge...	['2168436', '2168437', '2168438', '2168439', '...
1	2168101	Amazon.com Gift Card in a Greeting Card (Vano...	4.672981	Amazon.com Gift Cards are the perfect way to g...	['2168465', '2168466', '2168467', '2168103', '...
2	2168102	Amazon.com Gift Card in a Greeting Card	4.619449	Amazon.com Gift Cards are the perfect way to g...	['2168502', '2168525', '2168526', '2168527', '...
3	2168103	Amazon.com Gift Card in a Black Gift Box (Holi...	4.673174	Amazon.com Gift Cards are the perfect way to g...	['2168467', '2168470', '2168469', '2168490', '...
4	2168104	Amazon.com Gift Cards, Pack of 10 (Various Car...	4.703655	Amazon Gift Cards are the perfect way to give ...	['2168643', '2168644', '2168618', '2168645', '...

5.2 Data Cleaning

The five rating scales that were used in our experiment were 1 star, 2 stars, 3 stars, 4 stars, and 5 stars. It was created using Amazon product information. The first dataset is often messy and challenging to model. There were a few blank rows that were causing the analytical process to get confused. The datasets before and after cleaning are listed in Figure 1. After cleaning, the datasets are separated in order to employ the sentiment classification classifiers.

5.3 Parsing

The first phase in parsing was generating an items graph from the meta data, which was used to add items and edges between goods if they were bought together. We next looked through the reviews dataset to find out more about the customers and the goods they had assessed. Then, if two people shared a purchase and both gave it a rating of three, we created two connections in the user graph linking their respective nodes. Using the reviews to determine what each user had assessed; we were also able to combine the person and item graphs to create a third graph.

5.4 Obtaining Clusters

After evaluating other clustering methods, we found that Infomap offered the best communities for both individuals and items since practically every node in the cluster was connected to every other node. Since Infomap only provided the nodes in the clusters, we had to map these nodes with the original graph in order to extract the subgraph corresponding to the nodes.

5.5 Time Comparison

This section will provide the time assessment of the seven alternative methods used to identify community structure utilising data sets from Amazon copurchases that already have node memberships. We assessed three graph sizes based on time:

- 351 nodes and 4900 edges
- 1097 nodes and 34754 edges
- 4099 nodes and 135190 edges

In this work, the state-of-the-art algorithms Louvain, KLB, Infomap, Girvan Newman, K-clique, Label Propagation, and Walktrap are assessed. Using a network dataset from Amazon with various product architectures, we compare the time efficacy of the three graph sizes mentioned above. We have discussed time complexity of all ground community detection algorithms and also clustering/ community detection algorithms where number of communities are specified priorly in table 2 and shown in graphical form in Figure 2.

Figure 2. Time complexity analysis

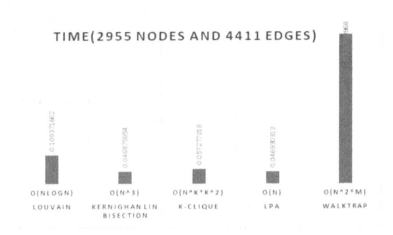

Table 2. Time complexity analysis of various community detection algorithms

Algorithm	Time Complexity	Time (2955 Nodes and 4411 Edges)
Louvain	O(nlogn)	0.109372
Kernighan Lin Bisection	O(n^3)	0.046876
GNM	O(m^2*n)	16.37799
K-Clique	O(n^k*k^2)	0.057278
LPA	O(n)	0.04693
Walktrap	O(n^2*m)	0.567884

6 CONCLUSION AND FUTURE WORK

Community discovery in social network analysis is a challenging task, especially when the network is large. To improve the efficacy of community identification in social networks, this study aims to identify the most successful community recognition technique for a network of this size. The experimental results show that when it comes to extracting community structures, the LPA surpasses the other algorithms in terms of time. Due to its advantages of linear time complexity and the absence of the need to beforehand characterise the goal function or the number of communities, the label propagation algorithm (LPA) has received a lot of attention. However, it also has a disadvantage in that we are effectively characterising the number of communities rather than naming communities. K-clique executes clustering in a manner like KLB if the number of communities is known beforehand; as a consequence, they have good time performance. Girvan Newman, Walktrap, and Louvain are the three ground-level settlements being investigated here. When it comes to modularity and community identification, Louvain does better in this situation. because of the community discovery methods in Luxembourg that are focused on modularity. The graph compression-based Louvain approach is only suitable for undirected networks, although it may boost effectiveness while maintaining efficiency for large networks. Thus, future research will focus on figuring out how to apply the graph compression approach to the neighbourhood discovery of attribute networks and multilayer networks.

REFERENCES

Alotaibi, N., & Rhouma, D. (2022). A review on community structures detection in time evolving social networks. *Journal of King Saud University - Computer and Information Sciences, 34*(8, Part B), 5646–5662. https://doi.org/https://doi.org/10.1016/j.jksuci.2021.08.016

Chen, Q., Wu, W., Zhao, T., Tan, W., Tian, J., & Liang, C. (2019). Complex Gene Regulation Underlying Mineral Nutrient Homeostasis in Soybean Root Response to Acidity Stress. *Genes, 10*(5), 402. Advance online publication. doi:10.3390/genes10050402 PMID:31137896

Clauset, A., Newman, M. E. J., & Moore, C. (2004). Finding community structure in very large networks. *Physical Review E: Statistical Physics, Plasmas, Fluids, and Related Interdisciplinary Topics, 70*(6), 6. doi:10.1103/PhysRevE.70.066111 PMID:15697438

Huang, X., Chen, D., Ren, T., & Wang, D. (2021). A survey of community detection methods in multilayer networks. *Data Mining and Knowledge Discovery, 35*(1), 1–45. doi:10.100710618-020-00716-6

Khan, M. S., Wahab, A. W. A., Herawan, T., Mujtaba, G., Danjuma, S., & Al-Garadi, M. A. (2016). Virtual Community Detection Through the Association between Prime Nodes in Online Social Networks and Its Application to Ranking Algorithms. *IEEE Access : Practical Innovations, Open Solutions*, *4*, 9614–9624. doi:10.1109/ACCESS.2016.2639563

Lancichinetti, A., & Fortunato, S. (2009). Benchmarks for testing community detection algorithms on directed and weighted graphs with overlapping communities. *Physical Review E: Statistical, Nonlinear, and Soft Matter Physics*, *80*(1), 16118. doi:10.1103/PhysRevE.80.016118 PMID:19658785

Li, S., Jiang, L., Wu, X., Han, W., Zhao, D., & Wang, Z. (2021). A weighted network community detection algorithm based on deep learning. *Applied Mathematics and Computation*, *401*, 126012. doi:10.1016/j.amc.2021.126012

Li, S., Zhao, D., Wu, X., Tian, Z., Li, A., & Wang, Z. (2020). Functional immunization of networks based on message passing. *Applied Mathematics and Computation*, *366*, 124728. doi:10.1016/j.amc.2019.124728

Liu, Q., Wei, J., Liu, H., & Ji, Y. (2023). A Hierarchical Parallel Graph Summarization Approach Based on Ranking Nodes. *Applied Sciences (Basel, Switzerland)*, *13*(8), 4664. Advance online publication. doi:10.3390/app13084664

Palla, G., Der'enyi, I., Farkas, I., & Vicsek, T. (2005). Uncovering the overlapping community structure of complex networks in nature and society. *Nature*, *435*(7043), 814–818. doi:10.1038/nature03607 PMID:15944704

Zare, H., Hajiabadi, M., & Jalili, M. (2021). Detection of Community Structures in Networks with Nodal Features based on Generative Probabilistic Approach. *IEEE Transactions on Knowledge and Data Engineering*, *33*(7), 2863–2874. doi:10.1109/TKDE.2019.2960222

Zhang, X.-K., Ren, J., Song, C., Jia, J., & Zhang, Q. (2017). Label propagation algorithm for community detection based on node importance and label influence. *Physics Letters. [Part A]*, *381*(33), 2691–2698. doi:10.1016/j.physleta.2017.06.018

Zhang, Y., Wu, B., Ning, N., Song, C., & Lv, J. (2019). Dynamic Topical Community Detection in Social Network: A Generative Model Approach. *IEEE Access : Practical Innovations, Open Solutions*, *7*, 74528–74541. doi:10.1109/ACCESS.2019.2921824

Zhao, D., Wang, L., Wang, Z., & Xiao, G. (2019). Virus Propagation and Patch Distribution in Multiplex Networks: Modeling, Analysis, and Optimal Allocation. *IEEE Transactions on Information Forensics and Security*, *14*(7), 1755–1767. doi:10.1109/TIFS.2018.2885254

Zhao, D., Wang, L., Xu, S., Liu, G., Han, X., & Li, S. (2017). Vital layer nodes of multiplex networks for immunization and attack. *Chaos, Solitons, and Fractals*, *105*, 169–175. doi:10.1016/j.chaos.2017.10.021

Zhao, D., Xiao, G., Wang, Z., Wang, L., & Xu, L. (2021). Minimum Dominating Set of Multiplex Networks: Definition, Application, and Identification. *IEEE Transactions on Systems, Man, and Cybernetics. Systems*, *51*(12), 7823–7837. doi:10.1109/TSMC.2020.2987163

Zhu, P., Wang, X., Jia, D., Guo, Y., Li, S., & Chu, C. (2020). Investigating the co-evolution of node reputation and edge-strategy in prisoner's dilemma game. *Applied Mathematics and Computation*, *386*, 125474. doi:10.1016/j.amc.2020.125474

Chapter 10
Python Libraries Implementation for Brain Tumor Detection Using MR Images Using Machine Learning Models

Eman Younis

https://orcid.org/0000-0003-2778-4231
Minia University, Egypt

Mahmoud N. Mahmoud
Minia University, Egypt

Ibrahim A. Ibrahim
Minia University, Egypt

ABSTRACT

Cancer is the major cause of death after cardiovascular infections. In comparison to other sorts of cancer, brain cancer has the lowest survival rate. Brain tumors have many types depending on their shape and location. Diagnosis of the tumor class empowers the specialist to decide the optimal treatment and can help save lives. Over the past years, researchers started investigating deep learning for medical disease diagnosis. A few of them are concentrated on optimizing deep neural networks for enhancing the performance of conventional neural networks. This involves incorporating different network architectures which are obtained by arranging their hyperparameters. The proposed idea of this chapter is concerned

DOI: 10.4018/978-1-6684-8696-2.ch010

in providing implementation details of solutions for the problem of classifying brain tumors using classical and hybrid approaches combining convolutional neural networks CNN with classical machine learning. The authors assessed the proposed models using MRI brain tumor data set of three types of brain tumors (meningiomas, gliomas, and pituitary tumors).

INTRODUCTION

Brain tumors can emerge from anomalous growth of the cells interior the brain or can come from cells that have spread to the brain from a cancer somewhere else. There is a wide assortment of brain tumor sorts that are classified in accordance with their cell of root. The essential tumors are those begun inside the brain. The larger part of essential brain tumors starts from glial cells (named glioma) and are classified by their histopathological appearances utilizing the World Health Association (WHO) framework into low grade glioma (LGG) and high-grade glioma (HGG).

The World Health Association (WHO) has created an evaluating framework to show a tumor's danger or generosity based on its histological highlights beneath a magnifying lens as Most malignant Quick growth, aggressive Broadly infiltrative, Quick recurrence Corruption inclined.

At present, imaging innovation may be a must for understanding diagnosis. The different restorative pictures like attractive resonance imaging (MRI), ultrasound, computed tomography (CT), X-ray, etc. play a critical part in the method of malady, diagnosing and treating. The later insurgency in restorative imaging comes about from techniques such as CT and MRI, can give nitty gritty information almost malady, and can distinguish numerous pathologies.

Doctors are unable to accurately diagnose and predict patient survival. They can also decide the appropriate choice of treatment which can range from surgery, followed by chemotherapy and radiotherapy, to a "wait and see" approach which avoids invasive procedures. Hence, tumor grading is an important aspect of treatment planning and monitoring. Exact detection and precise detection of abnormal tissues are vital for diagnosis. This reality is completely upheld by the presence of successful approaches utilizing division or classification or their combination for brain characterization both quantitatively as well as subjectively. Based on human interactivity, MR pictures can be handled using manual, semi-automatic, and completely programmed procedures.

In medical picture processing, segmentation/classification ought to be accurate which is in this way commonly performed by specialists physically and consequently time devouring.

A correct diagnosis, on the other hand, helps patients begin the correct treatment sooner and live longer. Therefore, there is an urgent need in the field of artificial intelligence (AI) to develop and design new and innovative computer-aided diagnosis (CAD) systems. It is intended to reduce the burden of diagnosing and classifying tumors and to assist physicians and radiologists.

Convolutional Neural Networks (CNNs) are one of the most popular deep neural networks that rely on mathematical linear equations between matrices called convolutions. A CNN has multiple layers. There are classical layers, pooling layers, nonlinear layers, fully connected layers, etc. Nonlinear and pooling layers have no parameters, but conventional and fully connected layers have parameters. There are different types of deep CNNs, such as Visual Pure Mathematics Cluster Networks (VGG-Net), Residual Networks (ResNet), Inception, Inception Resent50, and Xception.

Many ML algorithms have been used to classify brain tumors. Classical methods such as SVM, KNN, NN were used. In addition, deep learning techniques have also been used with promising results. I will introduce it in this work. A hybrid approach that combines a deep learning CNN as a feature extractor. Conventional ML was then used for classification. We compared different deep learning architectures for feature extraction. We also compared the base model with a model built using data augmentation.

The organization of this chapter is as follows: Section II presents an introduction about the field and highlights the problem of the current available systems for brain tumor detection. Section III surveys current applications and research to clarify opportunities and new features of the proposed system. Sections (IV) present system architecture and software Implementation details and results are discussed in Section V. Finally, conclusion and future work are presented in Section VI.

LITERATURE REVIEW

The application of medical imaging to detect brain tumors has evolved over the past decades. Brain tumor imaging detects the area and size of the tumor. This supports clinical tasks such as closure, surgical treatment and radiotherapy. It is also used to assess whether treatment is being given. Classification of MR images should be highly effective for legitimate studies of brain tumors. Many studies have used the capabilities of image segmentation techniques to extract important material, such as tumors, from medical images to aid in better investigation of brain tumors. However, the laborious search for brain tumors is more complicated, especially by the inconsistency in tumor morphology and the presence of cerebrospinal fluid (CSF).

The focus of each system is to successfully distinguish tumor tissue by separating it from other brain tissue, which is usually color-coded. An additional color palette is included to allow the user to better visualize the colors associated with typical and tumor tissue for each MR image type. As for improving the MRT framework, it is now widely used for purposes of evaluating brain tumor patients. MRI Preferences compared to other techniques such as computed tomography (CT) imaging It can be shortened as a delicate tissue, higher resolution than CT, and a big difference for non-ionizing radiation. MRI is classified as "conventional" "Extended" and "Advanced". Subjective with conventional MRI (C-MRI) strategies Organization photo. Enhanced MRI images can be quantitative or semi- Quantitative estimation of brain tissue. MRI is used to form MR Signals are electromagnets, permanent magnets, and superconducting magnets. Communication network. Superconducting magnets are commonly used in today's MR scanners and can provide a very stable range up to 8 Tesla. Conventional MRI protocols are used using tissue properties, echo time (TE), and repetition time. There are different stages in detecting brain tumors using MRI images: Preprocessing, feature extraction, segmentation and classification. Collect and save images to evaluate. Standard brain tumor databases, particularly his BRATS, Harvard Medical School, Brain Web, and Internet Brain Segmentation Store (IBSR), are commonly used by analysts. Additionally, experts have identified approaches to data storage from a variety of clinical and pathology laboratories. The main challenge is obtaining MRI information. Subsequently, improved MRI rules were developed. Changes such as standardization, optimization, and unification of security protocols are expected to continue in the future. Productive identification, extraction, segmentation, and classification of tumors are just some of the challenging tasks for physicians and radiologists. Mechanizing these modules in this manner is a large part of research in the field of restorative imaging. Several existing detection techniques appear to achieve excellent performance across various tumor datasets. Regardless of the accuracy percentages reported by tumor localization systems programmed using the best performing segmentation approach, a second opinion is required in each case to make better decisions. Differentiation in MR images can be a noteworthy metric as it has a significant impact on how brain tumors are detected.

The main goal is to develop an automated system for brain tumor system, segmentation, and classification. This system can be used by neurosurgeons and medical professionals. The focus of this project is on MR brain imaging of tumor ectopy and presenting it in a simpler form so that everyone can understand it. The purpose of this work is to provide some useful information in a simple format to users, especially medical staff who care for patients. An accurate and fully automated framework with minimal preprocessing for brain tumor classification. Help patients get the right treatment right away. We provide an algorithm that combines multiple techniques to ensure tumor presence, providing a method for tumor detection in

MR brain imaging. Extract meaningful and accurate information from these images with minimal error. Helps in early detection and monitoring of tumor identification and localization.

Convolutional layers are the main layers in CNNs. This layer is responsible for feature extraction such as image edges and colors. This allows the network to visually understand the image dataset. This layer focuses on using learnable kernels. These kernels typically have small spatial dimensions, but are distributed across the depth of the input. A traditional layer contains each filter over the spatial dimension of the input and produces a feature map as output. The second type of layer is a pooling layer. This layer serves to reduce the dimensionality of related features. This reduces the number of parameters and computational complexity of the model. Conventional neural networks (CNNs) are the most commonly used species in image and video recognition, speech processing, and natural language processing. CNN was biologically inspired by how the visual cortex works in cats and spider monkeys. CNNs are mostly successfully applied to image processing due to their ability to recognize patterns in images. In general, CNNs mainly contain three types of layers: conventional layers, pooled layers, and fully connected layers.

Related Work

Most previous studies have used accuracy as a metric to evaluate model performance. However, using this metric alone for comparison can be misleading. Accuracy ignores sensitivity to imbalanced data, with some classes performing better than others. Other metrics such as precision, recall, f1 score, and average accuracy were used. Therefore, we can get a clear indication of the generalization of the model to the MRI image data set.

Ismael and Abdel-Qader (2018) presented a framework for classification of brain tumors in MRI images that combines statistical features and neural network algorithms, and obtained a total accuracy of 91.9. Pashaei et al. (2018) proposed framework for brain tumor classification, which takes the tumor coarse boundaries as extra inputs within its pipeline to increase the Caps Net's focus. The proposed approach noticeably 90.89 accuracy. Afshar et al. (2019) proposed classification system adopts the concept of deep transfer learning and uses a pre-trained Google Net to extract features from brain MRI images.

Gull et al. (2021) proposed model with two pre-trained conventional neural networks Alex Net and VGG-19 are used for classification using transfer learning. The transferred VGG-19 model achieved 98.50 accuracy and the transferred Alex Net model achieved 97.25 accuracy. The research work Mondal and Shrivastava (2022) compared the performance of our model with state-of-the-art deep CNN models like

DenseNet201, InceptionV3, MobileNetV2, ResNet50 and VGG19, they achieved 98.33 overall accuracy with 5-fold cross validation using record-wise data split.

SYSTEM ARCHITECTURE

In the proposed system, the input image is a sample from MRI Brain tumor data-set, which is the input of the system. First, the original training images were augmented (Brightness, and Contrast) after removing noise by using a median filter and then extracting CNN deep features with different CNN architectures. In the proposed work shown in fig. 1, the deep CNN feature extraction was tested on two sets of classifier models other than the usual soft max classifier within the deep CNN models. These are the SVM and k-nearest neighbors (KNN) classifiers. The choice of SVM and KNN for our experiments was a result of inspiration from previous work where SVM and KNN had shown promising performance in classifying CNN features.

Figure 1. System framework

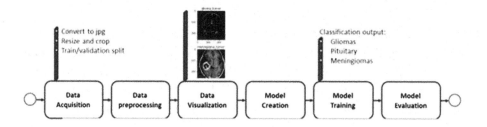

Data Set

In this work, using a public tumor dataset of 3064 MRI images containing three types of balanced brain tumors (meningioma, glioma, and pituitary tumor). This data set was not inherited from Southern Hospital, Guangzhou, China and General Hospital, Tianjin Medical University, China during the period 2005-2010. It contains images collected anonymously from his second tomography of 233 cancer patients. This dataset was originally compiled by Cheng et al. processed to create a tumor type classification model. I have some sample images of a dataset with category labels. The tumor dataset has tumor types as baseline truth: meningioma (708 slices), glioma (1426 slices), and pituitary tumor (930 slices). His CE-MRI image dataset of the brain can be accessed at (https://figshare.com/articles/brain_tumor_dataset/1512427/5).

Figure 2. Brain tumor data set

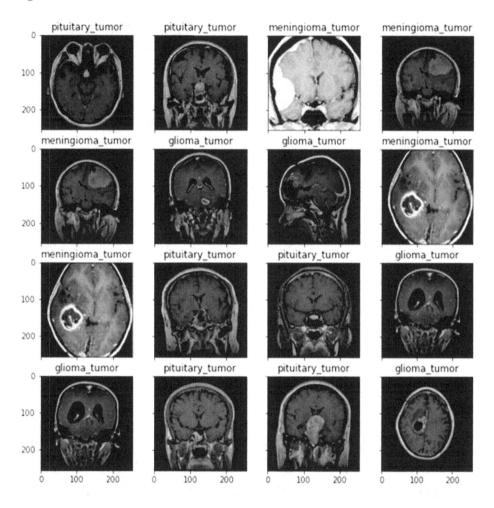

1. There is a lot of noise in the MRI image, this may be the cause from surroundings, equipment, or operator negligence. These possibilities It leads to great inaccuracies in MRI examinations. Therefore, the first step is to remove noise from the MRI image. The methods used for noise reduction can be linear or non-linear. For linear noise reduction filters, pixel values are updated by the weighted average of their neighbors. This method reduces image quality. On the other hand, the non-linear method preserves the page but reduces the fine structure. Here we used a median filter to remove noise from the image.

Figure 3. Applying median filter

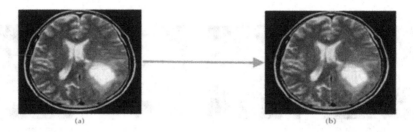

2. Data augmentation is a way to overcome the problem of lack of data. Sufficient amount of training data . data augmentation defined As a process that artificially increases the amount of data by creating New data points from existing data. This includes adding minor keys Modify data or use machine learning models to generate new models Data points within the latent space of the original data enrich the data set. Augmented data has proven effective in improving performance of a deep learning model by generating new and distinct instances of training dataset. Medical image datasets are limited in size and size difficult to collect

Figure 4. Augmentation of the brain images

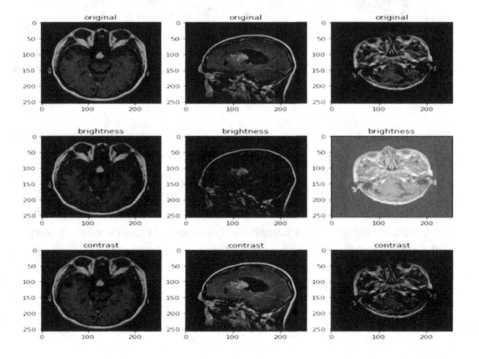

FEATURE EXTRACTION

In the experiments performed here, variants of CNN have been used for automated feature extraction as follows:

- VGG16, as the name suggests, is a 16-layer deep neural network. VGG16 is therefore a relatively large network with a total of 138 million parameters, huge even by today's standards. However, the simplicity of the VGGNet16 architecture is the main advantage. VGG16 has 3 fully connected layers and 13 convolution layers.
- VGG19 is a variant of the VGG model, in short It consists of 19 layers (16 convolutional layers, 3 fully connected layers, 5 max pool layers, 1 softmax layer). There are other variants of VGG such as VGG11, VGG16. VGG19 has 19.6 billion FLOPs.
- Xception is a deep conventional neural network architecture that involves Depth-wise Separable Convolutions. It was developed by Google researchers. Google presented an interpretation of Inception modules in conventional neural networks as being an intermediate step in-between regular convolution and the depth-wise separable convolution operation (a depth-wise convolution followed by a point-wise convolution).
- ResNet, short for Residual Network, is a special type of Convolutional Neural Network (CNN) introduced in the 2015 publication "Deep Residual Learning for Image Recognition" by HeKaiming, Zhang Xiangyu, Ren Shaoqing, and Sun Jian. CNNs are often used to support computer vision applications. ResNet-50 is a 50-layer convolutional neural network (48 convolution layers, max pool layer, average pool layer). A residual neural network is a type of artificial neural network (ANN) that stacks residual blocks to form a network. Regular networks were based on VGG neural networks (VGG-16 and VGG-19). Each traditional network had a 3x3 filter. However, ResNet has fewer filters and is less complex than VGGNet. A 34-layer ResNet can achieve 3.6 billion FLOPs of performance, while a smaller 18-layer Resent can achieve 1.8 billion FLOPs. This is significantly faster than the 19.6 billion FLOPs VGG-19 network.
- Inception-ResNet-v2 is a traditional neural architecture built on top of the Inception family of architectures. However, it contains the remaining connections (replaces the filter chain stage in the Inception architecture).

CLASSIFICATION METHODS

Two classification methods have been used for classifying the brain tumor images namely, SVM and KNN.

- A simple linear SVM classifier works by drawing a straight line between two classes. This means that all data points on one side of the line represent one category, and data points on the other side of the line fall into another category. This means you can choose from an infinite number of lines.
- K-Nearest Neighbor is one of the simplest machine learning algorithms based on supervised learning techniques. The K-NN algorithm assumes similarities between new cases/data and available cases and assigns new cases to the category that most closely resembles the available categories.

IMPLEMENTATION DETAILS

1. Reading Data Set From Drive

```
import os
import glob
    # List to be returned
    full_names_img = list()
    # check if the folder with images exists!
    prev_path = os.getcwd()
    if verbose:
        print('(1) Original path was:  {} \n'.format(prev_
path))
    if os.path.isdir(path_ima):
        if verbose:
            print('(2) The directory {} does exists!\n'.
format(path_ima))
    else:
        if verbose:
            print('(2) WARNING: There is not such directory\n')
    # 2_ Read all the files with the specified "extension" in
the current
    # working directory
    full_names_img = glob.glob(os.path.join(path_ima,img_ext))
    # glob.glob(os.path.join(path_img, img_ext))
```

```
    if verbose:
        print('(3) The "{0}" directory has {1} images with {2}
extension.\n'
                .format(os.getcwd(),len(full_names_img),img_ext))
    return full_names_img
import tensorflow as tf
from tensorflow.keras.utils import image_dataset_from_directory
# set to fixed image size 256x256
PATH = "/content/drive/MyDrive/datasets/brain2"
ds = image_dataset_from_directory(PATH,
                                    validation_split=0.2,
subset="training",
                                    image_size=(256,256),
interpolation="bilinear",
                                    crop_to_aspect_ratio=True,
                                    seed=42, shuffle=True, batch_
size=32)
import matplotlib.pyplot as plt
fig, ax = plt.subplots(4, 4, sharex=True, sharey=True,
figsize=(10,10))
for images, labels in ds.take(1):
    for i in range(4):
        for j in range(4):
            ax[i][j].imshow(images[i*3+j].numpy().
astype("uint8"))
            ax[i][j].set_title(ds.class_names[labels[i*3+j]])
plt.show()
Applying Median filter to remove noise from images
img = cv2.imread(args['image'])
        apply the 3x3 median filter on the image
        processed_image = cv2.mediafilter(img, 3)
         display image
        cv2.imshow('Median Filter Processing', processed_image)
         save image to disk
        cv2.imwrite('processed_image.png', processed_image)
Using augmentation of brain tumor images
brightness = tf.keras.layers.RandomBrightness([-0.8,0.8])
contrast = tf.keras.layers.RandomContrast(0.2)
#Visualize augmentation
fig, ax = plt.subplots(3, 3, figsize=(10,12))
```

```
for images, labels in ds.take(1):
    for i in range(3):
        ax[0][i].imshow(images[i].numpy().astype("uint8"))
        ax[0][i].set_title("original")
        # brightness
        ax[1][i].imshow(brightness(images[i]).numpy().
astype("uint8"))
        ax[1][i].set_title("brightness")
        # contrast
        ax[2][i].imshow(contrast(images[i]).numpy().
astype("uint8"))
        ax[2][i].set_title("contrast")
plt.show()
```

2. Using CNN Models as Feature Extraction

```
# create the pretrained models
    # check for pretrained weight usage or not
    # check for top layers to be included or not
    if model_name == "vgg16":
      base_model = VGG16(weights=weights)
      model = Model(inputs=base_model.input, outputs=base_
model.get_layer('fc1').output)
      image_size = (224, 224)
    elif model_name == "vgg19":
      base_model = VGG19(weights=weights)
      model = Model(inputs=base_model.input, outputs=base_
model.get_layer('fc1').output)
      image_size = (224, 224)
    elif model_name == "resnet50":
      base_model = ResNet50(weights=weights)
      model = Model(input=base_model.input, output=base_model.
get_layer('flatten').output)
      image_size = (224, 224)
    elif model_name == "inceptionresnetv2":
      base_model = InceptionResNetV2(include_top=include_top,
weights=weights, input_tensor=Input(shape=(299,299,3)))
      model = Model(inputs=base_model.input, outputs=base_
```

```
model.get_layer('conv_7b').output)
      image_size = (299, 299)
    elif model_name == "xception":
      base_model = Xception(weights=weights)
      model = Model(inputs=base_model.input, outputs=base_
model.get_layer('avg_pool').output)
      image_size = (299, 299)
    else:
      base_model = None
import tensorflow as tf
from keras.applications.vgg16 import VGG16, preprocess_input
from keras.applications.vgg19 import VGG19, preprocess_input
from keras.applications.xception import Xception, preprocess_
input
from keras.applications.inception_resnet_v2 import
InceptionResNetV2, preprocess_input
from keras.applications.mobilenet import MobileNet, preprocess_
input
from keras.applications.inception_v3 import InceptionV3,
preprocess_input
from keras.preprocessing import image
from keras.models import Model
from keras.models import model_from_json
from keras.layers import Input
model_name     = "inceptionresnetv2"
    weights        = "imagenet"
    include_top    = 0
    train_path     = "/content/drive/MyDrive/datasets/" +
dataset[ds]
    features_path = "/content/drive/MyDrive/output/" +
dataset[ds] + "/" + model_name + "/features.h5"
    labels_path    = "/content/drive/MyDrive/output/" +
dataset[ds] + "/" + model_name + "/labels.h5"
    results        = "/content/drive/MyDrive/output/" +
dataset[ds] + "/" + model_name + "/results" + dataset[ds] +
".txt"
    model_path     = "/content/drive/MyDrive/output/" +
dataset[ds] + "/" + model_name + "/model"
    test_size      = test_set[ds]
    # check if the output directory exists, if not, create it.
```

```
    check_if_directory_exists("/content/drive/MyDrive/output/")
    # check if the output directory exists, if not, create it.
    check_if_directory_exists("/content/drive/MyDrive/output/"
+ dataset[ds])
    # start time
    print ("[STATUS] start time - {}".format(datetime.datetime.
now().strftime("%Y-%m-%d %H:%M")))
    start = time.time()
base_model = InceptionResNetV2(include_top=include_top,
weights=weights, input_tensor=Input(shape=(256,256,3)))
      model = Model(inputs=base_model.input, outputs=base_
model.get_layer('conv_7b').output)
      image_size = (256, 256)
base_model = Xception(weights=weights)
      model = Model(inputs=base_model.input, outputs=base_
model.get_layer('avg_pool').output)
      image_size = (299, 299)
 # path to training dataset
    train_labels = os.listdir(train_path)
    # encode the labels
    print ("[INFO] encoding labels...")
    le = LabelEncoder()
    le.fit([tl for tl in train_labels])
    # variables to hold features and labels
    features = []
    labels   = []
    # loop over all the labels in the folder
    count = 1
    for i, label in enumerate(train_labels):
      cur_path = train_path + "/" + label
       # check how many files are, together with their
extensions
      list_files = os.listdir(cur_path)
      count = 1
      for image_path in range(0, len(list_files)):
        print ("[INFO] Processing - " + str(count) + " named "
+ list_files[image_path])
          img = tf.keras.utils.load_img(cur_path + "/" + list_
files[image_path], target_size=image_size)
 x = np.expand_dims(x, axis=0)
```

```
        ax[3][i].imshow(tf.image.central_crop(images[i],
x).numpy().astype("uint8"))
        x = preprocess_input(x)
        feature = model.predict(x)
        flat = feature.flatten()
        features.append(flat)
        labels.append(label)
        print ("[INFO] processed for image - " + list_
files[image_path])
        count += 1
      print ("[INFO] completed label - " + label)
    # encode the labels using LabelEncoder
    le = LabelEncoder()
    le_labels = le.fit_transform(labels)
Using KNN algorithm as classification layer.
from __future__ import print_function
from sklearn.neighbors import KNeighborsRegressor
import sklearn.metrics
from sklearn import svm
import numpy as np
from sklearn.metrics import classification_report
from sklearn.model_selection import train_test_split
(trainData, testData, trainLabels, testLabels) = train_test_
split(np.array(features),

np.array(labels),

test_size=test_size,

random_state=exp)
        print ("[INFO] splitted train and test data...")
        print ("[INFO] train data : {}".format(trainData.
shape))
        print ("[INFO] test data  : {}".format(testData.shape))
        print ("[INFO] train labels: {}".format(trainLabels.
shape))
        print ("[INFO] test labels: {}".format(testLabels.
shape))
        print ("[INFO] creating model...")
        model = KNeighborsRegressor(n_neighbors=49).
```

```
fit(trainData,trainLabels)
 f = open(results, "w")
    avg_acc = st.mean(avg_accuracy)
    std_acc= st.stdev(avg_accuracy)
    avg_rec = st.mean(avg_recall)
    std_rec= st.stdev(avg_recall)
    # write the classification report to file
    f.write("Averaged Accuracy: {:.2f}%\n\n".format(avg_acc))
    f.write("Std deviation (Accuracy): {:.2f}%\n\n".format(std_
acc))
    f.write("Averaged Recall: {:.2f}%\n\n".format(avg_rec))
    f.write("Std deviation (Recall): {:.2f}%\n\n".format(std_
rec))
    # write the classification report to file
    f.write("{}\n".format(classification_report(testLabels,
preds)))
    # dump classifier to file
    #print ("[INFO] saving model...")
    pickle.dump(classifier, open(classifier_path, 'wb'))
    f.close()
```

3. Using SVM Algorithm in Classification Layer

```
 print ("[INFO] training started...")
        # split the training and testing data
        (trainData, testData, trainLabels, testLabels) = train_
test_split(np.array(features),

np.array(labels),

test_size=test_size,

random_state=exp)
        print ("[INFO] splitted train and test data...")
        print ("[INFO] train data : {}".format(trainData.
shape))
        print ("[INFO] test data  : {}".format(testData.shape))
        print ("[INFO] train labels: {}".format(trainLabels.
shape))
```

```
        print ("[INFO] test labels: {}".format(testLabels.
shape))
        # use logistic regression as the model
        print ("[INFO] creating model...")
        #model = LogisticRegression(random_state=seed)
        model = svm.SVC(kernel='linear', probability=True,
class_weight='balanced')
        model.fit(trainData, trainLabels)
        # use rank-1 and rank-5 predictions
        print ("[INFO] evaluating model...")
    # evaluate the model of test data
        preds = model.predict(testData)
        accuracy = sklearn.metrics.accuracy_score(testLabels,
preds)
        accuracy = accuracy * 100
        avg_accuracy.append(accuracy)
        recall = sklearn.metrics.recall_score(testLabels,
preds, average='macro')
        recall = recall * 100
        avg_recall.append(recall)
    f = open(results, "w")
    avg_acc = st.mean(avg_accuracy)
    std_acc= st.stdev(avg_accuracy)
    avg_rec = st.mean(avg_recall)
    std_rec= st.stdev(avg_recall)
    # write the classification report to file
    f.write("Averaged Accuracy: {:.2f}%\n\n".format(avg_acc))
    f.write("Std deviation (Accuracy): {:.2f}%\n\n".format(std_
acc))
    f.write("Averaged Recall: {:.2f}%\n\n".format(avg_rec))
    f.write("Std deviation (Recall): {:.2f}%\n\n".format(std_
rec))
    # write the classification report to file
    f.write("{}\n".format(classification_report(testLabels,
preds)))
    f.close()
```

4. Computing and Drawing Confusion Matrix

```
from mlxtend.plotting import plot_confusion_matrix
import matplotlib.pyplot as plt
import numpy as np
import matplotlib
class_dict = {0: 'G',
              1: 'P',
              2: 'M'
              }
true_pos = np.diag(cmat)
false_pos = np.sum(cmat, axis=0) - true_pos
false_neg = np.sum(cmat, axis=1) - true_pos
precision = np.sum(true_pos / (true_pos + false_pos))
recall = np.sum(true_pos / (true_pos + false_neg))
fig, ax = plot_confusion_matrix(conf_mat=cmat,
                                colorbar=True,
                                show_absolute=False,
                                show_normed=True)
plt.show()
```

RESULTS

Several performance measures are defined for the standard evaluation of a classifier. Classification accuracy is the most extensively used quality index. Accuracy, in classification, is defined as the ratio of the number of correctly classified samples to the total number of data samples. The classification accuracy obtained in our experiments showed that the best method using inception Resent-v2 in feature extraction with KNN classifier using contrast augmented images with an average accuracy of 99.5%. Figure 5 shows a comparison among various methods in terms of accuracy. Figure 6 shows the confusion matrix for Inception Resent-v2 with different augmentation techniques.

Figure 5. Comparing various methods for tumor classification

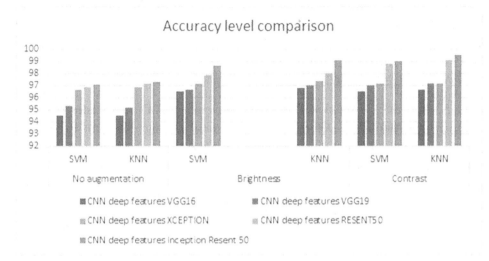

CONCLUSION

This chapter presented a framework for the automatic classification of brain tumors, with minimum pre-processing. The model was trained on a benchmark brain tumor MRI image data set of 3064 MRI images. It was evaluated using several performance metrics such as precision, recall, f1-score, and balanced accuracy. Experiments were run using different CNN models (VGG16, VGG19, XCEPTION, Resent50, Inception-Resent-v2) as feature extraction layers. The classification was then performed with SVM and KNN classifiers. We compared the obtained results of the original image Brightness, and contrast augmentation techniques. The best performance was achieved using Inception-Resent -v2 as a feature extractor with the KNN classifier and contrast as an augmentation method for improving the training process. It achieved an accuracy of "99.5%", improving state-of-the-art by 1.5%.

In future work, we plan to extend this work to experiment with larger datasets and more tumor types. In addition, developed models can be deployed in the cloud to assist doctors in their diagnosis. This should greatly reduce the burden on doctors. Overfitting has been observed with smaller training data. Future research in this area, perhaps with more data, will address these issues. Augmentation methods and further refinement of transfer learning models. We also believe that the proposed model can be used for other types of medical imaging, such as radiography (X-ray), ultrasound (ultrasound), endoscopy, thermos copy, and histological imaging.

REFERENCES

Afshar, P., Plataniotis, K. N., & Mohammadi, A. (2019). Capsule Networks for Brain Tumor Classification Based on MRI Images and Coarse Tumor Boundaries. *ICASSP 2019 - 2019 IEEE International Conference on Acoustics, Speech and Signal Processing (ICASSP),* 1368-1372. 10.1109/ICASSP.2019.8683759

Gull, S., Akbar, S., & Shoukat, I. A. (2021, November). A Deep Transfer Learning Approach for Automated Detection of Brain Tumor Through Magnetic Resonance Imaging. In *2021 International Conference on Innovative Computing (ICIC)* (pp. 1-6). IEEE. 10.1109/ICIC53490.2021.9692967

Ismael, R., & Abdel-Qader, I. (2018). Brain Tumor Classification via Sta-tistical Features and Back-Propagation Neural Network. *2018 IEEE International Conference on Electro/Information Technology (EIT),* 252-257. 10.1109/EIT.2018.8500308

Mondal, A., & Shrivastava, V. K. (2022). A novel Parametric Flatten-p Mish activation function based deep CNN model for brain tumor classification. *Computers in Biology and Medicine, 150,* 106183. doi:10.1016/j.compbiomed.2022.106183

Pashaei, A., Sajedi, H., & Jazayeri, N. (2018). Brain Tumor Classification via Convolutional Neural Network and Extreme Learning Machines. *2018 8th International Conference on Computer and Knowledge Engineering (ICCKE),* 314-319. 10.1109/ICCKE.2018.8566571

Chapter 11
Predicting the Severity of Future Earthquakes by Employing the Random Forest Algorithm

Mariana Marchenko
University of Wollongong in Dubai, UAE

Sandro Samaha
University of Wollongong in Dubai, UAE

ABSTRACT

Random forest regression is an ensemble, supervised learning algorithm capable of executing both classification and regression. Within this report, the use of the following algorithm will be implemented on an earthquake dataset which consists of all recorded occurrences of earthquakes from 1930 to 2018. Certain columns from the database will be used as target variables such as magnitude and depth to predict the following outcome based on trained data. Hyper parameter tuning will be performed to maximize the model's performance by increasing its accuracy, decreasing errors, and ensuring efficiency. The parameter in this model that contributed to the efficiency while performing hyper parameter tuning was number of estimators. Findings from the research report concluded that the model's accuracy levels were approximately 75%. Despite increasing the number of trees used, the model's accuracy did not significantly change and improve but rather significantly slowed down the run-time.

DOI: 10.4018/978-1-6684-8696-2.ch011

1. INTRODUCTION

Earthquakes are one of the most unpredictable natural disasters to occur. What can range from being a slight feeling of vibration to a catastrophe, earthquakes have many side effects and endanger humans and animals on a daily basis. This can be specifically applied to areas which are geographically located in active seismic zones. This includes countries such as Japan, Indonesia, Fiji, Tonga, Turkey, China and Iran. With that said, these countries suffered terrible catastrophes which have led to fatal damages which are still being repaired to this day (U.S. Geological Survey, 2016). Due to the lack of information on earthquakes as well as possible solutions which can aid in predicting them, a large number of individuals experience a fatal death, injuries, damages to their homes, and continue living in fear for this disaster to happen again. Not Predicting the Severity of Future Earthquakes by Employing the Random Forest Algorithm 3 only does this affect individuals on a personal level, but earthquakes significantly impact economies and cause countries/nations to spend millions and billions of dollars every year to repair damages caused by earthquakes.

According to the USGS, no scientist has been able to identify potential solutions to this issue. This is because, it isn't possible to predict earthquakes as they do not occur based on patterns and are completely out of human control. Currently, ways in which scientists and USGS are addressing the issue is by designing a system which can detect earthquakes once it has begun (U.S. Geological Survey, 2016) .By doing so, citizens in the area affected can be notified immediately. Another step that the USGS is taking is improving the durability of buildings and structures to ensure the safety of humans and reduce/ minimize damages (american geosciences institute, 2022). Although, there have not been successful forecasts in the past, it is believed that given the numerous advantages that technology has played, machine learning can play an undeniable role in geoscience and forecasting using algorithms (Papiya Debnath, 2021).

This research report explores the idea of using a machine learning algorithm to create a model which would be able to forecast earthquakes with a moderate level of accuracy. The model chosen for this exploration is Random Forest, a model which will use regression to predict the magnitude and depth of earthquakes based on existing data provided by the dataset used.

1.1 Random Forest Regressor

"Random Forest is a supervised learning algorithm that uses ensemble learning method for regression" (Chaya, 2020). By definition, ensemble learning method can be defined as a technique which uses a combination of predictions from numerous machine learning models to be able to develop an overall more accurate prediction compared to a single model (Chaya, 2020). By doing so, this allows the Random Forest algorithm to solve regression and classification problems. The algorithm is considered as one of the most powerful and effective algorithms available. Due to this reason, the algorithm is widely used in both classification and regression models.

The Random Forest Regression algorithm operates by using a mixture of numerous random decision trees which are trained on a portion of the data provided (Reader, 2021). By using multiple trees, this ensures that the algorithm remains secure and balanced as well as ensures that the algorithm reduces most/if not all deviation. An advantage of this algorithm is its ability to work with large sets of data as well as its ability to adapt to different types of data. The use of hyperparameter tuning is essential to this algorithm as different datasets have their own qualities and target variables.

Hyperparameter tuning is a concept of finding a set of hyperparameter values for a learning algorithm and applying this optimized algorithm to any dataset (Navas, 2022). These parameters are set prior to the commencement of model training. The use of multiple hyperparameters can substantially augment the model's performance and reduce the number of errors made, producing better overall results (Navas, 2022). Although this concept is encouraged to be used within machine learning models, it is important to note that since datasets are different from one another, the concept of hyperparameter tuning significantly relies on experimentation to attain a model with the best performance. Another important aspect to consider is that models should be evaluated on both training and test sets since solely focusing on one will lead to the issue of overfitting (Koehrsen, 2018). Overfitting means that the model excels and performs well on trained data however will struggle performing on other data (test data). This therefore indicates the model will be impractical and ineffective as it lacks the ability to adapt and apply itself to other data. The

Random Forest Regressor algorithm consists of many hyperparameters. Taken by sklearn, the most commonly tuned parameters are: **max_depth, min_samples_split, min_samples_leaf, and max_features.**

1.1.1 Max_depth

This parameter defines the splits that each decision tree is allowed to make. Within this parameter, it is important to ensure a correct number of splits is used based on the data set as this can avoid the model from overfitting and underfitting (Ram, 2020). It is recommended to use a depth of 3, 5 or, 7.

1.1.2 Min_samples_split

This parameter in the model "specifies the minimum number of samples an internal node must hold" to be able to split into more nodes (GeeksforGeeks, 2021). It is recommended that the value set remains between the values 2 to 6 as this ensures that the value remains high enough that it reduces the risk of overfitting and is not low enough that the model is underfitting. Having a number between 2 to 6 will "decrease the total number of splits, thus limiting the number of parameters in the model" (GeeksforGeeks, 2021).

1.1.3 Min_samples_leaf

This parameter will specify the minimum number of samples that a node leaf should contain after being split (GeeksforGeeks, 2021). Like other parameters, min_samples_leaf reduces overfitting when having an extensive number of parameters. This is accomplished through the technique of pre-pruning which uses max-depth, min_samples_leaf and min_samples split to tune and stop the growth of the tree, preventing the model from overfitting.

1.1.4 Max_features

This parameter represents the maximum number of columns shown to each decision tree (Ram, 2020). The Random Forest regressor will randomly consider subsets of features from the dataset to be able to find the best split. This parameter can take 4 different values: "auto", "sqrt", "log2", "none".

2. LITERATURE REVIEW

Earthquakes are categorized as a common natural disaster which is responsible for many tragedies across the world. According to the USGS, half a million earthquakes are detected worldwide on a yearly basis (Stasha, 2022). Despite their occurrence being common, the severity of earthquakes can range from subtle feelings of vibration to uncontrollable shaking in which disastrous catastrophes occur, causing tragedies from the loss of homes, painful injuries, or even death.

Unfortunately, earthquakes are not preventable and are challenging to detect as their occurrence is random and does not follow a recognizable pattern (Mondol, 2021). Despite this claim, several researchers and data scientists believed that creating an AI model would be able to detect earthquakes with a fair degree of accuracy. Earthquake prediction can be classified in two ways, short term and forecast. Most existing models opt to create a model which can detect earthquakes months and years in advance rather than short term as this information can be used more effectively within a larger amount of time, preventing causalities and allowing regions to prepare more effectively. By creating an earthquake forecast model, this would evidently alleviate the number of casualties, prevent further damage, alleviate the economic costs that countries would spend for repairs, and evidently find a sustainable solution. This would also ensure the safety of individuals, providing a much safer and secure life.

Within this section of the research report, an analysis and discussion take place in which an overview look of other research studies was done to see the approaches taken, the machine learning algorithm used, their findings, and the overall conclusion of the research study.

A research study conducted in 2019 by the Southern Methodist University, Dallas Texas use the Random Forest machine learning technique and Ada Boost Regressor algorithm to predict the time remaining before an earthquake. Within this research study, the university neglects historical earthquake data and use a dataset produced through a laboratory experiment which incorporates stick-slip displacements. Given that this laboratory experiment is used to study seismologic faults which depict related behavior to earthquakes, the dataset was used to complete this research. The university chose to use artificial earthquake data rather than historical/recorded data since the recurrences of earthquakes are not constant which causes results to be presented in broad ranges rather than specific values (Olha Tanyuk, 2019). This evidently causes the model to be less reliable and accurate. The data produced through their lab experiment consisted of finding patterns of aperiodic seismic signals within a given time of an artificial earthquake. Within an earthquake cycle, these patterns of aperiodic seismic signals would anticipate/foresee an occurrence of an earthquake. It was concluded that between the two algorithms, the Random Forest Algorithm calculated the most accurate results. Another conclusion that can be made from this research report was that despite the use of a regression algorithm, the university did not consider past or future data/information when calculating predictions (Olha Tanyuk, 2019).

Another research study made by HAL during 2020 predicts earthquakes using various machine learning algorithms. Within this study, HAL has an intention of predicting/ forecasting earthquakes from months to years in advance since this can ensure the safety of residents and avoid catastrophic deaths. To do this, eight different machine learning algorithms were applied (Random Forest, Naive Bayes, Logistic Regression, MultiLayer Perceptron, AdaBoost, K-nearest neighbors, Support Vector Machine, and Classification and Regression Trees) on a real-life dataset to predict for earthquakes using different parameters based on the model (Roxane Mallouhy, 2019). For each algorithm tested, values including the True Positive, False Positive,

True Negative, and False Negative rates were collected along with the Mean Absolute Error, Root Mean Squared Error and Percentage to determine the accuracy of each algorithm tested. The research paper concluded that the algorithm Random Forest performed with the best accuracy of 76.97% (Roxane Mallouhy, 2019) compared to the other algorithms. From looking at the results of the Random Forest algorithm, it can be deduced that the number of trees did not play a role on the overall prediction value, thus having no effect on the MSE or RMSE values.

The University of Twente, The Netherlands, conducted a research study in which aimed to find the most accurate method of predicting magnitude and depth of earthquakes. Various machine learning methods were used consisting of Random Forest, Linear Regression, Polynomial Regression, and Long Short-Term Memory. The intention of using multiple machine learning algorithms was to identify the most accurate model for earthquake detection through comparison of results and accuracy levels. The study uses realworld earthquake data to analyze and discover insights/patterns in the data (Mondol, 2021). This report provided many insights on the difficulty of predicting earthquakes accurately. Every machine learning model used within this investigation was able to provide different insights. When predicting the magnitude of an earthquake, Polynomial Regression, Random Forest and LSTM struggled with accurately predicting the magnitude of an earthquake compared to Linear regression. When calculating the R 2, Linear Regression was fully accurate, implying that it would be able to calculate the magnitude of an earthquake correctly without error. Despite Linear Regression accurately predicting the Root Squared value for magnitude, it was deduced that the Random Forest Model was able to predict the depth of an earthquake exceptionally better compared to other models. The RMS calculated an almost perfect value of approximately 86%, consequently keeping the RMSE the lowest (Mondol, 2021). The report concluded with mentioning that the model that was able to predict both magnitude and depth relatively accurately was Polynomial Regression; it is important to note that Random Forest was also mentioned as another method which would predict magnitude and depth with a fair degree of accuracy.

Within another study, an investigation was taken place which involved comparing predicted accuracies of various seismic vulnerability assessments and mapping methods on an earthquake (Jihye Han, 2020). Conducted by the Pukyong National University, Korea, this study focused on data from the Gyeonggi earthquake which occurred in 2016; and aimed to predict the damages on buildings caused by the earthquake. The study used different types of machine learning models to compare prediction accuracies. This consisted of both regression and classification models. The models used within this study included Frequency Ratio, Decision Tree, and Random Forest. Unlike other studies, this study aims to predict the amount of damage that would be done to buildings/ districts if an earthquake of the same magnitude and depth as the Gyeonggi earthquake were to occur again. By creating a model with such aim, this can allow countries and areas to prepare for natural disasters and minimize the damage and loss of homes. Given the studies aim, the parameters used were damaged buildings as the dependent variables and sub-indicators related to seismic vulnerability as the independent variable. By doing so, the study would be able to predict the level of damage based on building. The study concluded with mentioning that the Random Forest and Frequency Ratio algorithm were the most suitable algorithms used as they were able to identify the dangerous districts within their target area at a higher accuracy compared to others (Jihye Han, 2020).

Within this study, multiple classification models were used to identify the best fit machine learning algorithm to forecast earthquakes. Unlike most research reports identified, this was one of the few which used classification as the main method of forecasting earthquakes rather than regression models. This was achieved by categorizing earthquakes based on severity. The categories included fatal earthquakes, moderate earthquakes, and mild earthquakes (Papiya Debnath, 2021).A variety of classification models (The Bayes Net, Random Tree, Simple Logistic, Random Forest, Logistic Model Tree, ZeroR and Logistic Regression algorithms) were used on multiple datasets. The datasets in this report focused on areas in India along with nearby regions. Each classification and regression model were applied on every dataset to compare and contrast the difference in performance and identify the best model. This was determined based on the level of accuracy and precision. It was concluded that the best performing model was Simple Logistic and Logistic Model Tree classifiers (Papiya Debnath, 2021). This was because both classification models were able to perform the best for each dataset, having an accuracy and precision of 99%. Another conclusion deduced from this research report was that regression models performed the worst compared to all models tested.

3. METHODOLOGY

Within this portion of the report, the implementation and demonstration of the Random Forest Regressor algorithm will be executed with the aid of an earthquake activity dataset. Earthquake activity in the United States is monitored and recorded by the United States Geological Survey (USGS). All data pertaining to earthquakes of varying magnitudes and depths are recorded and made available to the public. The dataset being used in this research contains data recorded by the USGS and was acquired from Kaggle (Martins, 2021). This dataset includes the location, magnitude, and depth of various earthquakes recorded from the year 1930 up until 2018. Be that as it may, much of this research will include the data recorded as far as 1975, as any further values might prove to be redundant. Results pertaining to the model's performance will later be discussed. Python libraries such as seaborn, pandas, and matplotlib will be in use all throughout the process of implementing the Random Forest model.

3.1 Data Cleaning

The dataset that will be used contains several columns which are as follows: 'time', 'latitude', 'longitude', 'depth', 'mag', 'magType', 'nst', 'gap', 'dmin', 'rms', 'net', 'id', 'updated', 'place', 'type', 'horizontalError', 'depthError', magError', 'magNst', 'status', 'locationSource', 'magSource'.

Data cleaning is a crucial aspect of this research since no model can work well with bad data. Irrelevant data must be filtered out as it will hinder the algorithm's ability to predict accurate results. A further step taken when cleaning data is to dispense of the missing or null data. This is done simply due to the fact the machine learning models do not cooperate with missing data (finnstats, 2022). With that said, the data cleaning process began with holding on to key columns that will be used to perform the regression analysis using the Random Forest Regressor algorithm and discarding inconsequential ones. The 'latitude', 'longitude', 'depth', 'mag' columns were selected as well as the date belonging to each earthquake. Throughout the observation of the edited dataset, an abrupt discovery attributed to the time column was made. Seeing as the time column contained both the time and date of the earthquake, the column was split, and the date was taken and placed into a column of its own since the exact time of the earthquake occurring is counterproductive in the context of this research. Using pandas built-in functions .info(), data values in the dataset were displayed and examined for any null or missing values. The .dropna() function was exercised in pursuance of ridding the dataset of any null values.

3.2 Exploratory Data Analysis

With the dataset consisting of up to 30000 rows, visualizing the data was the next step to implement. Using the seaborn library, various histograms were implemented to display the data. A histogram is a very effective and handy tool which assists in the analysis of data, particularly for facilitating the visualization of sizeable data and its frequency (CFI Team, 2022).

From looking at the figure above (Figure 1), it can be inferred that the count of earthquakes occurred significantly drops when the magnitude value increases. This denotes an inverse relationship regarding the count of earthquakes occurring and their respective magnitude values.

Figure 1. Earthquake magnitude vs. earthquake count

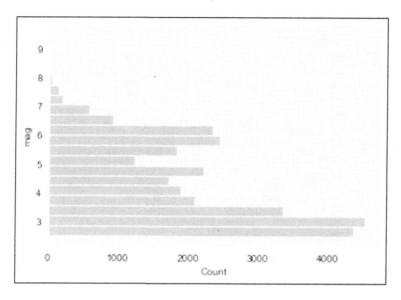

From looking at the figure above (Figure 1), it can be inferred that the count of earthquakes occurred significantly drops when the magnitude value increases. This denotes an inverse relationship regarding the count of earthquakes occurring and their respective magnitude values.

More specifically, earthquakes with a magnitude higher than 7.0 are highly improbable to occur. Given that earthquakes with a magnitude of over 7 are highly unlikely to occur, these values can be considered as outliers and will be removed from the dataset to prevent discouraging model accuracy scores. It can also be inferred that earthquakes with a magnitude of 6.0 and lower are more plausible and likely to occur. (Figure 1) also shows that most common earthquakes occur with a magnitude ranging from 2.5 - 3.5. This can conclude that the most frequent earthquakes are generally not extremely destructive in nature.

Adopting a similar histogram, the count of earthquakes with their respective depths are plotted in (Figure 2). A similar correlation to the one in (Figure 1) is recorded in the above (Figure 2), displaying a right-skewed distribution. An analysis of the histogram can conclude that there is once again an inverse relationship between the count of recorded earthquakes with their respective depth values. Earthquakes with a depth value less than 30 comprise 80% of the dataset, while having a depth value between 30 and 65 completes a further 18% of the values found in the dataset. The final 2% of earthquakes that form the dataset had a depth value recorded at over 65 and can be considered as outlying values. This ascertains that shallower earthquakes are generally more likely to occur than deeper ones.

Figure 2. Earthquake depth vs. earthquake count

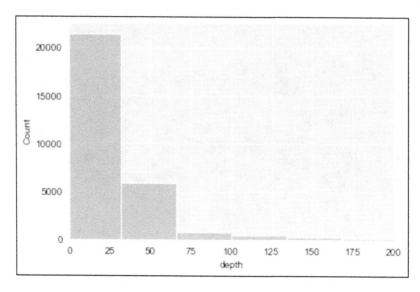

Figure 3. All earthquake-affected areas

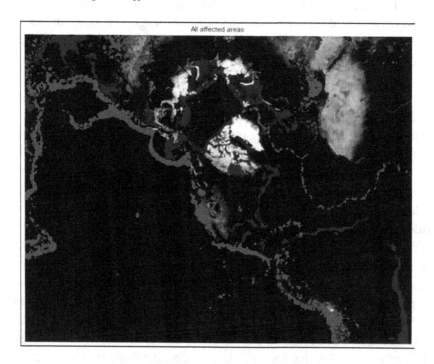

To better visualize the earthquake occurrences based on their latitude and longitude coordinates, a map was implemented. Each red dot that can be found on the map in (Figure 3) is a recorded earthquake with latitude and longitude coordinates that can be found in the dataset being used. The map also exhibits intriguing data that could not otherwise be replicated by use of normal graphs, said data being that most of the earthquakes are being recorded on the outskirts of the land closer to the coast. The main reason for these numerous occurrences along the coast is due to "stress accumulating in the plates which eventually exceeds some failure criterion on a fault plane found on the outskirts of the land" (Brodsky, 2004).

3.3 Feature Engineering

Outliers found in datasets can often lead to inaccurate values presenting themselves when predicting outcomes. The presence of outliers can deceive a machine learning algorithm into predicting false and inaccurate results, hampering its performance, and increasing the error variance. The data analysis demonstrated in (Figure 1), and (Figure 2) revealed outliers all throughout the higher magnitude and depth values found in the dataset. Data found in the dataset including magnitude values of over 6.5 and depth values of over 65 were consequently dropped following their detection. The elimination of these outliers will prove vital in developing a better more accurate model with a significantly smaller margin of error.

3.4 Train-Test-Split

Prior to commencing the model training and prediction, the extensive data must be split up accordingly. This will be done using Train-Test-Split- a method in which part of the data will be set to train the model and then later tested against the remaining data. Firstly, the data is split and assigned to x and y variables containing the independent and dependent columns respectively.

Studies have shown that the declaration of the training sample size can have a greater impact on increasing accuracy and reducing margins of error than the algorithm being utilized (Borkowski, 2020). A standard that can be followed when splitting data is an 80-20 train-test split (Afshin Gholamy, 2018). As is used in this research, 80% of the data is assigned to the training variables that will later be used in training the model, the results will then be tested against the remaining 20% of the data to investigate the accuracy of the model when used to predict the target variables, being the magnitude and depth of earthquakes here.

The data is split 80-20 for training then testing to combat the problem of overfitting. Overfitting occurs when "the algorithm in question learns the detail in the training data too well." In other words, the model will be able to predict training data with immense accuracy but will fail to predict the test data with any sort of relevant accuracy (Brownlee, 2019). This can negatively impact the performance and accuracy of the model and essentially render it useless, hence why a train-test-split of 80-20 is used.

3.5 Random Forest Regressor

The Random Forest Algorithm from Scikit Learn will be utilized. The choice to proceed with the RF Regressor was made due to its performance being a match for other algorithms with the added benefit of it being straightforward and more forgiving to use (Horning, 2010). The model is created with the default decision tree value of 50 to begin with. RF then selects several features to be considered when looking for the best split at each node. The number of features selected can be specified, however RF will select random values if not specified to complete the process of splitting the trees (Caifeng Zou, 2021).

When using RF, the number of decision trees enforced will heavily impact the result of the accuracy score. A value in the hundreds is most commonly the optimum value. Despite that, the optimum value is almost impossible to guess. Be that as it may, consistently increasing the number of decision trees being utilized can have a negative effect. The addition of decision trees beyond the optimum value is considered redundant and will cost in heavy computational resources with nothing of value to display.

3.6 Hyperparameter Tuning

To answer the question of what the most optimum decision tree value is to be used with the RF model, GridSearchCV from Scikit Learn will be implemented. "A hyperparameter is a parameter whose value is used to control the learning process of a model" (Mondol, 2021).

Hyperparameter tuning is an essential step to take to control the behaviour of a model as it aids in finding the optimum set of hyperparameters to use when predicting outcomes. The process of predicting outcomes without the use of hyperparameter tuning can needlessly increase the risk of error variance with the model.

An array containing numbers ranging from 400 all the way to 800 is created, then applying GridSearchCV, the process of fitting and predicting is underway utilizing the numbers found in the aforementioned array. This process is reiterated and cross validated 5 times. The practice of cross validation is imperative as it ensures the most optimum data is sent for training. It is worth noting that the RF model performed best when utilizing 800 decision trees, however with the original 50 decision trees showing similar results too. This implies that there is a limit to how many decision trees can be used since any value over 50 may be considered redundant.

3.7 Evaluation Metrics

Within this section of the report, the evaluation of the model will be concluded. The evaluation metrics that will be in use are the Mean Squared Error, Root Mean Squared Error, and the Coefficient of Determination; all made available through Scikit Learn.

3.7.1 Mean Squared Error

The Mean Squared Error (also referred to as MSE) in simple terms is "the average of the square of the difference between the actual and predicted values" (Great Learning Team, 2022). This evaluation metric is widely applied in today's world as it measures the number of errors a machine learning algorithm produces. The MSE is also favoured over other evaluation metrics due its natural ability to punish errors, since the value is squared, larger errors are more profound (Frost, 2022). The equation below is the formula used to calculate the MSE (Equation 1).

$$MSE = \frac{1}{n} \sum_{i=1}^{n} \left(Y_i - \hat{Y}_i \right)^2 \tag{1}$$

3.7.2 Root Mean Squared Error

Root Mean Squared Error shows how far predictions fall from measured true values using Euclidean distance (c3.ai, 2022). From the name, it can be inferred RMSE is calculated the same way as the MSE, but with the addition of the square root. (Refer to Equation 2). RMSE is used in this research due its efficacy in analyzing regression models. The RMSE focuses on displaying a numerical measure which illuminates how far off the prediction errors are from the regression line (Statistics How To, 2022).

$$RMSE = \sqrt{\frac{1}{n} \sum_{i=1}^{n} \left(Y_i - \hat{Y}_i \right)^2} \tag{2}$$

3.7.3 Coefficient of Determination (R^2)

The coefficient of determination (R^2) is an equation used when evaluating machine learning models. R^2 develops a numerical value between 0 and 1 which can be used to derive the model's accuracy when predicting outcomes. (See Figure 4)

$$R^2 = \frac{RSS}{TSS} = \frac{\Sigma\left(\hat{Y} - \bar{Y}\right)^2}{\Sigma\left(Y - \bar{Y}\right)^2} \tag{3}$$

The coefficient of determination can be calculated using the equation shown above (Equation 3). The RSS denotes the residual sum of squares, while the TSS denotes the total sum of squares (Enders, 2022).

Figure 4. Coefficient of determination
Source: Turney (2022)

Coefficient of determination (R^2)	Interpretation
0	The model **does not** predict the outcome.
Between 0 and 1	The model **partially** predicts the outcome.
1	The model **perfectly** predicts the outcome.

4. RESULTS AND DISCUSSION

This segment of the report will observe the findings of the model and the results gathered by the evaluation metrics.

As displayed in the table above (Table 1), it can be deduced that the model's accuracy score increased with every iteration. The greater the number of decision trees adapted, the greater the accuracy score. A further analysis of the data can show the redundancy that comes with the addition of decision trees after the optimum count is reached. An increase of 2.54% is shown in the table with a 750-decision tree count gap between the first and last iteration. Utilizing 800 decision trees comes with a great increase on computational resources when compared with 50 decision trees, and with a measly 2.54% percent increase on accuracy, it can be debated whether proceeding with 800 decision trees is the appropriate response.

276

Table 1. Results obtained from the GridSearchCV

Number of Trees	Accuracy (%)	MSE	RMSE
50	72.52	31.03	6.13
400	73.78	30.14	5.89
500	74.35	29.92	5.65
600	74.65	29.75	5.58
700	74.92	29.56	5.43
800	75.06	29.30	5.32

The MSE and RMSE contained within the table above (Table 1) does not show promising scores. With a RMSE value ranging between 5 and 6, it can be implied that the model is predicting values with a significant margin of error. This can be attributed to the lack of correlation between the dependent and independent variables used in this study (Figure 4)

Figure 5. Heat map denoting correlation

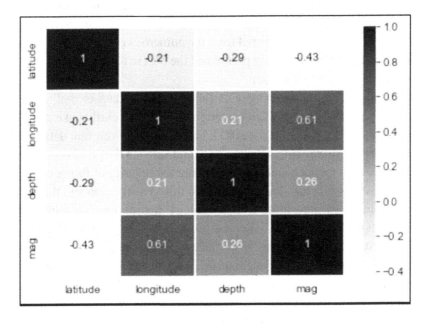

Data such as magnitude and longitude show somewhat positive correlation. Unfortunately, almost all other columns are not correlated. A slightly positive correlation between depth and magnitude can be understood. Despite that, the correlation scores obtained from (Figure 5) simply do not grant the conditions necessary for a random forest regression model to acquire an excellent accuracy score.

5. CONCLUSION

Throughout the course of this report, an investigation took place where the implementation of machine learning algorithms was explored to solve a recurring issue. In this case, the issue at hand was detecting as well as predicting the severity of future earthquakes by identifying the magnitude and depth levels. The Random Forest Algorithm was used to perform regression analysis on the dataset acquired.

The investigation commenced with analysing existing research reports, identifying the methods/algorithms used, the implementation of such algorithms, recorded findings, and the conclusions made. Many of the reports chosen for this section used numerous algorithms to detect the magnitude and depth of future earthquakes to essentially compare results and determine which machine learning algorithm can predict with the highest degree of accuracy. By doing so, this provided a better understanding on why Random Forest was the best algorithm to implement using regression analysis. Insights gathered from the numerous reports concluded that the Random Forest algorithm not only performed the best in terms of accuracy but was also the simplest algorithm to use.

Perhaps the most important part of this study, the dataset that was applied included a significant amount of information on recorded earthquake activity. The dataset, found on Kaggle (Martins, 2021), had all kinds of relevant data pertaining to earthquakes all the way from the year 1930 and aided in the process of developing a machine learning model capable of predicting the severity of future earthquakes.

After analysing existing studies relating to this investigation and the utilization of the random forest algorithm, a methodology was planned and implemented. The dataset in use was cleaned and processed before being employed in any model training or testing. Outlier detection was adapted and proved to be a very effective tool in handling outliers all throughout the dataset. From there on, the data was employed in the process of training the model in question, then testing it against real values found in the dataset. Hyperparameter tuning was enforced towards the end of the study to eliminate all sub-optimum hyperparameters being exploited by the model and produce the highest accuracy. The model was tested and evaluated based on various evaluation metrics, which painted the picture of how error prone the model was when utilizing the dataset pertaining to this study.

Through the implementation of the model, results showed that the models accuracy levels were approximately 75%. Results also concluded that despite increasing the number of trees used, the model's accuracy did not significantly change and improve. The main reason as to why the accuracy level is lower than anticipated, is due to the lack of correlation found between columns from the dataset used. When plotting the Heatmap (Shown in Figure 5), it was evident that the dataset lacked any significant correlation which would otherwise aid the model in producing a higher accuracy score.

REFERENCES

Afshin Gholamy, V. K. (2018). *Why 70/30 or 80/20 Relation Between Training and Testing Sets:A Pedagogical Explanation*. University of Texas at El Paso.

American Geosciences Institute. (2022, November 29). *Can earthquakes be predicted?* Retrieved from American Geosciences Institute: americangeosciences.org/ critical-issues/faq/can-earthquakes-be-predicted#:~:text=U.S.%20Geological%20 Survey%20FAQs%3A,time%20in%20the%20foreseeable%20future.

Borkowski, K. P.-F. (2020). On the Importance of Train–Test Split Ratio of Datasets in Automatic Landslide Detection by Supervised Classification. *Remote Sensing of Natural Hazards*, 3054.

Brodsky, H. K. (2004). The physics of earphquakes. *Reports on Progress in Physics*, 69.

Brownlee, J. (2019, August 12). *Overfitting and Underfitting With Machine Learning Algorithms*. Retrieved from machinelearningmastery: https://machinelearningmastery. com/overfitting-and-underfitting-with-machine-learning-algorithms/

c3.ai. (2022, November 23). *Root Mean Square Error (RMSE)*. Retrieved from c3.ai: https://c3.ai/glossary/data-science/root-mean-square-error-rmse/

Chaya. (2020, June 9). *Random Forest Regression*. Retrieved from Level Up Coding: https://levelup.gitconnected.com/random-forest-regression-209c0f354c84#:~:text=Random%20Forest%20Regression%20is%20a%20 supervised%20learning%20algorithm%20that%20uses,prediction%20than%20a%20 single%20model

Enders, F. B. (2022, October 4). *coefficient of determination*. Retrieved from Encyclopedia Britannica: https://www.britannica.com/science/coefficient-of-determination

finnstats. (2022, September 7). *Importance of Data Cleaning in Machine Learning.* Retrieved from R-bloggers: https://www.r-bloggers.com/2022/09/importance-of-data-cleaning-in-machine-learning/#:~:text=Data%20cleansing%20is%20essential%20because,every%20situation%20you%20might%20encounter

Frost, J. (2022, November 21). *Mean Squared Error (MSE).* Retrieved from Statstics By Jim: https://statisticsbyjim.com/regression/mean-squared-error-mse/

Great Learning Team. (2022, November 18). *Mean Squared Error – Explained | What is Mean Square Error?* Retrieved from Great learning: https://www.mygreatlearning.com/blog/mean-square-error-explained/

Horning, N. (2010). *Random Forests: An algorithm for image classification and generation of continuous fields data sets.* American Museum of Natural History Center for Biodiversity and Conservation.

Jihye Han, J. K. (2020, September). Seismic Vulnerability Assessment and Mapping of Gyeongju, South Korea Using Frequency Ratio, Decision Tree, and Random Forest. *MDPI*, 22.

Martins, G. (2021). *Earthquakes for ML prediction.* Retrieved from Kaggle: https://www.kaggle.com/datasets/gustavobmgm/earthquakes-for-ml-prediction

Mondol, M. (2021). *Analysis and Prediction of Earthquakes using different Machine Learning techniques.* University of Twente.

Olha Tanyuk, D. D. (2019). Machine Learning Predicts Aperiodic Laboratory Earthquakes. *SMU Data Science Review*, 20.

Papiya Debnath, P. C. (2021, January 19). Analysis of Earthquake Forecasting in India Using Supervised Machine Learning Classifiers. *MDPI*, 13.

Reader, T. C. (2021, October 19). *Random Forest Regression Explained with Implementation in Python.* Retrieved from The Medium: https://medium.com/@theclickreader/random-forest-regression-explained-with-implementation-in-python-3dad88caf165

Roxane Mallouhy, C. A. (2019). *Major earthquake event prediction using various machine learning algorithms.* Paris: HAL Open Science.

Stasha, S. (2022, September 29). *Earthquake Statistics And Facts For 2022.* Retrieved from Policy Advice: https://policyadvice.net/insurance/insights/earthquake-statistics/

Statistics How To. (2022, November 15). *RMSE: Root Mean Square Error.* Retrieved from Statistics How To: https://www.statisticshowto.com/probability-and-statistics/ regression-analysis/rmse-root-mean-square-error/

Team, C. F. I. (2022, November 27). *Histogram.* Retrieved from Corporate Finance Institute: https://corporatefinanceinstitute.com/resources/excel/histogram/

Turney, S. (2022, September 14). *Coefficient of Determination (R²) | Calculation & Interpretation.* Retrieved from scribbr: https://www.scribbr.com/statistics/coefficient-of-determination/#:~:text=What%20is%20the%20definition%20of,predicted%20 by%20the%20statistical%20model

U.S. Geological Survey. (2016, November 30). *Predicting Earthquakes.* Retrieved from USGS: https://pubs.usgs.gov/gip/earthq1/predict.html#:~:text=The%20 goal%20of%20earthquake%20prediction,the%20likelihood%20of%20future%20 earthquakes

Zou, L. Z. (2021). Porosity Prediction With Uncertainty Quantification From Multiple Seismic Attributes Using Random Forest. *Journal of Geophysical Research: Solid Earth,* (7).

Compilation of References

Abadi, M., Barham, P., Chen, J., Chen, Z., Davis, A., Dean, J. M., Devin, M., Ghemawat, S., Irving, G., Isard, M., Kudlur, M., Levenberg, J., Monga, R., Moore, S., Murray, D. G., Steiner, B., Tucker, P. A., Vasudevan, V., Warden, P., . . . Zheng, X. (2016). TensorFlow: A system for large-scale machine learning. *Operating Systems Design and Implementation*, 265–283. https://doi.org/ doi:10.5555/3026877.3026899

Abiramasundari, S., Ramaswamy, V., & Sangeetha, J. (2021). *Spam filtering using Semantic and Rule Based model via supervised learning*. Retrieved from https://www.annalsofrscb.ro/index.php/journal/article/view/1405/1174

Adjabi, I., Ouahabi, A., Benzaoui, A., & Taleb-Ahmed, A. (2020). Past, Present, and Future of Face Recognition. *RE:view*, *9*(8), 1188. Retrieved June 20, 2023, from https://www.mdpi.com/2079-9292/9/8/1188

Afshar, P., Plataniotis, K. N., & Mohammadi, A. (2019). Capsule Networks for Brain Tumor Classification Based on MRI Images and Coarse Tumor Boundaries. *ICASSP 2019 - 2019 IEEE International Conference on Acoustics, Speech and Signal Processing (ICASSP)*, 1368-1372. 10.1109/ICASSP.2019.8683759

Afshin Gholamy, V. K. (2018). *Why 70/30 or 80/20 Relation Between Training and Testing Sets: A Pedagogical Explanation*. University of Texas at El Paso.

Ahmad, H., Ahmad, S., Asif, M., Rehman, M., Alharbi, A., & Ullah, Z. (2021). Evolution-based performance prediction of star cricketers. *Computers, Materials & Continua*, *69*(1), 1215–1232. doi:10.32604/cmc.2021.016659

Ahmed, W. (2015). *A Multivariate Data Mining Approach to Predict Match Outcome in One-Day International Cricket* [Doctoral dissertation]. Karachi Institute of Economics and Technology.

Ahuja, M. K., & Singh, A. (2015, July). Hand Gesture Recognition Using PCA. *International Journal of Computer Science and Engineering Technology*, *5*(7), 267–27.

Akinyelu, A., Zaccagna, F., Grist, J., Castelli, M., & Rundo, L. (n.d.). *Brain Tumor Diagnosis Using Machine Learning, Convolutional Neural Networks, Capsule Neural Networks and Vision Transformers, Applied to MRI: A Survey*. Retrieved December 1, 2022, from https://www.mdpi.com/2313-433X/8/8/205

Alotaibi, N., & Rhouma, D. (2022). A review on community structures detection in time evolving social networks. *Journal of King Saud University - Computer and Information Sciences, 34*(8, Part B), 5646–5662. https://doi.org/https://doi.org/10.1016/j.jksuci.2021.08.016

American Geosciences Institute. (2022, November 29). *Can earthquakes be predicted?* Retrieved from American Geosciences Institute: americangeosciences.org/critical-issues/faq/can-earthquakes-be-predicted#:~:text=U.S.%20Geological%20Survey%20FAQs%3A,time%20in%20the%20foreseeable%20future.

Andre, L. (2021, June 15). *You are on the internet almost daily. You check your email, send replies, maybe browse websites and even click.* https://financesonline.com/how-much-data-is-created-every-day/

Anuraj, A., Boparai, G. S., Leung, C. K., Madill, E. W., Pandhi, D. A., Patel, A. D., & Vyas, R. K. (2023, March). Sports data mining for cricket match prediction. In *International Conference on Advanced Information Networking and Applications* (pp. 668-680). Cham: Springer International Publishing. 10.1007/978-3-031-28694-0_63

Azizur Rahman, S. (2020). Mobile for health: A digital intervention to reduce smoking in the United Arab Emirates. *2020 IEEE 44th Annual Computers, Software, and Applications Conference (COMPSAC).* 10.1109/COMPSAC48688.2020.0-171

Bag, A. K., Tudu, B., Roy, J., Bhattacharyya, N., & Bandyopadhyay, R. (2011). Optimization of sensor array in electronic nose: A rough set-based approach. *IEEE Sensors Journal, 11*(11), 3001–3008. doi:10.1109/JSEN.2011.2151186

Bahgat, E. M., Rady, S., Gad, W., & Moawad, I. F. (2018). Efficient email classification approach based on semantic methods. *Ain Shams Engineering Journal, 9*(4), 3259–3269. doi:10.1016/j.asej.2018.06.001

Bajaj, A. (2022, November 14). *Performance Metrics in Machine Learning* [Complete Guide]. Neptune.ai. Retrieved December 5, 2022, from https://neptune.ai/blog/performance-metrics-in-machine-learning-complete-guide#:~:text=Performance%20metrics%20are%20a%20part,a%20metric%20to%20judge%20performance

Banerji, J. N. (1928). *India International Reports of Schools for the Deaf. Washington City.* Volta Bureau.

Baranwal, S., Jaiswal, K., Vaibhav, K., Srikantaswamy, R., & Kumar, A. (2020, September 1). *Performance analysis of Brain Tumour Image Classification using CNN and SVM.* IEEE Xplore. doi:10.1109/ICIRCA48905.2020.9183023

Beheshti, N. (2022). *Guide to Confusion Matrices & Classification Performance Metrics.* Medium. Available at: https://towardsdatascience.com/guide-to-confusion-matrices-classification-performancemetrics-a0ebfc08408e#:~:text=Confusion%20matrices%20can%20be%20used

Benouis, M. (2019). Behavioural smoking identification via hand-movement dynamics. *2019 IEEE SmartWorld, Ubiquitous Intelligence & Computing, Advanced & Trusted Computing, Scalable Computing & Communications, Cloud & Big Data Computing, Internet of People and Smart City Innovation (SmartWorld/SCALCOM/UIC/ATC/CBDCom/IOP/SCI)*. doi:10.1109/SmartWorld-UIC-ATC-SCALCOM-IOP-SCI.2019.00309

Borkowski, K. P.-F. (2020). On the Importance of Train–Test Split Ratio of Datasets in Automatic Landslide Detection by Supervised Classification. *Remote Sensing of Natural Hazards*, 3054.

Borole, V., Nimbhore, S., & Kawthekar, S. (2015, September). Image Processing Techniques for Brain Tumor Detection: A Review. *International Journal of Emerging Trends & Technology in Computer Science*. Retrieved December 4, 2022, from https://www.ijettcs.org/Volume4Issue5(2)/IJETTCS-2015-10-01-7.pdf

Brill, R. (1986). *The Conference of Educational Administrators Serving the Deaf: A History.* Gallaudet University Press.

Brodsky, H. K. (2004). The physics of earphquakes. *Reports on Progress in Physics*, 69.

Brownlee, J. (2017). *A Gentle Introduction to Transfer Learning for Deep Learning.* Machine Learning Mastery. Retrieved April 2, 2023, from https://machinelearningmastery.com/transfer-learning-for-deep-learning

Brownlee, J. (2019, August 12). *Overfitting and Underfitting With Machine Learning Algorithms.* Retrieved from machinelearningmastery: https://machinelearningmastery.com/overfitting-and-underfitting-with-machine-learning-algorithms/

c3.ai. (2022, November 23). *Root Mean Square Error (RMSE).* Retrieved from c3.ai: https://c3.ai/glossary/data-science/root-mean-square-error-rmse/

Chaudhri, S. N. (2022). *Novel intelligent signal processing approaches for performance enhancement of gas sensor nodes suitable for near real-time resource-constrained scenarios* [Doctoral dissertation]. IIT (BHU).

Chaudhri, S. N., & Rajput, N. S. (2021). Mirror Mosaicking: A Novel Approach to Achieve High-performance Classification of Gases Leveraging Convolutional Neural Network. SENSORNETS, 86-91. doi:10.5220/0010251500860091

Chaudhri, S. N., & Rajput, N. S. (2022). Multidimensional Multiconvolution-Based Feature Extraction Approach for Drift Tolerant Robust Classifier for Gases/Odors. *IEEE Sensors Letters*, 6(4), 1–4. doi:10.1109/LSENS.2022.3153832

Chaudhri, S. N., Rajput, N. S., Alsamhi, S. H., Shvetsov, A. V., & Almalki, F. A. (2022). Zero-padding and spatial augmentation-based gas sensor node optimization approach in resource-constrained 6G-IoT paradigm. *Sensors (Basel)*, 22(8), 3039. doi:10.339022083039 PMID:35459024

Chaudhri, S. N., Rajput, N. S., & Mishra, A. (2022). A novel principal component-based virtual sensor approach for efficient classification of gases/odors. *Journal of Electrical Engineering*, 73(2), 108–115. doi:10.2478/jee-2022-0014

Chaudhri, S. N., Rajput, N. S., & Singh, K. P. (2020). The Novel Camouflaged False Color Composites for the Vegetation Verified by Novel Sample Level Mirror Mosaicking Based Convolutional Neural Network. *IEEE India Geoscience and Remote Sensing Symposium (InGARSS)*, 237-240. 10.1109/InGARSS48198.2020.9358926

Chaudhri, S. N., Rajput, N. S., Singh, K. P., & Singh, D. (2021). Mirror Mosaicking Based Reduced Complexity Approach for the Classification of Hyperspectral Images. *IEEE International Geoscience and Remote Sensing Symposium IGARSS*, 3657-3660. 10.1109/IGARSS47720.2021.9554276

Chaya. (2020, June 9). *Random Forest Regression*. Retrieved from Level Up Coding: https://levelup.gitconnected.com/random-forest-regression-209c0f354c84#:~:text=Random%20Forest%20Regression%20is%20a%20supervised%20learning%20algorithm%20that%20uses,prediction%20than%20a%20single%20model

Chen, Q., Wu, W., Zhao, T., Tan, W., Tian, J., & Liang, C. (2019). Complex Gene Regulation Underlying Mineral Nutrient Homeostasis in Soybean Root Response to Acidity Stress. *Genes*, *10*(5), 402. Advance online publication. doi:10.3390/genes10050402 PMID:31137896

Choden, P., Seesaard, T., Dorji, U., Sriphrapradang, C., & Kerdcharoen, T. (2017). Urine odor detection by electronic nose for smart toilet application. *IEEE 14th International Conference on Electrical Engineering/Electronics, Computer, Telecommunications and Information Technology (ECTI-CON)*, 190-193. 10.1109/ECTICon.2017.8096205

Chollet, F. (2017). *Deep Learning with Python*. http://cds.cern.ch/record/2301910

Chowdhury, M. (2022). *Limitations Of Facial Recognition In Today's World*. Retrieved October 31, 2022, from https://www.analyticsinsight.net/limitations-of-facial-recognition-technology-in-todays-world/

Chowdhury, S., & Schoen, M. P. (2020, October 2). *Research Paper Classification using Supervised Machine Learning Techniques*. ResearchGate. https://www.researchgate.net/publication/346853360_Research_Paper_Classification_using_Supe rvised_Machine_Learning_Techniques?enrichId=rgreq-1c98526e9543b39049d181d973ede8c2- XXX&enric hSource=Y292ZXJQYWdlOzM0Njg1MzM2MDtBUzoxMDUxMTgzNTY1MjY2OTQ1Q DE2Mjc2MzMxMDA0ODI%3D&el=1_x_3&_esc=publicationCoverPdf

Clauset, A., Newman, M. E. J., & Moore, C. (2004). Finding community structure in very large networks. *Physical Review E: Statistical Physics, Plasmas, Fluids, and Related Interdisciplinary Topics*, *70*(6), 6. doi:10.1103/PhysRevE.70.066111 PMID:15697438

Cock, P. J. A., Antao, T., Chang, J. T., Chapman, B., Cox, C. J., Dalke, A., Friedberg, I., Hamelryck, T., Kauff, F., Wilczyński, B., & De Hoon, M. (2009). Biopython: Freely available Python tools for computational molecular biology and bioinformatics. *Bioinformatics (Oxford, England)*, *25*(11), 1422–1423. doi:10.1093/bioinformatics/btp163 PMID:19304878

Cole, M., Covington, J. A., & Gardner, J. W. (2011). Combined electronic nose and tongue for a flavour sensing system. *Sensors and Actuators. B, Chemical, 156*(2), 832–839. doi:10.1016/j.snb.2011.02.049

Cukierski, W. (2015). *The Enron Email Dataset.* Kaggle.com. https://www.kaggle.com/datasets/wcukierski/enron-email-dataset

Dakhel, A. M., Majdinasab, V., Nikanjam, A., Khomh, F., Desmarais, M. C., & Jiang, Z. M. J. (2023). Github copilot ai pair programmer: Asset or liability? *Journal of Systems and Software, 203*, 111734. doi:10.1016/j.jss.2023.111734

Das, B., & Chakraborty, S. (n.d.). *An Improved Text Sentiment Classification Model Using TF IDF and Next Word Negation. https://arxiv.org/pdf/1806.06407.pdf*

Das, N. R., Mukherjee, I., Patel, A. D., & Paul, G. (2023). An intelligent clustering framework for substitute recommendation and player selection. *The Journal of Supercomputing*, 1–33. doi:10.100711227-023-05314-z PMID:37359323

de Arriba-Pérez, F., Caeiro-Rodríguez, M., & Santos-Gago, J. (2016). Collection and processing of data from wrist wearable devices in heterogeneous and multiple-user scenarios. *Sensors (Basel), 16*(9), 1538. doi:10.339016091538 PMID:27657081

Dhole, N., & Dixit, V. (2022). *Review of brain tumor detection from MRI images with hybrid approaches.* Springer Link. Retrieved December 2, 2022, from https://linkspringer-com.ezproxy.uow.edu.au/article/10.1007/s11042-022-12162-1

Divya Khyani, & S, S. B. (2021, January 7). *An Interpretation of Lemmatization and Stemming in Natural Language Processing.* ResearchGate. https://www.researchgate.net/publication/348306833_An_Interpretation_of_Lemmatization_and_ Stemming_in_Natural_Language_Processing#:~:text=What%20is%20Lemmatization%3F,adds%20meaning%20to%20particular%20words

Drobot, A. T. (2020). Industrial Transformation and the Digital Revolution: A Focus on Artificial Intelligence, Data Science and Data Engineering. IEEE, ITU Kaleidoscope: Industry-Driven Digital Transformation (ITU K), 1-11.

Dua, D., & Graff, C. (2019). *UCI machine learning repository.* School of Information and Computer Science, University of California. Available http://archive.ics.uci.edu/ml

Dulčić, L. (2019). *Face Recognition with FaceNet and MTCNN.* Retrieved November 1, 2022, from https://arsfutura.com/magazine/face-recognition-with-facenet-and-mtcnn/

Enders, F. B. (2022, October 4). *coefficient of determination.* Retrieved from Encyclopedia Britannica: https://www.britannica.com/science/coefficient-of-determination

Engineering Statistics Handbook. (2019). *7.1.6. What are outliers in the data?* Nist.gov. Available at: https://www.itl.nist.gov/div898/handbook/prc/section1/prc16.htm

Estakhroueiyeh, H. R., & Rashedi, E. (2015). Detecting moldy Bread using an E-nose and the KNN classifier. *IEEE 5th International Conference on Computer and Knowledge Engineering (ICCKE),* 251-255. 10.1109/ICCKE.2015.7365836

Finkelstein, J., & Wood, J. (2013). Interactive Mobile System for Smoking Cessation. *2013 35th Annual International Conference of the IEEE Engineering in Medicine and Biology Society (EMBC).* Available at: 10.1109/EMBC.2013.6609714

finnstats. (2022, September 7). *Importance of Data Cleaning in Machine Learning.* Retrieved from R-bloggers: https://www.r-bloggers.com/2022/09/importance-of-data-cleaning-in-machine-learning/#:~:text=Data%20cleansing%20is%20essential%20because,every%20situation%20you%20might%20encounter

Fonollosa, J., Fernandez, L., Gutiérrez-Gálvez, A., Huerta, R., & Marco, S. (2016). Calibration transfer and drift counteraction in chemical sensor arrays using Direct Standardization. *Sensors and Actuators. B, Chemical, 236,* 1044–1053. doi:10.1016/j.snb.2016.05.089

freeCodeCamp.org. (2018). *An intuitive guide to Convolutional Neural Networks.* Available at: https://www.freecodecamp.org/news/an-intuitive-guide-to-convolutional-neural-networks260c2de0a050/#:~:text=The%20term%20convolution%20refers%20to

Frost, J. (2022, November 21). *Mean Squared Error (MSE).* Retrieved from Statstics By Jim: https://statisticsbyjim.com/regression/mean-squared-error-mse/

Gardner, J. W. (1991). Detection of vapours and odours from a multisensor array using pattern recognition Part 1. Principal component and cluster analysis. *Sensors and Actuators. B, Chemical, 4*(1-2), 109–115. doi:10.1016/0925-4005(91)80185-M

Garg, B. (2022). *Design and Development of Naive Bayes Classifier.* Ndsu.edu. https://doi.org/ http://hdl.handle.net/10365/23048

Ghaffari, R., Zhang, F., Iliescu, D., Hines, E., Leeson, M., Napier, R., & Clarkson, J. (2010). Early detection of diseases in tomato crops: An electronic nose and intelligent systems approach. *IEEE International Joint Conference on Neural Networks (IJCNN),* 1-6. 10.1109/IJCNN.2010.5596535

Ghamisi, P., Benediktsson, J. A., & Ulfarsson, M. O. (2013). Spectral–spatial classification of hyperspectral images based on hidden Markov random fields. *IEEE Transactions on Geoscience and Remote Sensing, 52*(5), 2565–2574. doi:10.1109/TGRS.2013.2263282

Gholam Hosseini, H., Luo, D., Liu, H., & Xu, G. (2007). Intelligent processing of E-nose information for fish freshness assessment. *IEEE 3rd International Conference on Intelligent Sensors, Sensor Networks and Information,* 173-177.

Goldbloom, A. (2010, October 1). *Kaggle.* Kaggle. Retrieved February 27, 2023, from https:// www.kaggle.com/

Great Learning Team. (2022, November 18). *Mean Squared Error – Explained | What is Mean Square Error?* Retrieved from Great learning: https://www.mygreatlearning.com/blog/mean-square-error-explained/

Grogan, M. (2021). *CNN-LSTM: Predicting Daily Hotel Cancellations*. Medium. Available at: https://towardsdatascience.com/cnn-lstm-predicting-daily-hotel-cancellations-e1c75697f124#:~:text=Forecasting%20without%20LSTM%20layer

Gull, S., Akbar, S., & Shoukat, I. A. (2021, November). A Deep Transfer Learning Approach for Automated Detection of Brain Tumor Through Magnetic Resonance Imaging. In *2021 International Conference on Innovative Computing (ICIC)* (pp. 1-6). IEEE. 10.1109/ICIC53490.2021.9692967

Gunawardhana, L. G. U. P. (2022). *Optimising Cricket Team Selection for One Day International Series Based on Match Conditions* [Doctoral dissertation].

Guo, T., Dong, J., Li, H., & Gao, Y. (2020, March 10). *Simple Convolutional Neural Network on Image Classification*. IEEE Xplore. Retrieved December 28, 2022, from doi:10.1109/ICBDA.2017.8078730

Haralabopoulos, G., Anagnostopoulos, L., & McAuley, D. (2020). *Ensemble Deep Learning for Multilabel Binary Classification of User-Generated Content*. Retrieved May 6, 2023, from https://www.mdpi.com/1999-4893/13/4/83

Hassan, D. (2017). Investigating the Effect of Combining Text Clustering with Classification on Improving Spam Email Detection. In Intelligent Systems Design and Applications (Vol. 557, pp. 120–128). essay, Springer International Publishing AG 2017. doi:10.1007/978-3-319-53480-0_10

Hassan, H., Shafri, H., & Habshi, M. (2019). A Comparison Between Support Vector Machine (SVM) and Convolutional Neural Network (CNN) Models For Hyperspectral Image Classification. *IOP Conference Series: Earth and Environmental Science*. Retrieved December 20, 2022, from 10.1088/1755-1315/357/1/012035

Hassan, M., Mirza, W., & Hussain. (2017). Header Based Spam Filtering Using Machine Learning Approach. *International Journal of Emerging Technologies in Engineering Research, 5*. https://www.ijeter.everscience.org/Manuscripts/Volume-5/Issue-10/Vol-5-issue-10-M-21.pdf

Hoffheins, B. S. (1990). *Using sensor arrays and pattern recognition to identify organic compounds (No. ORNL/TM-11310). Oak Ridge National Lab*. ORNL. doi:10.2172/6875143

Horning, N. (2010). *Random Forests: An algorithm for image classification and generation of continuous fields data sets*. American Museum of Natural History Center for Biodiversity and Conservation.

Huang, X., Chen, D., Ren, T., & Wang, D. (2021). A survey of community detection methods in multilayer networks. *Data Mining and Knowledge Discovery, 35*(1), 1–45. doi:10.100710618-020-00716-6

Hunter, J. (2007). MatPlotLib: A 2D Graphics environment. *Computing in Science & Engineering, 9*(3), 90–95. doi:10.1109/MCSE.2007.55

IMAGENET. (2014). *Large Scale Visual Recognition Challenge 2014*. Retrieved May 2, 2023, from https://image-net.org/challenges/LSVRC/2014/results

Ismael, R., & Abdel-Qader, I. (2018). Brain Tumor Classification via Sta-tistical Features and Back-Propagation Neural Network. *2018 IEEE International Conference on Electro/Information Technology (EIT),* 252-257. 10.1109/EIT.2018.8500308

Jarvis, R. M., Broadhurst, D., Johnson, H. E., O'Boyle, N. M., & Goodacre, R. (2006). PYCHEM: A multivariate analysis package for python. *Bioinformatics (Oxford, England), 22*(20), 2565–2566. doi:10.1093/bioinformatics/btl416 PMID:16882648

Jia, Z., & Chen, D. (n.d.). *Brain Tumor Identification and Classification of MRI images using deep learning techniques.* IEEE Xplore. Retrieved December 5, 2022, from https://ieeexplore.ieee.org/stamp/stamp.jsp?arnumber=9166580

Jihye Han, J. K. (2020, September). Seismic Vulnerability Assessment and Mapping of Gyeongju, South Korea Using Frequency Ratio, Decision Tree, and Random Forest. *MDPI, 22.*

Joseph, R. (2018, December 30). *Grid Search for model tuning.* Towards Data Science. Retrieved December 1, 2022, from https://towardsdatascience.com/grid-search-for-model-tuning-3319b259367e

Kaluarachchi, A., & Aparna, S. V. (2010, December). CricAI: A classification based tool to predict the outcome in ODI cricket. In *2010 Fifth International Conference on Information and Automation for Sustainability* (pp. 250-255). IEEE. 10.1109/ICIAFS.2010.5715668

Kang, S., Zhang, Q., Li, Z., Yin, C., Feng, N., & Shi, Y. (2023). Determination of the quality of tea from different picking periods: An adaptive pooling attention mechanism coupled with an electronic nose. *Postharvest Biology and Technology, 197,* 112214. doi:10.1016/j.postharvbio.2022.112214

Karlos, S., Kostopoulos, G., & Kotsiantis, S. (2020). *A Soft-Voting Ensemble Based Co-Training Scheme Using Static Selection for Binary Classification Problems.* Retrieved May 6, 2023, from https://www.mdpi.com/1999-4893/13/1/26

Khan, A., Nazarian, H., Golilarz, N., Addeh, A., Li, J., & Khan, G. (2021, January 15). *Brain Tumor Classification Using Efficient Deep Features of MRI Scans and Support Vector Machine.* IEEE Xplore. Retrieved December 5, 2022, from https://ieeexplore.ieee.org/abstract/document/9317509

Khan, M. S., Wahab, A. W. A., Herawan, T., Mujtaba, G., Danjuma, S., & Al-Garadi, M. A. (2016). Virtual Community Detection Through the Association between Prime Nodes in Online Social Networks and Its Application to Ranking Algorithms. *IEEE Access: Practical Innovations, Open Solutions, 4,* 9614–9624. doi:10.1109/ACCESS.2016.2639563

Khan, M., & Shah, R. (2015). Role of external factors on outcome of a One Day International cricket (ODI) match and predictive analysis. *International Journal of Advanced Research in Computer and Communication Engineering, 4*(6), 192–197.

Kim, S.-W., & Gil, J.-M. (2019). Research paper classification systems based on TF-IDF and LDA schemes. *Human-Centric Computing and Information Sciences, 9*(1). doi:10.1186/s13673-019-0192-7

Kumar, T., Rashmi, K., Ramadoss, S., Sandhya, L., & Sangeetha, T. (2017, October 19). *Brain tumor detection using SVM classifier*. IEEE Xplore. Retrieved December 3, 2022, from https://ieeexplore-ieee-org.ezproxy.uow.edu.au/stamp/stamp.jsp?tp=&arnumber=8071613

Kumari, A., & Shashi, M. (2019, August). *Vectorization of Text Documents for Identifying Unifiable News Articles*. SAI Organization. https://www.researchgate.net/publication/334884108_Vectorization_of_Text_Documents_for_Iden tifying_Unifiable_News_Articles

Lancichinetti, A., & Fortunato, S. (2009). Benchmarks for testing community detection algorithms on directed and weighted graphs with overlapping communities. *Physical Review E: Statistical, Nonlinear, and Soft Matter Physics*, *80*(1), 16118. doi:10.1103/PhysRevE.80.016118 PMID:19658785

LeCun, Y., Bottou, L., Bengio, Y., & Haffner, P. (1998). Gradient-based learning applied to document recognition. *Proceedings of the IEEE*, *86*(11), 2278–2324. doi:10.1109/5.726791

Li, S., Jiang, L., Wu, X., Han, W., Zhao, D., & Wang, Z. (2021). A weighted network community detection algorithm based on deep learning. *Applied Mathematics and Computation*, *401*, 126012. doi:10.1016/j.amc.2021.126012

Li, S., Zhao, D., Wu, X., Tian, Z., Li, A., & Wang, Z. (2020). Functional immunization of networks based on message passing. *Applied Mathematics and Computation*, *366*, 124728. doi:10.1016/j.amc.2019.124728

Liu, Q., Wei, J., Liu, H., & Ji, Y. (2023). A Hierarchical Parallel Graph Summarization Approach Based on Ranking Nodes. *Applied Sciences (Basel, Switzerland)*, *13*(8), 4664. Advance online publication. doi:10.3390/app13084664

Llobet, E., Brezmes, J., Vilanova, X., Sueiras, J. E., & Correig, X. (1997). Qualitative and quantitative analysis of volatile organic compounds using transient and steady-state responses of a thick-film tin oxide gas sensor array. *Sensors and Actuators. B, Chemical*, *41*(1-3), 13–21. doi:10.1016/S0925-4005(97)80272-9

Lutins, E. (2017). *Ensemble Methods in Machine Learning: What are They and Why use Them?* Retrieved April 2, 2023, from https://towardsdatascience.com/ensemble-methods-in-machine-learning-what-are-they-and-why-use-them-68ec3f9fef5f

Martins, G. (2021). *Earthquakes for ML prediction*. Retrieved from Kaggle: https://www.kaggle.com/datasets/gustavobmgm/earthquakes-for-ml-prediction

Matthew, A., Tan, K., Suharyo, P., & Gunawan, A. (2022, July 25). *A Systematic Literature Review: Image Segmentation on Brain MRI Image to Detect Brain Tumor*. IEEE Xplore. Retrieved December 1, 2022, from https://ieeexplore-ieee-org.ezproxy.uow.edu.au/stamp/stamp.jsp?tp=&arnumber=9829177

McKinney, W. (2011). Pandas: A Foundational Python Library for Data Analysis and Statistics. *Python High Performance Science Computer*. https://www.dlr.de/sc/en/Portaldata/15/Resources/dokumente/pyhpc2011/submissions/pyhpc2011_submission_9.pdf

McKinney, W. (2012). *Python for data analysis*. O'Reilly Media, Inc. eBooks. http://ci.nii.ac.jp/ncid/BB11531826

McKinney, W. (2010). Data structures for statistical computing in Python. *Proceedings of the Python in Science Conferences*. 10.25080/Majora-92bf1922-00a

Metsis, V., & Paliouras, G. (2006). *Spam Filtering with Naive Bayes -Which Naive Bayes?* https://userweb.cs.txstate.edu/~v_m137/docs/papers/ceas2006_paper_corrected.pdf

Miglani, A., Madan, H., Kumar, S., & Kumar, S. (2021). *A Literature Review on Brain Tumor Detection and Segmentation*. IEEE Xplore. Retrieved December 3, 2022, from https://ieeexplore-ieee-org.ezproxy.uow.edu.au/stamp/stamp.jsp?tp=&arnumber=9432342

Mishra, A., & Rajput, N. S. (2018). A novel modular ANN architecture for efficient monitoring of gases/odours in real-time. *Materials Research Express*, 5(4), 045904. doi:10.1088/2053-1591/aabe09

Mishra, A., Rajput, N. S., & Han, G. (2017). NDSRT: An efficient virtual multi-sensor response transformation for classification of gases/odors. *IEEE Sensors Journal*, 17(11), 3416–3421. doi:10.1109/JSEN.2017.2690536

Mishra, A., Rajput, N. S., & Singh, D. (2018). Performance evaluation of normalized difference-based classifier for efficient discrimination of volatile organic compounds. *Materials Research Express*, 5(9), 095901. doi:10.1088/2053-1591/aad3dd

Mittal, H., Rikhari, D., Kumar, J., & Singh, A. K. (2021). *A study on machine learning approaches for player performance and match results prediction*. arXiv preprint arXiv:2108.10125.

Mohan, B. A. (2021). Breatheasy - An Android application to quit the smoking. *2021 IEEE International Conference on Distributed Computing, VLSI, Electrical Circuits and Robotics (DISCOVER)*. Available at: 10.1109/DISCOVER52564.2021.9663588

Mohanakrishnan, R. (2021). *Top 11 Facial Recognition Software in 2021*. Retrieved June 20, 2023, from https://www.spiceworks.com/it-security/identity-access-management/articles/facial-recognition-software/

Mondal, A., & Shrivastava, V. K. (2022). A novel Parametric Flatten-p Mish activation function based deep CNN model for brain tumor classification. *Computers in Biology and Medicine*, 150, 106183. doi:10.1016/j.compbiomed.2022.106183

Mondol, M. (2021). *Analysis and Prediction of Earthquakes using different Machine Learning techniques*. University of Twente.

Moore, S. W., Gardner, J. W., Hines, E. L., Göpel, W., & Weimar, U. (1993). A modified multilayer perceptron model for gas mixture analysis. *Sensors and Actuators. B, Chemical*, 16(1-3), 344–348. doi:10.1016/0925-4005(93)85207-Q

Muhammad, A. N., Bukhori, S., & Pandunata, P. (2019). Sentiment Analysis of Positive and Negative of YouTube Comments Using Naïve Bayes – Support Vector Machine (NBSVM) Classifier. *2019 International Conference on Computer Science, Information Technology, and Electrical Engineering (ICOMITEE)*. 10.1109/ICOMITEE.2019.8920923

Munib, Q., Habeeb, M., Takruri, B., & Al-Malik, H. A. (2007). American Sign Language (ASL) recognition based on Hough transform and neural networks. *Expert Systems with Applications*, *32*(1), 24–37. doi:10.1016/j.eswa.2005.11.018

Nagpal, Mitra, & Agrawal. (n.d.). Design Issue and Proposed Implementation of Communication Aid for Deaf & Dumb People. *International Journal on Recent and Innovation Trends in Computing and Communication, 3*(5), 147-149.

Nur, Marthasari, & Nuarini. (2020). Optimization of Sentiment Analysis for Indonesian Presidential Election using Naïve Bayes and Particle Swarm Optimization. *Jurnal Online Informatika, 5*(1), 81–88. https://join.if.uinsgd.ac.id/index.php/join/article/view/558/148

Olha Tanyuk, D. D. (2019). Machine Learning Predicts Aperiodic Laboratory Earthquakes. *SMU Data Science Review*, 20.

Ortis, A., Caponnetto, P., Polosa, R., Urso, S., & Battiato, S. (2020). A report on smoking detection and quitting technologies. *International Journal of Environmental Research and Public Health*, *17*(7), 2614. doi:10.3390/ijerph17072614 PMID:32290288

Palla, G., Der'enyi, I., Farkas, I., & Vicsek, T. (2005). Uncovering the overlapping community structure of complex networks in nature and society. *Nature*, *435*(7043), 814–818. doi:10.1038/nature03607 PMID:15944704

Pannakkong, W., Thiwa-Anont, K., Singthong, K., Parthanadee, P., & Buddhakulsomsiri, J. (2022, January). Hyperparameter Tuning of Machine Learning Algorithms Using Response Surface Methodology: A Case Study of ANN, SVM, and DBN. *Mathematical Problems in Engineering*, *2022*, 1–17. doi:10.1155/2022/8513719

Pan, X., Chen, J., Wen, X., Hao, J., Xu, W., Ye, W., & Zhao, X. (2023). A comprehensive gas recognition algorithm with label-free drift compensation based on domain adversarial network. *Sensors and Actuators. B, Chemical*, *387*, 133709. doi:10.1016/j.snb.2023.133709

Papiya Debnath, P. C. (2021, January 19). Analysis of Earthquake Forecasting in India Using Supervised Machine Learning Classifiers. *MDPI*, 13.

Parmar, N., Sharma, A., Jain, H., & Kadam. (2020). Email Spam Detection using Naïve Bayes and Particle Swarm Optimization. *International Journal of Innovative Research in Technology*, 1–7.

Pashaei, A., Sajedi, H., & Jazayeri, N. (2018). Brain Tumor Classification via Convolutional Neural Network and Extreme Learning Machines. *2018 8th International Conference on Computer and Knowledge Engineering (ICCKE)*, 314-319. 10.1109/ICCKE.2018.8566571

Pedregosa, F., Varoquaux, G., Gramfort, A., Michel, V., Thirion, B., Grisel, O., Blondel, M., Prettenhofer, P., Weiss, R., Dubourg, V., Vanderplas, J., Passos, A., Cournapeau, D., Brucher, M., Perrot, M., & Duchesnay, E. (2011). SciKit-Learn: Machine Learning in Python. *HAL (Le Centre Pour La Communication Scientifique Directe)*. https://hal.inria.fr/hal-00650905

Piatetsky-Shapiro, G. (2013). *KDnuggets*. Data Science and AI Consulting. http://www.kdnuggets.com/2013/06/kdnugg ets-annual-software-poll-rapidminer-r-viefor-first-place. html

Pintelas, P., & Livieris, L. E. (2020). *Special Issue on Ensemble Learning and Applications.* Retrieved May 6, 2023, from https://www.mdpi.com/1999-4893/13/6/140

Prakash, C. D., Patvardhan, C., & Lakshmi, C. V. (2016). Data analytics based deep mayo predictor for IPL-9. *International Journal of Computer Applications, 152*(6), 6–10. doi:10.5120/ijca2016911080

Preetha, R., & Suresh, G. (2014). *Performance Analysis of Fuzzy C Means Algorithm in Automated Detection of Brain Tumor.* IEEE Xplore. Retrieved December 1, 2022, from https://ieeexplore-ieee-org.ezproxy.uow.edu.au/stamp/stamp.jsp?tp=&arnumber=6755100

Priya, S., Gupta, A. K., Dwivedi, A., & Prabhakar, A. (2022, April). Analysis and Winning Prediction in T20 Cricket using Machine Learning. In *2022 Second International Conference on Advances in Electrical, Computing, Communication and Sustainable Technologies (ICAECT)* (pp. 1-4). IEEE. 10.1109/ICAECT54875.2022.9807929

Rajput, N. S., Das, R. R., Mishra, V. N., Singh, K. P., & Dwivedi, R. (2010). A neural net implementation of SPCA pre-processor for gas/odor classification using the responses of thick film gas sensor array. *Sensors and Actuators. B, Chemical, 148*(2), 550–558. doi:10.1016/j.snb.2010.05.051

Raschka, S. (2014). *Naive Bayes and Text Classification I Introduction and Theory.* https://arxiv.org/pdf/1410.5329.pdf

Rasmussen, B. (2010, October 1). *ESPNcricinfo*. ESPNcricinfo. Retrieved February 27, 2023, from https://www.espncricinfo.com/

Reader, T. C. (2021, October 19). *Random Forest Regression Explained with Implementation in Python.* Retrieved from The Medium: https://medium.com/@theclickreader/random-forest-regression-explained-with-implementation-in-python-3dad88caf165

Reback, J., & McKinney, W. (2020). pandas-dev/pandas: Pandas 1.0.5. Zenodo. doi:10.5281/zenodo.3898987

Reback J. McKinney W. Van Den Bossche J. Augspurger T. Cloud P. Klein A. Seabold S. (2020). pandas-dev/pandas: Pandas 1.0. 5. Zenodo.

RECFACES BLOG. (n.d.). *What Is AI Facial Recognition Tech and How does It Work?* Retrieved October 23, 2022, from https://recfaces.com/articles/ai-facial-recognition

Rehman, A. U., Belhaouari, S. B., Ijaz, M., Bermak, A., & Hamdi, M. (2020). Multi-classifier tree with transient features for drift compensation in electronic nose. *IEEE Sensors Journal*, *21*(5), 6564–6574. doi:10.1109/JSEN.2020.3041949

Rish, I. (2001). *An Empirical Study of the Naïve Bayes Classifier*. ResearchGate. https://www.researchgate.net/publication/228845263_An_Empirical_Study_of_the_Naive_Bayes_Classifier

Rodriguez-Lujan, I., Fonollosa, J., Vergara, A., Homer, M., & Huerta, R. (2014). On the calibration of sensor arrays for pattern recognition using the minimal number of experiments. *Chemometrics and Intelligent Laboratory Systems*, *130*, 123–134. doi:10.1016/j.chemolab.2013.10.012

Rossant, C. (2014). *IPython Interactive Computing and Visualization Cookbook*. https://scholarvox.library.inseec-u.com/catalog/book/docid/88851238?_locale=fr

Roxane Mallouhy, C. A. (2019). *Major earthquake event prediction using various machine learning algorithms*. Paris: HAL Open Science.

Sahmoud, T., & Mikki, M. (2022). *Spam Detection Using BERT*. Retrieved November 30, 2022, from https://arxiv.org/ftp/arxiv/papers/2206/2206.02443.pdf

Sanaeifar, A., Mohtasebi, S., Ghasemi-Varnamkhasti, M., Ahmadi, H., & Lozano Rogado, J. S. (2014). *Development and application of a new low-cost electronic nose for the ripeness monitoring of banana using computational techniques (PCA, LDA, SIMCA, and SVM)*. Available: (http://hdl.handle.net/10662/4367

Santos, D., & Santos, E. (2022, January 25). *Brain Tumor Detection Using Deep Learning*. Medrxiv. Retrieved December 5, 2022, from https://www.medrxiv.org/content/medrxiv/early/2022/01/25/2022.01.19.22269457.full.pdf

Sari, I. M., Wijaya, D. R., Hidayat, W., & Kannan, R. (2021). An approach to classify rice quality using electronic nose dataset-based Naïve bayes classifier. *IEEE International Symposium on Electronics and Smart Devices (ISESD)*, 1-5. 10.1109/ISESD53023.2021.9501909

Satyanarayan, A., Moritz, D., Wongsuphasawat, K., & Heer, J. (2017). Vega-Lite: A grammar of interactive Graphics. *IEEE Transactions on Visualization and Computer Graphics*, *23*(1), 341–350. doi:10.1109/TVCG.2016.2599030 PMID:27875150

Senyurek, V., Imtiaz, M., Belsare, P., Tiffany, S., & Sazonov, E. (2019). Cigarette smoking detection with an inertial sensor and a smart lighter. *Sensors (Basel)*, *19*(3), 570. doi:10.339019030570 PMID:30700056

Serengil. (2023). *RetinaFace: Deep Face Detection Library for Python*. Retrieved April 2, 2023, from https://github.com/serengil/retinaface

Shekhar, S., Bansode, A., & Salim, A. (2022, January). *A Comparative study of Hyper-Parameter Optimization Tools*. https://arxiv.org/pdf/2201.06433.pdf

Simonyan, K., & Zisserman, A. (2015). *Very deep convolutional networks for large-scale image recognition*. Retrieved May 2, 2023, from https://arxiv.org/pdf/1409.1556.pdf

Simplilearn. (2021). *What Is Keras: The Best Introductory Guide To Keras*. Retrieved October 31, 2022, from https://www.simplilearn.com/tutorials/deep-learning-tutorial/what-is-keras

Soni, A. N. (2019). Spam e-mail detection using advanced deep convolution neural network algorithms. Journal for Innovative Development in Pharmaceutical and Technical Science.

Srivastava, S., Chaudhri, S. N., Rajput, N. S., Alsamhi, S. H., & Shvetsov, A. V. (2023). Spatial Upscaling-Based Algorithm for Detection and Estimation of Hazardous Gases. *IEEE Access : Practical Innovations, Open Solutions*, *11*, 17731–17738. doi:10.1109/ACCESS.2023.3245041

Srivastava, S., Chaudhri, S. N., Rajput, N. S., & Mishra, A. (2023). A novel data-driven technique to produce multi-sensor virtual responses for gas sensor array-based electronic noses. *Journal of Electrical Engineering*, *74*(2), 102–108. doi:10.2478/jee-2023-0013

Staff, N. C. I. (2020, February 12). *Artificial Intelligence Expedites Brain Tumor Diagnosis during Surgery*. National Cancer Institution. Retrieved December 5, 2022, from https://www.cancer.gov/news-events/cancer-currents-blog/2020/artificial-intelligence-brain-tumor-diagnosis-surgery

Stasha, S. (2022, September 29). *Earthquake Statistics And Facts For 2022*. Retrieved from Policy Advice: https://policyadvice.net/insurance/insights/earthquake-statistics/

Statistics How To. (2022, November 15). *RMSE: Root Mean Square Error*. Retrieved from Statistics How To: https://www.statisticshowto.com/probability-and-statistics/regression-analysis/rmse-root-mean-square-error/

Sunasra, M. (2017, November 11). *Performance Metrics for Classification problems in Machine Learning*. Medium. Retrieved December 4, 2022, from https://medium.com/@MohammedS/performance-metrics-for-classification-problems-in-machine-learning-part-i-b085d432082b

Suneratech. (2021). *What Is AI, ML & How They Are Applied to Facial Recognition Technology*. Retrieved October 23, 2022, from https://www.suneratech.com/blog/ai-ml-and-how-they-are-applied-to-facial-recognition-technology/

Sungheetha, A., & Sharma, R. R. (2020). GTIKF- Gabor-Transform Incorporated K-Means and Fuzzy C Means Clustering for Edge Detection in CT and MRI. *Journal of Soft Computing Paradigm*. doi:10.36548/jscp.2020.2.004

Sunitha, K. A. (2016). Deaf Mute Communication Interpreter-A Review. *International Journal of Applied Engineering Research*, *11*, 290–296.

Suryapriya, A. K., Sumam, S., & Idicula, M. (2009). Design and Development of a Frame based MT System for English to ISL. *World Congress on Nature and Biologically Inspired Computing*, 1382-1387.

Tan, M., & Le, Q. (2019). EfficientNet: Rethinking Model Scaling for Convolutional Neural Networks. *Proceedings of Machine Learning Research*. Retrieved May 2, 2023, from https://proceedings.mlr.press/v97/tan19a.html.

Tatman, R. (2017). *Fraudulent E-mail Corpus*. Kaggle.com. https://www.kaggle.com/datasets/rtatman/fraudulent-email-corpus

Team, C. F. I. (2022, November 27). *Histogram*. Retrieved from Corporate Finance Institute: https://corporatefinanceinstitute.com/resources/excel/histogram/

Text Classification. (2014). What it is And Why it Matters. *MonkeyLearn*. https://monkeylearn.com/text- classification/

Turney, S. (2022, September 14). *Coefficient of Determination (R²) | Calculation & Interpretation*. Retrieved from scribbr: https://www.scribbr.com/statistics/coefficient-of-determination/#:~:text=What%20is%20the%20definition%20of,predicted%20by%20the%20statistical%20model

U.S. Geological Survey. (2016, November 30). *Predicting Earthquakes*. Retrieved from USGS: https://pubs.usgs.gov/gip/earthq1/predict.html#:~:text=The%20goal%20of%20earthquake%20prediction,the%20likelihood%20of%20future%20earthquakes

Ucuzal, H., Yasar, S., & Colak, C. (2019, December 16). *Classification of brain tumor types by deep learning with convolutional neural network on magnetic resonance images using a developed web-based interface*. IEEE Xplore. Retrieved December 5, 2022, from https://ieeexplore-ieee-org.ezproxy.uow.edu.au/stamp/stamp.jsp?tp=&arnumber=8932761

Vanderplas, J. (2016). *Python Data Science Handbook: Essential Tools for Working with Data*. http://cds.cern.ch/record/2276771

Vani, N., Sowmya, A., & Jayamma, N. (2017, July 7). Brain Tumor Classification using Support Vector Machine. *International Research Journal of Engineering and Technology*. Retrieved December 5, 2022, from https://www.irjet.net/archives/V4/i7/IRJET-V4I7367.pdf

Vergara, A., Vembu, S., Ayhan, T., Ryan, M. A., Homer, M. L., & Huerta, R. (2012). Chemical gas sensor drift compensation using classifier ensembles. *Sensors and Actuators. B, Chemical*, *166*, 320–329. doi:10.1016/j.snb.2012.01.074

Vestly, D. J., Hariharan, S., Kukreja, V., Prasad, A. B., Swaraj, K., & Gopichand, D. (2023, May). Parametric Analysis of a Cricketer's Performance using Machine Learning Approach. In *2023 7th International Conference on Intelligent Computing and Control Systems (ICICCS)* (pp. 344-348). IEEE. 10.1109/ICICCS56967.2023.10142664

Vistro, D. M., Rasheed, F., & David, L. G. (2019). The cricket winner prediction with application of machine learning and data analytics. *International Journal of Scientific & Technology Research*, *8*(09).

Wang, P. (2012, July 17). *Download and Install Anaconda*. Anaconda. Retrieved February 27, 2023, from https://www.anaconda.com/

Waskom, M. (2021). seaborn: Statistical data visualization. *Journal of Open Source Software*, *6*(60), 3021. doi:10.21105/joss.03021

Who.int. (2022). *Tobacco*. Available at: https://www.who.int/news-room/fact-sheets/detail/tobacco

Wickham, H. (2009). *ggplot2: Elegant Graphics for Data Analysis*. http://ndl.ethernet.edu.et/bitstream/123456789/60263/1/107.pdf

Wisam, Ameen, & Ahmed. (2019, June). *An Overview of Bag of Words: Importance, Implementation, Applications, and Challenges*. ResearchGate. https://www.researchgate.net/publication/338511771_An_Overview_of_Bag_of_WordsImportance_Implementation_Applications_and_Challenges

Wu, X., Sun, K., & Cao, M. (2023). A New Regularized Spatiotemporal Attention-Based LSTM with Application to Nitrogen Oxides Emission Prediction. *ACS Omega*, *8*(14), 12853–12864. doi:10.1021/acsomega.2c08205 PMID:37065070

Yang, X., Yang, K., Cui, T., & He, L. (2022, February 11). *A Study of Text Vectorization Method Combining Topic Model and Transfer Learning*. ResearchGate. https://www.researchgate.net/publication/358585623_A_Study_of_Text_Vectorization_Method_Combining_Topic_Model_and_Transfer_Learning

Yegulalp, S. (2022). *What is TensorFlow? The machine learning library explained*. Retrieved November 1, 2022, from https://www.infoworld.com/article/3278008/what-is-tensorflow-the-machine-learning-library-explained.html

Ying, X., Liu, W., Hui, G., & Fu, J. (2015). E-nose based rapid prediction of early mouldy grain using probabilistic neural networks. *Bioengineered*, *6*(4), 222–226. doi:10.1080/21655979.2015.1022304 PMID:25714125

YoungWonks. (2021). *What is OpenCV, what does it do and where is it used?* Retrieved November 1, 2022, from https://www.youngwonks.com/blog/What-is-OpenCV

Zach. (2021, August 9). *How to Interpret a ROC Curve (With Examples)*. Statology. https://www.statology.org/interpret-roc-curve/

Zare, H., Hajiabadi, M., & Jalili, M. (2021). Detection of Community Structures in Networks with Nodal Features based on Generative Probabilistic Approach. *IEEE Transactions on Knowledge and Data Engineering*, *33*(7), 2863–2874. doi:10.1109/TKDE.2019.2960222

Zhang, S., Cheng, Y., Luo, D., He, J., Wong, A. K., & Hung, K. (2021). Channel attention convolutional neural network for Chinese baijiu detection with E-nose. *IEEE Sensors Journal*, *21*(14), 16170–16182. doi:10.1109/JSEN.2021.3075703

Zhang, W., Wang, L., Chen, J., Bi, X., Chen, C., Zhang, J., & Hans, V. (2021). A Novel Gas Recognition and Concentration Estimation Model for an Artificial Olfactory System with a Gas Sensor Array. *IEEE Sensors Journal*, *21*(17), 18459–18468. doi:10.1109/JSEN.2021.3091582

Zhang, X.-K., Ren, J., Song, C., Jia, J., & Zhang, Q. (2017). Label propagation algorithm for community detection based on node importance and label influence. *Physics Letters. [Part A]*, *381*(33), 2691–2698. doi:10.1016/j.physleta.2017.06.018

Zhang, Y., Wu, B., Ning, N., Song, C., & Lv, J. (2019). Dynamic Topical Community Detection in Social Network: A Generative Model Approach. *IEEE Access : Practical Innovations, Open Solutions, 7*, 74528–74541. doi:10.1109/ACCESS.2019.2921824

Zhao, D., Wang, L., Wang, Z., & Xiao, G. (2019). Virus Propagation and Patch Distribution in Multiplex Networks: Modeling, Analysis, and Optimal Allocation. *IEEE Transactions on Information Forensics and Security, 14*(7), 1755–1767. doi:10.1109/TIFS.2018.2885254

Zhao, D., Wang, L., Xu, S., Liu, G., Han, X., & Li, S. (2017). Vital layer nodes of multiplex networks for immunization and attack. *Chaos, Solitons, and Fractals, 105*, 169–175. doi:10.1016/j.chaos.2017.10.021

Zhao, D., Xiao, G., Wang, Z., Wang, L., & Xu, L. (2021). Minimum Dominating Set of Multiplex Networks: Definition, Application, and Identification. *IEEE Transactions on Systems, Man, and Cybernetics. Systems, 51*(12), 7823–7837. doi:10.1109/TSMC.2020.2987163

Zhu, P., Wang, X., Jia, D., Guo, Y., Li, S., & Chu, C. (2020). Investigating the co-evolution of node reputation and edge-strategy in prisoner's dilemma game. *Applied Mathematics and Computation, 386*, 125474. doi:10.1016/j.amc.2020.125474

Ziyatdinov, A., Fonollosa, J., Fernandez, L., Gutierrez-Galvez, A., Marco, S., & Perera, A. (2015). Bioinspired early detection through gas flow modulation in chemo-sensory systems. *Sensors and Actuators. B, Chemical, 206*, 538–547. doi:10.1016/j.snb.2014.09.001

Zou, L. Z. (2021). Porosity Prediction With Uncertainty Quantification From Multiple Seismic Attributes Using Random Forest. *Journal of Geophysical Research: Solid Earth*, (7).

Zuccarelli, E. (2020, December 29). *Performance Metrics in Machine Learning — Part 1: Classification.* Towards Data Science. Retrieved December 5, 2022, from https://towardsdatascience.com/performance-metrics-in-machine-learning-part-1-classification-6c6b8d8a8c92

Zvarevashe, K., & Olugbara, O. (2020). *Ensemble Learning of Hybrid Acoustic Features for Speech Emotion Recognition.* Retrieved May 6, 2023, from https://www.mdpi.com/1999-4893/13/3/70

About the Contributors

Soly Mathew Biju has been in the field of academic and IT industry for a total of 25 years. She has a Ph.D. in Computer Science and also an MBA in IT management. She is currently an Associate Professor at the Faculty of Engineering and Information Sciences, University of Wollongong in Dubai. Dr Biju has achieved the CEng status awarded by Engineering Council (UK). She also has achieved the Chartered IT Professional status which is a symbol of excellence in the field of IT and is also an ISTQB-certified software testing professional. She is also a Fellow Higher Education Academy, UK. She was nominated for the Teaching Excellence and Research Excellence awards at UOWD on numerous occasions and received the prestigious Teaching Excellence Award in 2012, 2015 and 2019. She was also awarded the prestigious Amity Global Academic Excellence award in 2020. She spearheads the 'Global Health and Wellbeing ' cluster at UOWD. Her research interests include machine learning, data security, software testing, cryptography, e-learning, innovations in teaching, agile software development, online teaching, network security and programming techniques. She has papers published in reputed journals and books and presented and reviewed papers at national and international conferences and journals. She has been a scientific and organizing committee member and session chair and content chair on various reputed national and international conferences. She was nominated for the Teaching Excellence and Research Excellence awards at UOWD on numerous occasions and received the prestigious Teaching Excellence Award in 2012, 2015 and 2019. She was also awarded the prestigious Amity Global Academic Excellence award in 2020. Her research interests include machine learning, data security, software testing, cryptography, e-learning, innovations in teaching, agile software development, online teaching, network security and programming techniques. She has papers published in reputed journals and books and presented and reviewed papers at national and international conferences and journals. She has been a scientific and organizing committee member and session chair and content chair on various reputed national and international conferences.

* * *

Haseeb Ahmad is serving as an Assistant Professor at Department of Computer Science, National Textile University, Faisalabad, Pakistan. He received the BS degree from G.C. University, Faisalabad, Pakistan in 2010 and the Master's degree from the Virtual University of Pakistan in 2012. He has obtained his Ph.D. degree from Beijing University of Posts and Telecommunications, Beijing, China in 2017. He has published several papers in esteemed journals and conferences. His current research interest includes data mining, information retrieval, and information security.

Harishchander Anandaram completed a PhD in bioengineering, an M.Tech., and a B.Tech. in bioinformatics from the Sathyabama Institute of Science and Technology, Chennai, in 2020, 2011, and 2009. In his bachelor's and master's theses, he worked on analyzing resistance in HIV protease inhibitors based on molecular mechanics and machine learning studies, a collaborative project with IIT Madras. In his PhD thesis, he worked on pharmacogenomics and miRNA-regulated networks in psoriasis, a collaborative project with Georgetown University, USA, JIPMER, India, CIBA, India, and ILS, India. His thesis illustrated a multi-disciplinary approach by combining computational biophysics and molecular biology machine learning. While doing a PhD, He had the opportunity to collaborate with international researchers and have publications in reputed international journals in bioinformatics and systems biology. He has received the prestigious "Young Scientist Award" from "The Melinda Gates Foundation" for his research abstract on "The Implications of miRNA Dynamics in Infectious Diseases". To date, he has reviewed more than 200 manuscripts in systems biology.

Manivasagan C. is an assistant professor of Department of BCA. He accomplished the State Eligiblity Test (S.E.T) and pursuing 11 years experience in campus. His research interests are in the field of Data Mining.

Shiv Nath Chaudhri received the B.Sc. degree and the B.Tech. degree in electronics and communication engineering from the Madan Mohan Malaviya Engineering College, Gorakhpur, in 2009 and 2013, respectively, and the M.Tech. and Ph.D. degrees in electronics engineering from the Department of Electronics Engineering, Indian Institute of Technology (Banaras Hindu University) Varanasi, Varanasi, in 2017 and 2022, respectively. His current research interests include intelligent sensor signal processing for electronic noses, gas sensor array, hyperspectral image, and LiDAR using artificial intelligence, machine learning, and deep learning.

Haseeb Imdad is a highly accomplished individual who holds a BSCS degree from National Textile University (NTU), Pakistan, where he earned the prestigious gold medal in his program. Currently pursuing an MSCS from NTU, his research interests lie in Data Mining, Explainable AI, and NLP. Additionally, Haseeb is skilled in web development using Django in Python. With his outstanding academic achievements and expertise, he is a valuable asset to the computer science community.

Sujith Jayaprakash is currently the Head of NIIT in Accra, Ghana.

Gowri K. is currently an Assistant Professor in the Faculty of Computer Science with Cognitive Systems at the Sri Ramakrishna College of Arts and Science in Coimbatore, Tamilnadu.

Manoj Kumar obtained his Ph.D. Computer Science from The Northcap University, Gurugram. He did his B. Tech in computer science from Kurukshetra University. He obtained M. Sc. (Information Security and Forensics) degree from ITB, Dublin in and M. Tech from ITM University. Mr. Kumar has 9.5+ years of experience in research and academics. He published over 29 publications in reputed journals and conferences. He published 2 books and 5 patents with his team. Presently, Mr. Kumar is working on the post of assistant professor (SG), (SoCS) in university of petroleum and energy studies, Dehradun. He is a member of various professional bodies and reviewed for many reputed journals. He is Editorial Board Member in The International Arab Journal of Information Technology (IAJIT), Jordon and Journal of Computer Science Research, Singapore. He is recognized as Quarterly Franklin Member (QFM) by London Journal Press from March 2019 onwards and Bentham Ambassador (India) on behalf of Bentham Science Publisher. He delivered various key speech and talks in national and international forums. He got best researcher award 2020 from ScenceFather research community.

Thenmozhi M., Assistant Professor, Department of Computer Science and Engineering, Sri Eshwar College of Engineering, Coimbatore. Published papers in Scopus Journals and attended various international conferences.

Rahul Manwani recently graduated with a Bachelor's degree in Computer Science from the University of Wollongong in Dubai, where he specialized in Cyber Security. Rahul is currently working as a Full-stack software developer at a fintech startup. He is committed to staying up to date with the latest technologies and has a keen interest in working with AI technologies and projects. Rahul is always passionate about coding and problem-solving. Outside work, he likes spending his free time with family and friends, watching football and cricket, and binging TV shows.

Gokuldev S. has more than 18 years of academic, research and administrative experiences, served in various engineering colleges, technical Universities, Arts and Science colleges in and around Tamilnadu and Karnataka with various academic positions. Currently serving as Professor in the Department of Computer Science, Rathinam College of Arts and Science, Coimbatore and also associated with iNurture Education Solution, Bangalore as Zonal Head (South) – IT Academics. He has authored more than 25 publications in reputed International journals and more than 15 publications in National and International Conferences. He has been an active member in several professional bodies such as IEEE, CSI, IAENG, CSTA, IACSIT etc. and served as the reviewer for few reputed journals of IEEE, EAI Endorsed Journals, Springer – Publons, PLOS ONE, Inderscience Journal / IJICT, ETRI Journal etc. He has been the Session Chair and Panelist in several International Conferences.

Devaraju Sellappan received the B.Sc degree in Chemistry in 1997 from the University of Madras, Chennai, and the M.C.A. degree in Computer Applications in 2001 from the Periyar University, Salem, and the M.Phil. degree in Computer Science in 2004 from Periyar University, Salem and also received M.B.A. degree in Human Resource from Madurai Kamaraj University, Madurai in 2007. He received Ph.D degree in Computer Applications from Anna University, Chennai in 2017. Dr.S.Devaraju has 20+ years of teaching experience and 2 years industry experience. He is an Senior Assistant Professor, School of Computing Science and Engineering (SCSE), VIT Bhopal University, Sehore, Madhya Pradesh, India. Dr.S.Devaraju has published 4 patents, 6 Book Chapters and Reviewer for various reputed Journals and Conferences. He has published more than 40+ papers in international journals and conference proceedings. His area of research includes Network Security, Intrusion Detection, Soft Computing, and Wireless Communication.

Index

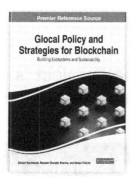
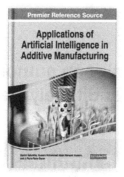
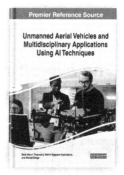

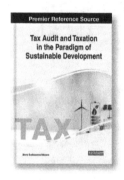

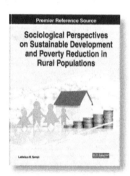

Printed in the United States
by Baker & Taylor Publisher Services